An
**Outdoor
Family
Guide** to

Yellowstone
& Grand Teton
National Parks

An Outdoor Family Guide to

Yellowstone & Grand Teton
National Parks

Second Edition

LISA GOLLIN EVANS

THE MOUNTAINEERS BOOKS

To Frank, with love and gratitude

THE MOUNTAINEERS BOOKS
*is the nonprofit publishing arm of The Mountaineers Club, an organization
founded in 1906 and dedicated to the exploration, preservation, and
enjoyment of outdoor and wilderness areas.*

1001 SW Klickitat Way, Suite 201, Seattle, Washington 98134

First edition: first printing 1996, revised 1998, third printing 2000, fourth printing 2002;
Second edition 2006

Manufactured in the United States of America

Project Editor: Kathleen Cubley
Copy Editor: Paula Thurman
Mapmaker: Moore Creative Designs
Cover and Book Design by The Mountaineers Books
Layout: Mayumi Thompson

All photos by the author unless otherwise noted.

Cover photograph: © National Park Service

Library of Congress Cataloging-in-Publication Data
Evans, Lisa Gollin, 1956-
  An outdoor family guide to Yellowstone and Grand Teton National Parks / Lisa Gollin Evans.-- 2nd ed.
    p. cm.
  Includes bibliographical references and index.
  ISBN 0-89886-972-2 (pbk.)
  1. Hiking--Yellowstone National Park--Guidebooks. 2. Hiking--Wyoming--Grand Teton National Park-
-Guidebooks. 3. Cycling--Yellowstone National Park--Guidebooks. 4. Cycling--Wyoming--Grand Teton
National Park--Guidebooks. 5. Boats and boating--Yellowstone National Park--Guidebooks. 6. Boats
and boating--Wyoming--Grand Teton National Park--Guidebooks. 7. Family recreation. 8. Yellowstone
National Park--Guidebooks. 9. Grand Teton National Park (Wyo.)--Guidebooks. I. Title.
  GV199.42.Y45E92 2006
  917.87'52--dc22
                    2005035678

CONTENTS

MAP LEGEND

(395) (50)	U.S. Highway	⌣	Bridge
(28) (260)	State or County Road	$	Store
540	Forest Service Road	⛽	Gas
▬▬▬	Paved Road	FS	Full services
═══	Unpaved Road	🛏	Lodging
----------	Main Trail	↟	Visitor center/ Ranger station
----------	Other Trail	🚻	Restroom
— · — · —	Wilderness/Park Boundary	↺	Turnaround
∿	River/Stream	△	Camping
∿≈	Falls	⛩	Picnic Area
🝰	Lake	▣	Point of Interest
✾ ✾ ✾	Wetland	Ⓟ	Parking
🛶	Boat ramp	Ⓣ	Trailhead
✕	Canoe portage	▲	Peak
Ⓟ️ⓘ	Put-In	◖🍂	Hike
Ⓣⓞ	Take-Out	⌒	Bike
❶	Trip Number	◣◢	Paddle
▬	Camping Zone		

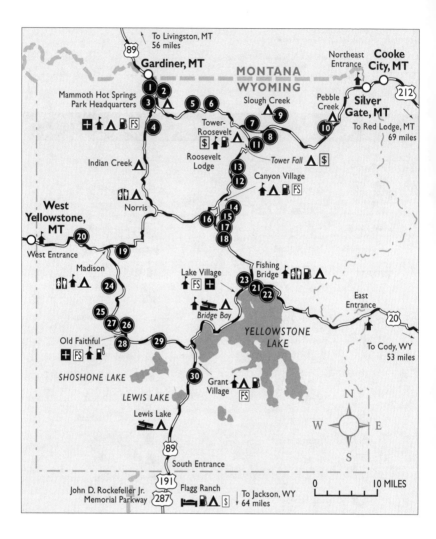

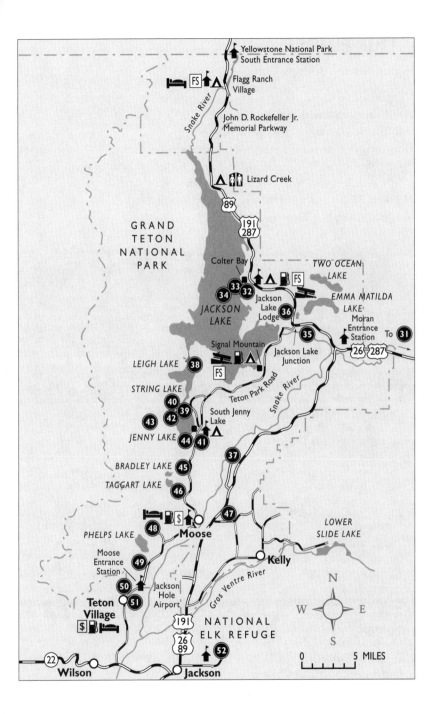

TRIP FINDER

	Difficulty	Mileage	Biking	Paddling	Usage	Backcountry Campsite	Fishing	Wildlife	Point of Interest
North Yellowstone National Park									
1. Beaver Ponds Loop	M	5 RT			M			Sp, F	
2. Boiling River	VE	0.5 OW			H		•	Sp, F	G, S
3. Mammoth Hot Springs Lower Terraces	VE	0.75 OW			H			•	G, SG
4. Bunsen Peak	S	2.2 OW			M			Sp, F	P
5. Blacktail Deer Creek	S	3.7 OW			M	•	•	•	
6. Forces of the Northern Range Self-Guiding Trail (H*)	VE	0.5 RT			L				SG, H
7. Yellowstone River Overlook	E	2 OW			L			•	G, H
8. Petrified Forest	S	1.75 OW			L			•	H
9. Slough Creek Meadows	E	2 OW			M	•	•		
10. Trout Lake	E	0.5 OW			H		•	•	
11. Tower Fall	VE	0.5 OW			H		•		W, H
Central Yellowstone National Park									
12. Mount Washburn	S	3 OW			H			•	P
13. Mount Washburn	S	3 OW	•		H			•	P
14. Seven-Mile Hole	S	5.5 OW			M	•	•		W, G
15. Lookout Point to Red Rock Point	E	0.4 OW			H				W

	Difficulty	Mileage	Biking	Paddling	Usage	Backcountry Campsite	Fishing	Wildlife	Point of Interest
Central Yellowstone National Park (continued)									
16. Brink of Lower Falls Trail	E	0.75 OW			H				W
17. Clear Lake Loop	M	3.75–6.8 RT			M	●	●	●	W, G
18. Uncle Tom's Trail	M	0.25+ OW			H				W
19. Artist Paint Pots Trail	VE	0.5 OW			M				G
20. Two Ribbons Trail (H*)	VE	0.75 RT			L		●	Sp, F	
South Yellowstone National Park									
21. Pelican Creek Loop	E	1 RT			L		●	●	S
22. Storm Point Nature Trail Loop	M	3–5 RT			M		●	●	
23. Elephant Back Mountain Loop	M	3.5 RT			M			Sp, F	P
24. Fountain Flat Road and Fairy Falls	E	5 OW	●		M		●	Sp, F	W, G
25. Mystic Falls Loop	M	3.2 RT			M			Sp, F	W, G
26. Observation Point	E	1.9 OW			H			Sp, F	G
27. Upper Geyser Basin	E	1.5–3.4 OW	●		H			Sp, F	G
28. Lone Star Geyser	M	2.3 OW	●		M	●	●	Sp, F	G
29. Shoshone Lake	M	3 OW			M	●	●	●	
30. Riddle Lake	M	2.5 OW			L			●	
North Grand Teton National Park									
31. Jade Lakes	E	2 OW			L	●	●	●	
32. Swan Lake and Heron Pond Loop	E	3 RT			H			●	
33. Hermitage Point Loop	S	8.8 RT			L	●	●	●	
34. Colter Bay	M	2 OW		●	H		●	Sp, F	
35. Snake River Float	M	5–6 OW		●	M		●	●	
36. Willow Flats Overlook	VE	0.5 OW			H			●	H
37. Schwabacher's Landing	VE	0.5 OW			M		●		
South Grand Teton National Park									
38. Leigh and Bearpaw Lakes	M	2.3–3.7 OW		●	H	●	●	●	S
39. String Lake to Jenny Lake's West Shore	E	1.7 OW			M		●	●	S
40. String Lake Loop	E	3.5 RT			M	●		Sp, F	S
41. Hidden Falls	E	0.5 OW**			H			●	W
42. Inspiration Point	M	0.9 OW**			H			●	W

	Difficulty	Mileage	Biking	Paddling	Usage	Backcountry Campsite	Fishing	Wildlife	Point of Interest
South Grand Teton National Park (continued)									
43. Forks of Cascade Canyon	S	4.5 OW**			H	●	●	●	W
44. Jenny Lake Paddle	M	4.5 RT		●	H		●		
45. Surprise and Amphitheater Lakes	VS	9.6 RT			H			●	
46. Taggart and Bradley Lakes Loop	M	4.7 RT			M	●	●	●	W
47. Mormon Row/Kelly Loop	M	14.75 RT	●		M		●	●	S, H
48. Phelps Lake Overlook and Death Canyon	M-S	0.9–3.7 OW			M	●	●	●	
49. Granite Canyon	M-S	3–6.2 OW			L	●	●	●	W
50. Rendezvous Peak/Rock Springs Bowl Loop	S	4.2 RT			M			●	P
51. Moose–Wilson Road Bike Trail (H*)	E	13 RT	●		H				
52. National Elk Refuge	M	6.8 OW	●		M			●	W, F

CHOOSE YOUR OWN ADVENTURE

	Easy	Moderate	Strenuous
Seeking Solitude			
6. Forces of the Northern Range (YNP)	●		
7. Yellowstone River Overlook (YNP)	●		
8. Petrified Forest (YNP)			●
20. Two Ribbons Trail (YNP)	●		
21. Pelican Creek Loop (YNP)	●		
30. Riddle Lake (YNP)		●	
31. Jade Lakes (GTNP)	●		
33. Hermitage Point Loop (GTNP)			●
49. Granite Canyon (GTNP)		●	●
Wild for Wildlife			
1. Beaver Ponds Loop (YNP)		●	
2. Boiling River (YNP)	●		
5. Blacktail Deer Creek (YNP)			●
7. Yellowstone River Overlook (YNP)	●		
8. Petrified Forest (YNP)			●
10. Trout Lake (YNP)	●		
12. Mount Washburn (YNP)			●
13. Mount Washburn (YNP)			●
17. Clear Lake Loop (YNP)		●	
21. Pelican Creek Loop (YNP)	●		
22. Storm Point Nature Trail Loop (YNP)		●	
29. Shoshone Lake (YNP)		●	
30. Riddle Lake (YNP)		●	
31. Jade Lakes (GTNP)	●		
32. Swan Lake and Heron Pond Loop (GTNP)	●		
33. Hermitage Point Loop (GTNP)			●
35. Snake River Float (GTNP)		●	
38. Leigh and Bearpaw Lakes (GTNP)		●	
43. Forks of Cascade Canyon (GTNP)			●
47. Mormon Row/Kelly Loop (GTNP)		●	
49. Granite Canyon (GTNP)		●	●
52. National Elk Refuge (GTNP)		●	
Reach a Peak			
4. Bunsen Peak (YNP)			●
12. Mount Washburn (YNP)			●
13. Mount Washburn (YNP)			●
23. Elephant Back Mountain Loop (YNP)		●	
Self-Guided Nature Trail			
6. Forces of the Northern Range (YNP)	●		

	Easy	Moderate	Strenuous
Take a Stroller (wheelchairs with assistance)			
6. Forces of the Northern Range (YNP)	●		
20. Two Ribbons Trail (YNP)	●		
Hot on the Trail: Geysers and Other Geothermal Features			
2. Boiling River (YNP)	●		
3. Mammoth Hot Springs Lower Terraces (YNP)	●		
17. Clear Lake Loop (YNP)		●	
19. Artist Paint Pots Trail (YNP)	●		
26. Observation Point (YNP)	●		
27. Upper Geyser Basin (YNP)	●		
28. Lone Star Geyser (YNP)		●	
Take a Swim			
2. Boiling River (YNP)	●		
38. Leigh and Bearpaw Lakes (GTNP)		●	
39. String Lake to Jenny Lake's West Shore (GTNP)	●		
40. String Lake Loop (GTNP)	●		
47. Mormon Row/Kelly Loop (GTNP)		●	
Hike into History			
6. Forces of the Northern Range (YNP)	●		
7. Yellowstone River Overlook (YNP)	●		
8. Petrified Forest (YNP)			●
11. Tower Fall (YNP)	●		
47. Mormon Row/Kelly Loop (GTNP)		●	
Visit a Waterfall			
11. Tower Fall (YNP)	●		
15. Lookout Point to Red Rock Point (YNP)	●		
16. Brink of Lower Falls Trail (YNP)	●		
17. Clear Lake Loop (YNP)		●	
18. Uncle Tom's Trail (YNP)		●	
24. Fountain Flat Road and Fairy Falls (YNP)	●		
25. Mystic Falls Loop (YNP)		●	
41. Hidden Falls (GTNP)	●		
42. Inspiration Point (GTNP)	●		
43. Forks of Cascade Canyon (GTNP)			●
Goin' Fishin'			
2. Boiling River (YNP)	●		
5. Blacktail Deer Creek (YNP)			●
9. Slough Creek Meadows (YNP)	●		
10. Trout Lake (YNP)	●		
11. Tower Fall Trail (YNP)	●		
14. Seven-Mile Hole (YNP)			●

	Easy	Moderate	Strenuous
Goin' Fishin' (continued)			
17. Clear Lake Loop (YNP)		●	
20. Two Ribbons Trail (YNP)	●		
21. Pelican Creek Loop (YNP)	●		
22. Storm Point Nature Trail Loop (YNP)		●	
24. Fountain Flat Road and Fairy Falls (YNP)	●		
28. Lone Star Geyser (YNP)		●	
29. Shoshone Lake (YNP)		●	
35. Snake River Float (GTNP)		●	
38. Leigh and Bearpaw Lakes (GTNP)		●	
39. String Lake to Jenny Lake's West Shore (GTNP)	●		
44. Jenny Lake Paddle (GTNP)		●	
46. Taggart and Bradley Lakes Loop (GTNP)		●	
48. Phelps Lake Overlook and Death Canyon (GTNP)		●	●
Take a Bike			
13. Mount Washburn (YNP)			●
24. Fountain Flat Road and Fairy Falls (YNP)	●		
27. Upper Geyser Basin (YNP)	●		
28. Lone Star Geyser (YNP)		●	
47. Mormon Row/Kelly Loop (GTNP)		●	
51. Moose–Wilson Road Bike Trail (GTNP)	●		
52. National Elk Refuge (GTNP)		●	
Paddling			
34. Colter Bay (GTNP)		●	
35. Snake River Float (GTNP)		●	
38. Leigh and Bearpaw Lakes (GTNP)		●	
44. Jenny Lake Paddle (GTNP)		●	
Go Camping			
5. Blacktail Deer Creek (YNP)			●
14. Seven-Mile Hole (YNP)			●
17. Clear Lake Loop (YNP)		●	
28. Lone Star Geyser (YNP)		●	
29. Shoshone Lake (YNP)		●	
31. Jade Lakes (GTNP)	●		
33. Hermitage Point Loop (GTNP)			●
38. Leigh and Bearpaw Lakes (GTNP)		●	
40. String Lake Loop (GTNP)	●		
43. Forks of Cascade Canyon (GTNP)			●
46. Taggart and Bradley Lakes Loop (GTNP)		●	
48. Phelps Lake Overlook and Death Canyon (GTNP)		●	●
49. Granite Canyon (GTNP)		●	●

WILDLIFE LOCATOR

The following chart lists Yellowstone's and Grand Teton's most actively sought-after birds and mammals and describes their habitats and likely locations. Bear in mind that for the great majority, dawn and dusk are the most fruitful viewing times. Another tip for wildlife watchers is to be aware of other viewers. Cars in pullouts (with people gesturing wildly) often means a sighting of some significance. If there's room in the designated turnoff, stop and find out. (But never block the flow of traffic; you may cause an accident!) In addition, park rangers are an excellent resource for information on recent sightings. Most of all, remember to watch wildlife ethically and safely.

Animal	Habitat	Likely Locations: Yellowstone	Likely Locations: Grand Teton
Bald Eagle	Nests near lakes and rivers. Look in tall trees near water.	Yellowstone Lake, Yellowstone River at overlook (9 mi. north of Fishing Bridge); along Lamar River.	Near Snake River and Jackson Lake. Try Trips 34, 35, and 37. Best bet is a scenic float on the Snake River.
Bear (Black)	Mixed forest and adjacent meadows. Prefers more densely forested areas than grizzlies. In late summer, feeds on berries and whitebark pines.	Along Mammoth–Tower Rd. between Undine Falls and Petrified Tree Turnout; between Tower Jct. and Lamar River Bridge; the Lamar Valley; forest and meadows between Old Chittenden Rd. and Tower Fall; Grant Village area in spring. Be especially alert on Trips 8–10, 12, 13, 17, 29, and 30.	West shore of Jenny Lake; forested areas near String, Leigh, Phelps, Bradley, and Taggart lakes. Wide-ranging. Be especially alert on Trips 33, 38–46.
Bear (Grizzly)	Open country, including mountain meadows, open forests, and areas near streams.	High meadows of Lamar Valley; Antelope Creek drainage visible from pullouts on the Canyon–Tower Rd. between Old Chittenden Rd. and Tower Fall; Hayden Valley (overlook 9 mi. north of Fishing Bridge). Be especially alert on Trips 17, 21–33.	Not known to inhabit the park, although bears have been sighted near Emma Matilda/Two Ocean Lake near Teton Wilderness.
Bighorn Sheep	Remote and rocky cliffs and mountainsides.	Cliffs above Gardner River east of the Mammoth–Gardiner Rd.; cliffs above Yellowstone River across from Calcite Springs Overlook; on Mt. Washburn via Trips 12 and 13. Try also Trips 5 and 7.	None in park.

Animal	Habitat	Likely Locations: Yellowstone	Likely Locations: Grand Teton
Bison	Grasslands and meadows near rivers.	Plentiful in Lamar and Hayden valleys; Pelican Valley. In spring and fall at Upper, Midway, and Lower Geyser basins, and meadows of Firehole Canyon Dr. Try Trips 4, 20, 22, 24–27.	Snake River bottomlands; Antelope Flats and Kelly Warm Springs; and along U.S. 191–89–26 from Moose to Moran Jct. Try Trips 37–45 and especially Trip 47.
Coyote	Primarily grasslands and sagebrush meadows.	Common at lower and middle elevations, especially on northern shore of Yellowstone Lake; in the Lamar and Hayden valleys; and in Upper, Midway, and Lower Geyser basins.	Sagebrush meadows flanking park roads' Antelope Flats, and Kelly Warm Springs. Try Trips 32, 33, 38, and 47.
Elk (Wapiti)	Summer: meadows and grasslands, dusk to dawn, forests in daytime. Spring-fall: throughout valleys.	Meadows of Lamar Valley; Antelope Creek drainage; Gibbon Meadow; Elk Park; and in spring and fall along Firehole and Gardner rivers. Year-round at Mammoth Hot Springs. Try Trips 1–3, 19.	Meadows flanking Teton Park Rd., especially west of Timbered Island, southeast of Jenny Lake.
Moose	Near creeks, rivers, ponds, and in marshy areas, especially with willow and aspen.	Willow Park (between Norris and Mammoth); along the northern and northwestern shore of Yellowstone Lake. Try Trips 21, 22, 29, 30.	Along Snake River (especially near Moose Visitor Center, Moran Jct., and Oxbow Bend); at ponds along Moose–Wilson Rd.; and at Willow Flats and wetlands along Christian Creek (near Jackson Lake Lodge). Try Trips 32–37, 43, 46, 48, and 49.
Pronghorn (Antelope)	Open grassland and sagebrush communities.	Along Old Gardiner Rd., from Mammoth to Gardiner; near North Entrance; the meadows around Tower Jct.; along Northeast Entrance Rd. to Lamar Valley. Try Trips 1 and 2.	Grasslands flanking Teton Park Rd. (especially near Timbered Island, south of Jenny Lake), Moose–Wilson Rd., and Antelope Flats. Try Trip 47.
Trumpeter Swan	Ponds and waterways.	In fall, Madison River near Seven-Mile Bridge; on Swan Lake off Mammoth–Norris Rd.; along Yellowstone River between Fishing Bridge and Hayden Valley.	Swan Lake (Trips 32 and 33); Christian Pond near Jackson Lake Lodge; Oxbow Bend (Trip 35); and Flat Creek in National Elk Refuge (Trip 52).
Wolf (Gray)	Meadows, open forest.	Lamar Valley (view from pullouts at dawn and dusk) northwest of the Lamar Ranger Station.	None in park.

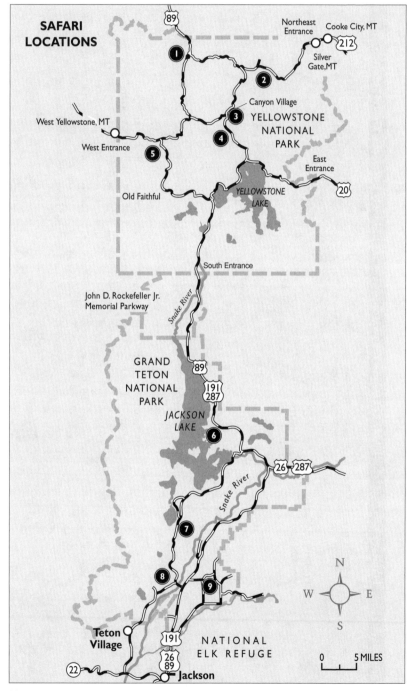

SAFARI LOCATIONS

89

Northeast Entrance
Cooke City, MT
212
Silver Gate, MT

1

2

West Yellowstone, MT

Canyon Village
3
YELLOWSTONE
NATIONAL
PARK

West Entrance

4

5

East Entrance
20

Old Faithful

YELLOWSTONE
LAKE

South Entrance

John D. Rockefeller Jr.
Memorial Parkway

Snake River

GRAND
TETON
NATIONAL
PARK

89

191
287

JACKSON
LAKE

6

26 287

Snake River

7

8

9

N
W   E
S

Teton
Village

191

NATIONAL
ELK REFUGE

0   5 MILES

22

26
89
Jackson

SELF-GUIDED WILDLIFE "SAFARIS"

The following "safaris" describe nine self-guided driving tours to places where particular animals are likely to be seen. For the best results, try these drives at dawn or dusk. Bring binoculars and keep your eyes moving!

Safari #1: Pronghorn in Yellowstone's Northwest Corner

From Mammoth Hot Springs, take the Old Gardiner Road (6 miles, one way) through the rolling sagebrush to the park's North Entrance. (For directions, see Trip 1.) The pronghorn make their home in these dry hills. Bring binoculars, and drive slowly, for the antelope's distinctive coloring is effective camouflage. At the end of the drive, turn right to circle back to Mammoth Hot Springs on the park's main road. On the return, look for elk, especially in spring, early and late summer, and fall. In spring, elk cows and their young often gather near the Gardner River. Other animals that may be seen are coyote, bighorn sheep (on the cliffs above the river), and birds of prey.

Safari #2: Wolves, Elk, Bison, and Bears in Yellowstone's Lamar Valley

The Lamar Valley is one of the most beautiful and fruitful places to "safari." In spring and fall, large predators are often seen. Drive east from Tower Junction on the Tower–Northeast Entrance Road about 6 miles to reach the beginning of the valley. A series of pullouts on the road's south side provide good places to park and set up spotting scopes. Bison graze in the meadows by the river. Elk are often seen in higher meadows. Scan the upper meadows, especially near the trees (the edge environments) for signs of predators. Wolves and grizzlies frequent the area in the spring and early summer to prey on elk calves. Look for flocks of ravens; they often appear with wolves at carcasses. Coyote and bald eagles may also be seen near the river.

Safari #3: Bears and Elk in Yellowstone's Antelope Creek Drainage

Antelope Creek Drainage is known for its grizzly bears. Spring and fall are the best viewing times. From Tower Junction, drive south about 6.2 miles on the Tower–Canyon Road to the pullouts overlooking the drainage. From Canyon Village, the pullouts begin just north of the Old Chittenden Road, about 11 miles north of Canyon Village. Elk are usually easy to locate in the meadows.

Scan the edge environment for grizzlies. An occasional moose may also be seen. The long viewing distances make binoculars or spotting scopes essential.

Safari #4: Bison, Elk, and Bald Eagles in Yellowstone's Hayden Valley

Hayden Valley is the stomping ground for large herds of bison. Visit in spring to see the cavorting calves, or in August to watch the rut's feisty bulls. To find Hayden Valley, drive south from Canyon Village on the Canyon–Fishing Bridge Road about 5 miles. There are numerous pullouts for viewing. At 7 miles south of Canyon and 9 miles north of Fishing Bridge, look for a pullout on the east side of the road. In early summer, when the trout are spawning, this is an excellent spot to see bald eagles. Coyote and elk also frequent the meadows on the far side of the river, visible from the overlook.

Safari #5: Bison Along Yellowstone's Firehole River

Take a drive down Firehole Canyon Drive to see the resident bison herd, usually congregated at the drive's northern end in a meadow near the road. Firehole Canyon Drive is located 15.3 miles north of Old Faithful on the Old Faithful–Madison Road and 0.4 mile south of Madison Junction. With or without bison, the one-way road makes an interesting trip. After watching the herd, ride by 800-foot-high lava cliffs and pass the 40-foot-high Firehole Falls. The popular Firehole River swimming hole, near the end of the drive, is a treat for youngsters. Finally, at the end of Firehole Canyon Drive, pass another 40-foot-high falls, Firehole Cascades.

Safari #6: Moose in North Grand Teton National Park

It's not hard to find moose in Grand Teton National Park. This safari visits several prime moose habitats, fortunately all in gorgeous locations with superb Teton views. First drive to Willow Flats Overlook, just south of Jackson Lake Lodge. Park in the overlook and look west over the willowed wetlands. Moose love willow and many come to feed in this large, soggy area. If no moose can be seen, walk a very short distance north on the road and look down to the left to the meadows surrounding Christian Creek. Next, return to your car and drive south about 0.5 mile to Jackson Lake Junction. Turn east at the Junction and drive 1.2 miles to the Oxbow Bend Turnout. Park in the turnout and resume your search along the riverbank and wetlands. If moose still elude you, enjoy the incredible wealth of birdlife found in Oxbow Bend (Trip 35).

Safari #7: Elk and Pronghorn in South Grand Teton National Park

Throughout the summer, elk and pronghorn are plentiful in the meadows west of Timbered Island at dawn and dusk. To find the "island" (actually a forested hill), drive north on the Teton Park Road about 2.7 miles to the Taggart Lake Trailhead. Just to the north and east, the trees of Timbered Island give shelter and shade to elk and pronghorn during the day. At dawn and dusk they leave the forest to graze on the sage-covered meadows. Drive this section slowly, for the animals frequently cross the road. From the north, start your safari just south of the Jenny Lake turnoff.

Safari #8: Moose on the Moose–Wilson Road in Grand Teton National Park

Find moose in the ponds along the Moose–Wilson Road at dawn and dusk. You may also see mule deer and elk grazing in meadows by the road. From the Park Headquarters at Moose, drive northwest on the Moose–Wilson Road. The road immediately curves southwest and parallels the out-of-sight Snake River. Try for moose first in the Sawmill Ponds Overlook, about 1 mile from the start of the road. From the overlook, there's a view of several spring-fed ponds. Next, continue southwest along the road another mile or so. Ponds and marshy areas, thick with aspen and willow provide perfect moose habitat. Look carefully on the east side of the road. Your safari ends at the turnoff for the White Grass Ranch and the Death Canyon Trailhead, about 3 miles from the start of the Moose–Wilson Road.

Safari #9: Bison, Bison, and More Bison on Antelope Flats Road (Pronghorn and Coyote, Too)

Find a herd of bison beside the Antelope Flats Road, as well as common sitings of pronghorn antelope and an occasional coyote. The bison herd has been hanging out near the picturesque cabins used in the 1953 Western *Shane*. Any time of day, bison are likely to be seen. Follow the driving directions for Trip 47 and use a car or bike to complete the loop described.

PREFACE

The Greater Yellowstone Ecosystem is one of the best destinations in the country for vacationing families. Within its borders, two national parks, Yellowstone and Grand Teton, offer rich recreation as well as unparalleled beauty. Limitless blue sky, wide open spaces, and abundant wildlife fill its wilderness. From eagles to bison, hot springs to waterfalls, precipitous peaks to plunging canyons, the parks' natural wonders are marvelously accessible.

Nevertheless, a word of warning: Don't attempt to "do" the whole of Yellowstone and Grand Teton in a day, or even two. Eight hours on a traffic-clogged road is a mind-numbing experience and a surefire way to generate cranky kids, headaches, and poor memories. This book offers an alternative to the "drive-thru" tour. It reveals incredibly beautiful places to stroll, hike, swim, bike, paddle, camp, view wildlife, and learn about the wilderness.

With the aid of this book, leave your car and discover a part of the earth largely unchanged by man. Enter a world where you are no longer the dominant predator; where hot, hissing steam rises from the ground; where you are watched by a hundred unseen eyes; where extremes of height and depth, hot and cold, beauty and ghastliness are beyond your control and imagination. This is a land of wonderment: of 25,000 elk, 4000 bison, 2000 mule deer, 171 wolves, and hundreds of grizzlies, black bear, pronghorn antelope, bighorn sheep, and moose.

But what about the hordes of humans? The traffic jams? The souvenir shops and sprawling campgrounds? Admittedly, these things are there, but it is easy to avoid them. Two hundred feet down any trail and the parking lot and traffic noise are unseen, unheard, and forgotten.

For families, the lure of a national park is not only its wildness but also the quality of its interpretive services and the accessibility of its adventures. The park service at Yellowstone and Grand Teton offers a rich array of ranger-led hikes, campfire programs, junior ranger opportunities, and informative visitor centers. For family adventures, the mix is broad and enticing, including well-marked trails, scenic campsites, world-famous trout streams, gentle lakes, and an abundance of horses, rafts, and kayaks for hire.

Take your family to Yellowstone. You won't regret it.

ACKNOWLEDGMENTS

I'd like to express special and sincere thanks to all those who made this book a joy to write; my favorite hiking partners, Frank, Sarah, Grace, and Lilly; my mother, Hannah Gollin, who is always a source of strength and wisdom; my father, Morton Gollin, who can still beat me in tennis and can still hike the trails; my wonderful father-in-law and mother-in-law, Frank and Anne Evans; two terrific nieces, Kerry Sullivan and Kristen O'Connell; and my most excellent friends: Ned, Julie, Peter, and Catherine Strong; Patty, Zack, and Sara Yoffe; and last (but not least) Dan, Allyn, Katie, and Nancy Carl.

I'd also like to thank the many helpful rangers and naturalists of Yellowstone and Grand Teton National Parks who provided invaluable assistance. Particularly, I'd like to express special thanks to park naturalist Peter Dederich of Grand Teton, who patiently and expertly answered my endless questions.

Appreciation is also due to Gene Ball, former director of the Yellowstone Institute, who taught me indispensable lessons on wildlife observation, and to the following outfitters, *par excellence:* O.A.R.S. and Far and Away Adventures, who introduced me to wonderful places I might never have seen. I also want to thank the gorgeous Snake River Lodge and Spa in Teton Village for the best massage I've ever had.

Lastly, I want to thank Dr. Patricia Moody for the generous and lengthy loan of her bear bells, which helped to keep me and my family safe and sound in the backcountry.

—*Lisa Gollin Evans*

INTRODUCTION

This book describes fifty-two hiking, biking, backpacking, and boating outings chosen specifically for families. Each outing introduces parents and children to natural features of the parks, and each description alerts them to animals, plants, thermal features, and more that they might otherwise miss. To get the most out of your visit, the book also includes detailed information on the parks' interpretive resources, camping, horseback riding, fishing, boating, wildlife viewing, and other activities in and near the parks. Yellowstone and Grand Teton are full of adventures for visiting families; this book is full of easy ways to make them happen.

HOW TO USE THIS BOOK

This book begins with the Trip Finder, a trip matrix that helps you quickly choose an outing that fits your needs. The matrix concisely lists information such as difficulty, distance, elevation gain, location, and attractions. Following the Trip Finder is the Choose Your Own Adventure chart that arranges the trips by interest, making it easy to locate an outing that offers just what you're look-ing for, whether it be a climb, a fishing hole, wildlife viewing, swimming, etc. A Wildlife locator and suggestions for self guided "Wildlife Safaris" follows and indicates the most likely places to view wildlife.

Before setting out on any outing, consult this Introduction for general tips on hiking, biking, and boating with children; safety considerations; wilderness ethics; park regulations; and essential equipment. More specific information on Yellowstone and Grand Teton, including campgrounds, lodging, weather, natural history, and recreational opportunities, is discussed in Chapter 1.

Following Chapter 1 are fifty-two detailed trip descriptions, organized by geo-graphic region. The outings are classified as easy, moderate, or strenuous, accord-ing to their length, starting elevation, elevation gain, and terrain. Generally, easy trips are 0.5 to 2 miles one way, moderate trips are 2 to 4 miles one way, and strenuous trips are over 4 miles one way. Also included in these descriptions are symbols that indicate whether the trip is a hike, bike, or paddle, and whether backcountry camping is available.

The trail descriptions do not provide estimates of walking or biking time. Hikers and bikers, especially children, travel at such variable speeds that general approximations would not be reliable. To roughly estimate the time required for a hike, use the average walking rate of two miles per hour on level ground for adults carrying packs, plus one hour for each 1,000 feet of elevation gained. Difficult terrain and hiking children obviously increase the time needed. After a few hikes, you can work out estimates for your own family. Generally, strenuous hikes require a full day; moderate hikes, a half day; and easy hikes, one to three hours.

Two useful appendixes follow the outing descriptions. Appendix A contains a bibliography for children and adults with recommended books on the area's natural and regional history. Appendix B provides information on conservation organizations working to protect the Greater Yellowstone Ecosystem.

TIPS ON HIKING, BIKING, AND PADDLING WITH CHILDREN

The key to a great outing is respect for the interests and needs of your children when exploring the outdoors. Below are some basic rules of thumb to make your trip fun and rewarding.

Choosing the Right Trip

Hiking, biking, or paddling a route that's too difficult for your children is sure to lead to frustration for all. Read trip descriptions carefully to find outings that match your children's abilities. If you are uncertain how far they can go, choose a trip that has intermediate points of interest, so that you can shorten it if necessary. Try also to match your youngsters' interests with an outing's particular attractions, whether they are fishing, rock climbing, swimming, or wildflowers.

Snacks

Let children snack liberally on their favorite treats while on an outing. They will be working hard, and snacks high in carbohydrates and sugar boost their energy. Also, salty snacks are good for replacing salts lost through perspiration. Good-tasting treats can also be used as a motivating force for reaching the next rest stop. Don't forget to bring plenty of water or juice, particularly in summer, when humidity is low and temperatures are high. Mild dehydration causes crankiness in children, and more severe cases can cause extreme discomfort.

Motivation

There are numerous ways to motivate children. The promise of a picnic or a treat is enough for some. For others, encouraging good-natured competition with siblings or peers does the trick. When a child's motivation wears thin, distraction can be the best solution. Songs, trail activities, games, and stories often invigorate sluggish youngsters. Consult Appendix A for books containing trail activities.

Leaders

Allow children to lead the group. When the novelty wears off, assign the lead role to another, rotating the honor among the youngsters. Let children determine the pace. Progress may be slower than desired, but the trip will be much more enjoyable. Adults will also benefit from slowing down: you may cover only half the distance, but you'll experience twice as much.

Positive Attitude

Praise children for all their achievements on the trail. Positive reinforcement for beginners is essential to build a solid base of good feelings about nature outings. Refrain from criticism if children disappoint you. Scolding won't improve their performance; it will only guarantee unhappiness.

The Right Stuff

Pack items in your backpack to keep children happy on the trail, especially when hiking. Magnifying glasses, binoculars, cameras, junior field guides, bug bottles, sketchbooks, or materials for simple projects like bark and stone rubbings provide welcome diversions for youngsters who need a break. A child-sized walking stick can also provide miles of enjoyment for a young hiker.

Relax

When hiking, biking, and paddling with children, the joy is in the process, in the small achievements and discoveries you share. To appreciate this, you must relax. You may miss the thrill of a peak or the rush of rapids, but the quiet rewards of sharing nature last a lifetime and build a foundation for your next trip.

WILDERNESS ETHICS

To keep the parks healthy and the wildlife safe, it is essential that visitors follow a simple code of wilderness ethics.

Make a Positive Impact

The rule of positive impact goes beyond the oft-repeated "Take only pictures; leave only footprints." That maxim falls short in today's overcrowded parks. My rule of positive impact asks that visitors leave the parks a *better* place. By picking up trash, for example, you enhance the beauty of the trail for the next visitor. Give children a small bag to stuff in their pocket for their own litter as well as for stray wrappers left by others. Parents should carry litter bags, too.

A second way to create a positive impact is to set a good example by hiking, biking, and paddling joyfully, attentively, and considerately. The model will be contagious. Just as a crowd gathers to look at a sight in which others show interest, other visitors will follow your lead if you find a trail interesting, fun, or exhilarating.

Do Not Feed the Animals

Do not feed the small mammals and birds that beg for handouts. Feeding is dangerous for you *and* the animals. Human food harms wildlife in several ways. First, snack foods are a poor nutritional substitute for an animal's natural diet. If handouts become a primary source of food, the animal may become malnourished and prey to disease and injury. Second, feeding an animal disrupts its natural foraging instincts. As a result, animals that depend on human feeding may not survive the winter. Third, human feeding unnaturally concentrates animal populations. An unusually large population of marmots or ground squirrels at a picnic area leaves that population vulnerable to epidemic disease.

Feeding wild animals is also dangerous for people. Small mammals may carry rabies, a potentially lethal disease. Rabies aside, a rodent's sharp

Yellow-bellied marmot, please do not feed!

incisors in your finger is painful. Second, fleas carrying bubonic plague have been found on the parks' rodents. Although rare, instances of human contraction of bubonic plague from flea bites have occurred.

Protect and Respect the Bears

Protect the parks' bears by storing your food correctly while camping. Bears that successfully raid campsites often end up dead. Once a bear associates people with food, it continues to frequent campgrounds. The park service relocates food-habituated bears, but they often return. Unnatural feeding behavior inevitably places bears in close proximity to people, where unfortunate encounters are likely. If a food-conditioned bear injures a person, the park service may be forced to destroy it. Avoid this sad chain of events by securing food and garbage properly. By hanging food, using backcountry storage boxes, and utilizing your car trunk, you can save a bear's life. (See the diagram on page 35.)

Respect closures and restrictions in Yellowstone's Bear Management Areas (BMAs). Periodically, the National Park Service (NPS) designates a backcountry area as a BMA to reduce human impact in high-density grizzly bear habitat.

The park service may close an area entirely or restrict it to day use. These periodic closures are essential to protect Yellowstone's threatened grizzly population. Before hiking, inquire about bear closures at a visitor center or ranger station. In addition, look for NPS postings at the trailhead. If a bear is sighted while hiking or camping, report your sighting at the nearest ranger station or visitor center.

Let Wildflowers Flourish

From May through September, wild gardens grace the Greater Yellowstone Ecosystem. To ensure that all have an opportunity to enjoy the flowers, visitors must refrain from picking even one blossom. At high elevations, picking wildflowers poses a particularly critical problem because plants have little time in which to set seed. Removing plants means removing seeds, thus preventing annuals from reproducing. This may have a dire impact on the food supply for the parks' wildlife.

Stay on the Trail

To maintain the integrity, beauty, and safety of trails, do not shortcut. Shortcuts are most tempting where a trail switchbacks down a steep slope. When hikers aim straight down a slope, they damage the vegetation between the switchbacks and cause erosion. If shortcutting occurs frequently, a trail may wash away, leaving a scarred and barren hillside. Also, abandoning a trail on a precipitous slope is dangerous and may cause you to fall or lose the trail entirely.

Observe Park Rules

Written copies of NPS regulations are available at ranger stations and visitor centers. A few of the most important, and most commonly violated, are the following:

- Carry out all refuse. Leave no litter on trails or in campsites. Do not attempt to burn or bury noncombustibles.
- Do not cut, remove, deface, or disturb any tree, shrub, wildflower, or other natural object. Carving on trees scars them permanently and can even kill them if the carving girdles the tree.
- Use only dead and downed wood for firewood. Never break branches from standing trees, even if they appear dead. The tree may still be living, and breaking a branch may injure it.
- Removal of rocks, minerals, fossils, or cultural artifacts from the parks is prohibited.
- Collecting antlers and animal bones is also prohibited. Bones and antlers are an important source of minerals for the parks' smaller animals.

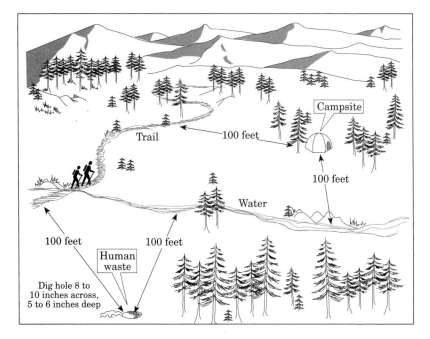

Backcountry Campsite Guidelines

- Edible plants, mushrooms, and berries may only be picked for your daily consumption. *Do not* eat any plants that you can't positively identify. Poisonous plants grow in both parks!
- All hunting is prohibited, as are firearms.
- Fishing requires a fishing permit for those over eleven years of age. Permits are available at ranger stations and visitor centers.
- Pets are prohibited on trails, in the backcountry, on boardwalks, and in thermal areas. Pets are allowed only within 25 feet of roads and parking areas and must be leashed.
- A permit is required for all boats (even nonmotorized) and a Coast Guard–approved flotation device is required for each person boating.
- Do not alter or put any objects in thermal features. These features are easily clogged and hence destroyed after tampering.

Builders Beware

Don't build *anything* in the parks. Don't build cairns, fireplaces, benches, or soft places to sleep. These structures linger long after you've left and blight the landscape. When camping, "naturalize" your camp before leaving by making the site look as if no one had camped there. Then make a positive impact by packing out any litter left by previous campers.

Get the Lead Out

Beginning in 1994, Yellowstone National Park began a lead-free fishing program. Wildlife such as loons, cranes, shorebirds, and trumpeter swans are particularly vulnerable to lead poisoning. As a result, the park prohibits fishing tackle such as leaded split-shot sinkers, weighted jigs (lead-molded to a hook), and soft lead-weighted ribbon.

Bike Responsibly

Bicycles are prohibited on backcountry trails and on boardwalks in the national parks. Bicycling is permitted only on established public roads and a few designated routes. Ask a ranger for a list of routes open to bicycles.

Light Stoves, Not Fires

In the backcountry, small fires are permitted at specific campsites within existing fire rings. Even where fires are allowed, the NPS discourages wood fires and recommends portable cooking stoves. Fires leave unsightly scars on the land,

Kayaking on Jackson Lake, Grand Teton National Park

rob forests of decomposing matter, present hazards in drought-stricken areas, and create haze in pristine skies. Also, ash carried by runoff contaminates lakes and streams. If you feel you can't camp without a fire, make it small, don't use it for cooking, limit its duration, and extinguish it carefully. Lastly, to make a positive impact, dismantle extra fire rings by scattering the rocks and condense overly large fire rings to discourage big fires.

Protect the Lakes

Backcountry lakes and streams are fragile and easily damaged by careless visitors. To protect them, set up camp, eliminate waste, and wash dishes at least 200 feet away. If picnicking on a lakeshore, choose a boulder or use areas already heavily impacted. It is unlikely that highly impacted areas will recover, and you will avoid spreading the damage. In addition, don't use any soaps in or near lakes and streams because *all* soaps pollute, even those that claim to be biodegradable.

SAFETY TIPS FOR YELLOWSTONE AND GRAND TETON NATIONAL PARKS

This section summarizes the basic precautions to be taken when visiting Yellowstone and Grand Teton National Parks. Be alert to the dangers described below and be prepared with the appropriate knowledge and gear to minimize hazardous situations. The checklist at the end of this section lists the essentials you need to take on *every* outing.

Bears

The Greater Yellowstone Ecosystem is home to black bears and grizzly bears. Sighting a bear is one of the parks' greatest thrills, but it also brings grave risks. All bears are unpredictable and potentially lethal. As a result, visitors should avoid bear confrontations and know what to do if one occurs.

Bear attacks are primarily caused by four occurrences: (1) surprising a bear; (2) getting between a sow and her cubs; (3) approaching a carcass or a bear with food; and (4) approaching a bear for a photo. To avoid placing yourself or your family in one of these dangerous situations, the NPS advises that visitors take the following precautions:

- **Be alert.** Learn how to recognize bear signs, including tracks, scat, and diggings. Use binoculars to scan the terrain while hiking. Fleeing wildlife may indicate the presence of bears; spotting a cub means a sow is nearby.
- **Make noise.** The more noise you make, the less likely you are to surprise a bear. Talk, sing, clap hands, and shake pebbles in a can. Don't rely on bear bells alone. Shout when entering dense and brushy vegetation, when traveling near noisy streams, and when hiking

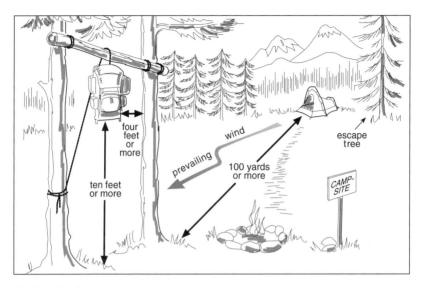

Guidelines for food storage in bear country

upwind. Whistling is not recommended because you may unwittingly sound like another animal and actually attract a bear!

- **Travel in groups of five or more.** Large parties are safer because they make more noise and are better able to effect a rescue in case of an emergency. Do not hike alone or allow children to be separated from the group.
- **Don't hike at night.** Bears travel and feed primarily at night. Plan your day so that your hiking is complete by dusk. Poor light increases your chances of surprising a bear.
- **Avoid carcasses.** Don't approach a dead elk, bison, or any other animal carcass. A bear may be out of sight guarding its food. Stop if you smell rotting meat while hiking. Other signs of carcasses include concentrations of ravens and/or coyotes. Never camp near a carcass. For the protection of others, report any dead animal near a trail or campsite to the nearest ranger station.
- **Avoid smelly food.** Don't bring odorous food into the backcountry. Bears have a legendary sense of smell and can even smell tuna in an unopened can! While camping, (1) keep a clean camp, (2) use food poles where provided, (3) don't sleep in the same clothes worn while cooking, (4) never store food or eat in your tent, (5) store food in airtight containers, (6) keep your sleeping area at least 100 yards from your cooking and food storage area, (7) bring at least fifty feet of rope

to hang food, (8) hang food ten feet off the ground and four feet out from tree trunks, and (9) don't bring large containers such as ice chests unless you're prepared to hang them. Also avoid wearing fragrant deodorants, sunscreens, or perfumes.

Despite all the above precautions, you might still see a bear. In that event, the NPS recommends the following:

- **If you see a bear at a distance:** Keep out of sight and detour as far away as possible. *Do not run.* By running, you will attract the attention of the bear, and you might be pursued. *You cannot outrun a bear.* Bears can sprint up to forty miles per hour. If the bear sees you but is still quite a distance away, you can climb a tree if you can climb at least fifteen feet up and preferably higher. Remember that all black bears, grizzly cubs, and even some adult grizzlies can climb trees if the spacing of the branches is right.

- **If you encounter a bear at close range:** Back away slowly, dropping gear or clothing if possible. Talk quietly to the bear. Do not run or make sudden movements. Avoid looking directly at the bear. Move your arms up and down slowly at your sides. Be prepared for a charge.

- **If a bear charges:** Freeze, never run. Many charges are "bluff charges." Bears may charge and then veer off or stop at the last second. If the bear does not stop, *play dead.* Drop to the ground, lift your legs to your chest, clasp the back of your neck, and protect your head. Your pack will shield your body. Bears have been known to inflict only minor injuries under these circumstances. Lie still and silent, for resistance would be useless. Be sure the bear is gone before moving.

- **Night attacks in your tent:** In this instance, *be aggressive and defend yourself. Do not play dead!* The bear in this situation is being predatory, so you must let the bear know that you are not easy prey. If the "prey" is too troublesome, the bear will give up. Develop a course of action with others in your party should this rare situation arise.

- **If you observe a bear prowling around the perimeter of your campsite:** Do not go to sleep. Climb a tree, if possible, and be prepared to stay in the tree until daylight. Then hike back to the trailhead and report the incident to a ranger immediately so that the campsite can be closed.

Lastly, for the safety of all park visitors, report all bear sightings and bear signs (scat, tracks, fresh carcasses) to the nearest park ranger.

Chemical bear repellents: Some professionals carry aerosol canisters of capsaicin, an irritant made from cayenne pepper. Tests have shown that when sprayed in the eyes, a bear will immediately retreat. This is not, by any means, a foolproof solution to bear encounters. Bears are highly unpredictable, and it is possible that spraying could incite a more aggressive attack. In addition, the spray has a very limited range, is subject to wind conditions, and must be aimed accurately in a moment of intense stress. If you're considering carrying a canister, read all warnings and practice before setting out.

Wildlife

Keep a safe distance from all wildlife. Park regulations prohibit approaching within 25 yards of wildlife and within 100 yards of bears. All park animals are unpredictable and dangerous. Bison are especially aggressive. Each year, bison inflict severe injuries on visitors who approach too closely. Be wary of any large animal with young. Elk, moose, and deer may also show aggression and cause grave injury during their mating seasons. In addition, for your safety, drive defensively on park roads, particularly between dusk and dawn. Large animals, especially bison, also use the roadways.

Thermal Features

Stay on boardwalks and designated trails when viewing thermal features. The crust around these features may be thin, and a misstep could plunge you into boiling water. Also, use extreme caution when frost glazes wooden boardwalks, for they become slippery.

Never swim in thermal pools or streams whose waters flow entirely from a thermal spring. It is illegal and hazardous. In addition, many thermal springs and pools are extremely acidic or alkaline. Each year some visitors are badly burned. Thermal waters may also contain organisms known to cause infections and/or amoebic meningitis, which can be fatal.

Hypothermia

To avoid hypothermia, hikers must always be prepared for sudden mountain storms. Hypothermia is the lowering of the body's core temperature to a degree sufficient to cause illness. The condition is serious and sometimes fatal. Signs of mild hypothermia include complaints of coldness, shivering, loss of coordination, and apathy. More severe hypothermia causes mental confusion, uncontrollable shivering, slurred speech, and a core temperature low enough to cause permanent damage or death.

Because small bodies lose heat more rapidly than large ones, children are more vulnerable to hypothermia than adults. Early signs of hypothermia in children may be crankiness and fussiness, which can also be caused by ordinary fatigue. A child might not even realize he or she is cold until serious shivering begins. Hikers, especially children, can become hypothermic when temperatures are well above freezing. Wind chill is a critical, and often over-looked, cause of hypothermia.

Parents can guard against dangerous chills by observing the following precautions:

- Carry an adequate supply of warm clothing, including wool sweaters, socks, gloves, and hats to insulate against heat loss. Gloves, hats, and scarves are particularly effective because they protect hands, heads, and necks—areas that are especially sensitive to heat loss. Carry these items even when the weather looks warm and sunny, especially at or above tree line. On cool rainy days, avoid cotton clothing, which is not warm when wet and wicks warmth away from the body.
- Dress in layers and remove unneeded layers to prevent excessive sweating, which lowers body temperature through evaporation. Parents must react quickly to temperature changes, whether occasioned by weather or changes in activity levels.
- Put on raingear *before* you get wet, and put on warm clothes before shivering begins.
- Avoid excessive exposure to wind and rain. *Always* carry raingear.
- Carry food high in carbohydrates and sugar that the body can quickly convert to heat.
- Carry warm liquids, such as hot cocoa, when hiking in cold weather.
- Avoid resting against ice, snow, or cold rocks, which draw heat away from the body. Place an insulating barrier, such as a foam pad, between the body and cold surfaces.
- Cover the mouth with a wool scarf to warm air entering the lungs.

If a member of your group shows signs of hypothermia, stop and take immediate steps to warm the person. Promptness is critical when treating hypothermia in children. Add layers of clothing. Replace wet clothes with dry ones. If possible, administer warm liquids or food. If necessary, build a small fire to warm the victim and dry wet clothing. Holding a cold child close to your body while wrapping a parka or blanket around the two of you is particularly effective. Crawling into a sleeping bag with the victim is recommended for cases that do not respond readily to other treatment.

Heat-Related Illness and Sun Exposure

Hiking, biking, or paddling at high altitudes, in warm weather, or in the open sun can cause excessive loss of water and salts (electrolytes). Failure to replace water and electrolytes can lead to dehydration, heat exhaustion, or even heat stroke. To prevent heat-related illnesses, consume adequate amounts of water and electrolytes. Avoid salt tablets in favor of salted snacks and liquids, which

Girl and horse, Yellowstone National Park

you should carry in amounts greater than you are likely to need. Flavored powders containing electrolytes may be added to water to replace those lost through perspiration. Remember that thirst is not a reliable indicator of the need for water. Schedule regular water stops to ensure against dehydration.

Precautions against overexposure to the sun are necessary in any season. During the dry, sunny summers, it is particularly important to avoid excessive exposure, especially on summit hikes. Harmful ultraviolet radiation increases with altitude. Also take additional precautions when in or near lakes, for radiation reflects off bodies of water.

Hazards of High Altitude—Mountain Sickness

Road elevations in Yellowstone National Park range from 5,300 to 8,860 feet. In Grand Teton National Park, most trails start around 6,800 feet. The decreased oxygen in the air at high altitudes can result in mountain sickness. Symptoms include headaches, fatigue, loss of appetite, weakness and dull pain in muscles, shortness of breath, nausea, and rapid heartbeat. If ignored or left untreated, mountain sickness can be fatal.

Mountain sickness strikes unpredictably. It affects both young and old, whether fit or not. Some people may experience no symptoms on one day but quickly develop them on another. In any case, the cardinal rule when the early symptoms of mountain sickness appear is to descend at once to a lower elevation.

To reduce the likelihood of mountain sickness, acclimate your family to high altitude gradually. At the beginning of your visit, choose trips at the lowest altitude, or at least those in the high country that are not strenuous. Because children are often inarticulate about their physical condition, be attuned to crankiness as a sign of altitude discomfort. If suspected, rest and retreat to lower elevations as soon as possible. To aid the family's acclimation, make sure everyone eats lightly, drinks plenty of fluids, gets sufficient rest, and limits physical activity for the first few days. Adults should limit their intake of alcohol at high elevations.

Lightning

Deep blue skies and low humidity are typical throughout the summer and fall in the Greater Yellowstone Ecosystem. The afternoons, however, are frequently interrupted by sudden thunderstorms, particularly in July and August. If you are hiking on an open ridge, above tree line, or in an open area with few trees, you

The Tetons

may be in danger of being hit by lightning, because lightning strikes at the highest object. If you do get caught in a thunderstorm, take the following precautions:

- Do *not* seek shelter under natural features, such as lone or tall trees, rock overhangs, or large boulders which project above their surroundings. Such large, exposed objects are more likely to be hit by lightning because of their height.
- Do *not* lie flat on the ground. To do so is to increase the body area exposed to electrical current in the event of a nearby strike.
- Assume the safest position—huddle on your knees with your head down. Crouch near medium-size boulders, if available.
- Safe places during thunderstorms include cars and large buildings, the larger, the better.
- Do *not* seek shelter in a tent because its metal rods conduct electricity. For the same reason, do not wear a metal-frame backpack during a lightning storm.
- Keep away from puddles, streams, and other bodies of water, because water conducts electricity.
- Do *not* remain on or next to a horse. Sitting on a horse increases your height; standing next to a horse gives lightning a larger target.
- If you are retreating to safety during a storm, stay as low as possible, remove children from back carriers, and walk with your legs wide apart.
- If you are boating, return to shore immediately.

Be aware of the fickleness of mountain weather. Storms can approach extremely rapidly. If you see a storm, the most prudent course is to retreat at once to a safe area. Don't proceed to a summit if you hear or see signs of an electrical storm.

Drinking Water—Giardiasis Prevention

Always carry a large quantity of safe drinking water—at least one quart per person. It is *not* safe to drink from any of the lakes and streams in the parks. The waters may be infested with *giardia,* a parasite that wreaks havoc in the human digestive system. *Giardia* infestation is caused when mammals such as muskrats defecate in or near the water, or when water has been contaminated by the careless disposal of human waste. Symptoms of giardiasis include diarrhea, abdominal distention, gas, and cramps, appearing seven to ten days after infection. If you suffer these symptoms, it is necessary to obtain treatment from a physician.

To purify water, boil it for three to six minutes. You may also disinfect the water chemically or by filtration, but these methods have not been proven to be as effective as heat. All water that might be swallowed must be treated, including water used for cooking, cleaning dishes, and brushing teeth.

To help prevent the spread of giardiasis and other harmful diseases, dig temporary latrines at least eight inches deep, eight to ten inches wide, and 200 feet away from water sources, trails, and campsites. After use, fill the hole with loose soil and tap down lightly. Do not bury the paper; pack it out. Of course, campers should wash hands thoroughly after use of the latrine. Parents should teach children safe toileting practices to protect their health and to keep lakes, streams, and rivers clean.

Ticks

Ticks can transmit Lyme disease. The symptoms of Lyme disease in advanced cases are severe, including arthritis, meningitis, neurological problems, and cardiac symptoms. These symptoms can occur a few weeks to over a year after the tick bite. Early signs can include a rash around the infected tick bite and flu-like symptoms. Timely diagnosis and treatment can cure or lessen the severity of the disease. If you or your family experiences these symptoms after a tick bite, immediately contact your physician.

Although there have been very few tick-related illnesses reported in Yellowstone and Grand Teton National Parks, it is prudent to take the following precautions:

- Use an insect repellent containing DEET or permethrin; spray on shoes and clothing, especially socks, pant legs and cuffs, and shirt sleeves and cuffs.
- Avoid direct application of DEET to the skin, for this potentially harmful chemical is easily absorbed. DEET can also damage rayon, acetate, and spandex, but is safe on nylon, cotton, and wool. When buying DEET, choose a formula containing no more than 35 percent DEET. Tests have shown that this amount provides as much protection as formulas containing higher concentrations. In addition, there are several repellents formulated especially for children.
- Tuck pants into boots, and button cuffs and collars.
- Wear light-colored clothing to spot ticks more easily.
- Check frequently for ticks on skin, scalp, and clothing. This may be done on rest breaks while hiking. Ticks often spend many hours on a body before they transmit the virus, so there is no need to panic if you find a tick. Infection can, nevertheless, be transmitted soon after the tick attaches, so check regularly.
- Use caution when visiting prime tick habitats: grassy, brushy, low elevation areas (4,000 to 6,500 feet) from mid-March until mid-July.

If you should discover a tick, remove it using tweezers, pulling it straight out. It is important to remove all head and mouth parts to prevent infection.

After removal, wash the area with soap and water. Even though ticks are rare in late summer and fall, you should still check your family regularly.

Snowfields, Ice Fields, Streams, and Waterfalls

Be extremely cautious when traveling over snow or ice. Snow and ice fields may persist in both parks until late summer at higher elevations. Never venture near the edge of snow or ice slopes or cornices. These areas can be treacherous and unstable. If you are hiking at high altitudes, check with rangers for snow conditions. If you do venture into areas where snow remains, be prepared with the necessary gear, such as crampons, ropes, and ice axes.

Streams and rivers can also be dangerous. The current of even small streams can be strong, especially in spring and early summer and particularly for children. Take appropriate precautions when crossing streams. Take the time to walk up- and downstream to find the safest place to ford. Hold hands or interlock arms when crossing, and undo the waist and chest straps of all packs. Never allow children to play unsupervised on stream banks. The frigid temperatures of snow- and groundwater-fed streams quickly disable even good swimmers.

The parks' waterfalls also present significant hazards. Slick rocks and steep drop-offs near waterfalls warrant an extra-close watch on children.

Falling Trees

The 1988 Yellowstone fires left many areas with standing dead trees. These trees may fall with little warning. In such areas, hike cautiously, be alert for falling trees, and don't stop to rest beneath a burned snag. If high winds develop, leave a burned area immediately, if possible.

Lost and Found

The parks' trails are generally well-marked and easy to follow. In Yellowstone, at frequent intervals along each trail, the NPS has nailed square orange metal markers to trailside trees. As an extra precaution, always carry current topographic maps for the area in which you are hiking. Visitor centers and local outdoor supply stores sell a variety of maps, including United States Geological Survey (USGS) maps. These are particularly useful because they show terrain and elevation by means of contour lines. If you have old maps, make sure they are up to date. Finally, buy waterproof maps, or carry maps in a waterproof pouch.

Also, carry a reliable compass and know how to use it in conjunction with your topographic map. If you don't feel confident, check with outing clubs in your area for instruction. Good books providing instruction in compass use are also available.

Signing the trail register, Yellowstone National Park

Children are particularly vulnerable to getting lost and are less able to care for themselves if they do. When hiking or biking, do not let children stray from your sight. Take the following preventive measures to guard against potentially traumatic or dangerous situations:

- Teach children to stay with the group.
- Instruct children never to leave designated trails.
- Give children whistles, with strict instructions to use the whistles only when lost.
- Instruct children to remain in one place if they become lost. That way, they can be found more easily.
- If children must move while lost, teach them how to build "ducks" by placing a smaller stone on top of a larger stone. By leaving a trail of ducks, the children will more easily be found.

Sign In, Please

In Yellowstone National Park, hikers should sign in at the trail register found at the beginning of each backcountry trail. In the event of an emergency, the date and time of your departure and your stated destination is critical information for park rangers.

Rattlesnakes

The only poisonous snake inhabiting the parks is the prairie rattlesnake occasionally found in the northwest corner of Yellowstone, near Gardiner, Montana. The snake can reach four feet long and has dark splotches on a brownish background with a rattle on its tail. Although certainly poisonous, its poison is rarely fatal to adults. The prairie rattlesnake usually inhabits cliffs or rocky outcrops, but it is uncommon in Yellowstone. Report sightings to the nearest ranger station.

The snakes most likely to be seen in the two parks are the rubber boa (brown with a yellow belly), the wandering garter (brownish green with three longitudinal stripes), and the valley garter snake (bright yellow and red lateral stripes with dark head). All are harmless to humans and usually measure less than two and a half feet long.

First-Aid Kit

Carry a first-aid kit on *every* outing. Commercially packaged kits are available in convenient sizes. If you purchase one, check its contents against the following list and supplement if necessary. To make your own first-aid kit, simply purchase the items listed below and place them in a nylon stuff bag, zippered container, or aluminum box.

- Adhesive bandage strips: Bring an abundant supply; their psychological value to children cannot be underestimated.
- Butterfly bandages for minor lacerations
- Sterile gauze pads (four by four inches) for larger wounds
- Adhesive tape to attach dressings
- Antibiotic ointment to treat wounds and cuts
- Moleskin for blisters
- Triangle bandages for slings
- Athletic tape for multiple uses
- Children's pain reliever
- Adult pain reliever
- Alcohol pads to cleanse skin
- Elastic bandage for sprains
- Knife with scissors and tweezers: Tweezers are needed to remove ticks and splinters.
- Space blanket for emergency warmth
- First-aid instruction booklet

CHECKLIST FOR SAFE HIKING
The Ten "Plus" Essentials

Use the following checklist before departing on each of your outings. It includes the Ten Essentials, a systems approach to safety compiled by The Mountaineers, and adds a few extra essentials specific to the needs of children. Bringing the following items prepares you for emergencies.

1. Navigation (map and compass). Carry a current map in a waterproof case, and know how to use your compass.
2. Sun protection (sunglasses and sunscreen). Hats with visors offer protection for youngsters too young to wear sunglasses.
3. Insulation (extra clothing). The extra weight ensures against cold, cranky children and hypothermia. A space blanket is also a useful and lightweight addition.
4. Illumination (headlamp or flashlight). A flashlight is needed to negotiate trails at night or to prepare a camp at unexpected hours.
5. First-aid supplies. Indispensable; see preceding list.
6. Fire (firestarter and matches/lighter). In an emergency, you may need to make a fire for warmth or for signaling. Containers for matches are available at outdoor supply stores or use a 35mm film canister.
7. Repair kit and tools (including knife). A knife has multiple uses in emergency situations.

8. Nutrition (extra food). Extra food is useful as a hiking incentive and essential in emergencies.
9. Hydration (extra water). An ample supply of water or sport drinks is the most important "essential" due to the high altitude and low humidity of the GYE.
10. Emergency shelter. Snowstorms and hailstorms can occur in *any* season. Mylar or kelvalite plastic blankets (space blankets), ultra-light tarps, or bivvy sacks, along with rope or duct tape, can provide temporary shelter.
11. Whistles. These are to be used only in the event children become lost.
12. Water purification tablets. The tablets ensure a source of emergency drinking water.
13. Bike repair kit. A necessary item for bicyclists.
14. Bike helmets. One for each rider and passenger.
15. Personal flotation devices. One for each passenger.
16. Small roll of duct tape. Great for repairing backbacks and boots and for making temporary splints.
17. Small mirror. For signaling in emergencies.

Frolicking in String Lake, Grand Teton National Park

A NOTE ABOUT SAFETY

Safety is an important concern in all outdoor activities. No guidebook can alert you to every hazard or anticipate the limitations of every reader. Therefore, the descriptions of roads, trails, routes, and natural features in this book are not representations that a particular place or excursion will be safe for your party. When you follow any of the routes described in this book, you assume responsibility for your own safety. Under normal conditions, such excursions require the usual attention to traffic, road and trail conditions, weather, terrain, the capabilities of your party, and other factors. Keeping informed on current conditions and exercising common sense are the keys to a safe, enjoyable outing.

—*The Mountaineers*

Opposite: Jumping for joy in the Tetons

CHAPTER I

YELLOWSTONE AND GRAND TETON NATIONAL PARKS
AN OVERVIEW

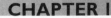

THE GREATER YELLOWSTONE ECOSYSTEM

Yellowstone National Park is the second-largest national park in the continental United States. At nearly 3,500 square miles, it exceeds the size of Rhode Island and Delaware combined. Just to the south, Grand Teton National Park encompasses another 40 miles of alpine peaks. Together, the parks provide a tremendous amount of wilderness to explore.

Yet to understand these wild lands, it is necessary to grasp a still larger picture. Grand Teton and Yellowstone constitute the heart of the Greater Yellowstone Ecosystem (GYE), the largest relatively intact temperate ecosystem on earth. Within the borders of the GYE are two national parks, seven national forests, three national wildlife refuges, and over 1 million acres of privately owned land. The GYE is more than six times the size of Yellowstone itself.

The scope of the GYE is most easily grasped by imagining an aerial view of the Yellowstone region. From the air, the GYE is discernable as an island of green; a high, rolling, forested plateau bordered by spectacular mountains and surrounded by arid plains and basins. Described another way, the GYE encompasses the migration routes and winter ranges of the greater Yellowstone ungulates (elk, bison, deer, antelope, bighorn sheep), the reaches of Yellowstone's extensive geothermal system, and the watersheds of the three major rivers born in the mountains of Yellowstone.

What is the importance of the GYE? The very health of the parks' wildlife, rivers, and geothermal features depends on the protection of the greater ecosystem. In the area surrounding the GYE, development has fundamentally changed the land, so that little of the original flora and fauna remains. Within the GYE, however, most of the plants and animals found in pre-Columbian times still survive. The GYE is one of the last strongholds in the Lower 48 for numerous species listed as threatened and endangered, including the grizzly bear, the peregrine falcon, the whooping crane, and the bald eagle.

Yet every year since 1999, the National Parks Conservation Association has placed Yellowstone National Park on its annual list of America's ten most endangered parks. Timber harvesting, oil and gas development, forest road building, hard rock mining, recreation development, and rural subdivisions endanger water quality, wildlife habitat, and scenic values. As you travel through the parks, you will hear and read much about the GYE. Hiking, biking, and paddling take you seamlessly from national park, to national forest, to private land, to national wildlife refuge. The realization that all these lands are integrally connected and equally worthy of protection is the essence of the GYE. The parks' wildlife, including its trout, grizzlies, eagles, and bison cannot survive on islands of preservation. Maintenance of the age-old ecosystem is the key to their survival, and it must be the goal of all who love this region.

YELLOWSTONE NATIONAL PARK

In the summer of 1988, extraordinary drought conditions and gale-force winds fueled ferocious fires in Yellowstone. Despite $120 million spent to stop the fires, six uncontrollable blazes swept through almost 50 percent of the park. Yet the fires' effect was not catastrophic. The fires burned in a mosaic pattern, taking patches of forest in some places but leaving adjacent acres untouched. Soil was sterilized in less than 1 percent of the forests burned. Almost half of the total 1.1 million acres burned endured only surface burn, in which only the understory was consumed. By the spring of 1989, dramatic rejuvenation had already begun. Green grasses and bright pink fireweed blanketed the fire-touched areas. Today, post-fire trees stand ten feet high and charred snags shine silver in the sun. Visitors enjoy panoramic vistas not seen in a century and the open forests greatly increase your chance of seeing wildlife.

Yellowstone's wildlife escaped relatively unscathed. Less than 1 percent of the park's large animals were killed by the fires. In fact, bison and elk ignored the inferno, grazing as close as 50 yards to the burning forest. The fires also had positive effects. Post-fire plant growth today provides richer grazing and browsing for the park's ungulates. Birds, such as woodpeckers and mountain bluebirds, are thriving, for burned snags provide homes and insects. In addition, the fires' removal of forest debris and creation of new meadows aid birds of prey, such as eagles, hawks, and owls, and larger predators, such as grizzlies. In general, experts believe that plant and animal diversity will noticeably increase in the quarter century following the fire.

Two-thirds of the earth's geothermal features are found in Yellowstone National Park. While the earth's molten rock layer (magma) normally lies 6 miles beneath the surface, in Yellowstone, the magma sits only 3 miles deep (In places, it is only 1 mile beneath the surface.) This molten rock heats water from rain and snow that seeps through fissures in the subsurface rock. The magma's heat turns the water to steam, and a buildup of pressure eventually brings it to the surface. The result is a wondrous collection of over ten thousand colorful hot springs, hissing fumaroles, roiling mud pots, and more than two hundred explosive geysers. Many are easily observed from boardwalks at the Upper, Middle, and Lower Geyser Basins, at beautiful Norris Geyser Basin, at Mammoth Hot Springs, and on backcountry trails.

One of the most awesome but underrated sights in Yellowstone National Park is the Grand Canyon of the Yellowstone River. Its yellow, orange, and pink rock walls rise 1,200 vertical feet above the river's whitewater. Two magnificent waterfalls roar at its head. The larger of the two, the Lower Falls, stands almost three times as tall as Niagara Falls. Rock pinnacles on the canyon walls support osprey nests five feet in diameter. From the riverbanks, clouds

Fishing on Yellowstone Lake

of steam rise from thermal activity beneath the canyon floors. This fascinating place can be experienced from a variety of vantage points and trails.

Yellowstone has been called America's Serengeti for its tens of thousands of highly visible elk, bison, antelope, moose, and deer. Although bears no longer beg along the roads, hundreds of grizzlies and black bears roam the backcountry. Since their historic reintroduction in 1995, wolves also make up a small but thriving population in Yellowstone! Nowhere else in the continental United States is wildlife so awesome and visible.

GRAND TETON NATIONAL PARK

Author-naturalist Gary Ferguson wrote that the Tetons "are to mountains what the Grand Canyon is to gorges; what Chartres is to cathedrals; what dark chocolate is to desserts." Ferguson aptly describes the awesome sweep of glistening rock rising 7,000 feet from the valley floor in a singular, magnificent gesture, wholly without foothills. This triumphant uplift is the result of a fault block, wherein enormous rock masses rose and slipped along a fault line on the eastern base of the Teton Range.

The movement of glaciers over the course of 200,000 years sculpted the Teton peaks into the jagged mountains we admire today. During the last Ice Age, approximately 10,000 years ago, immense tongues of ice, thousands of feet high, slid from its peaks, tearing knife-edge ridges and grinding U-shaped canyons. The glaciers pushed thousands of tons of debris down to the base of the range. When the glaciers melted, lakes were created at the foot of the mountains. These lakes reflect in heartbreaking perfection the chiseled peaks towering above them. Glaciers still hang high above the valley. The scene is postcard-perfect.

In the brief Teton summer, magnificent gardens of wildflowers grace the valley, mountainsides, and alpine meadows of the park. Hikers find fields of lavender lupine and rock gardens graced with electric-blue alpine forget-me-nots. Glorious flowers are a fine reward for hiking the park's steep trails.

PLANNING YOUR TRIP

Because of the overwhelming number of park visitors each summer (over 4 million), it is necessary to make camping and lodging reservations as early as possible.

Preplanning Is Essential

It is not unusual to make reservations for park accommodations one year in advance. For lodging in Grand Teton and Yellowstone, it is best to firm up your plans at least six months prior to arrival. Reservations are also accepted for popular activities such as horseback riding and Western cookouts.

Backpackers must plan ahead also. Grand Teton National Park accepts requests (free of charge) for summer backcountry campsites from January through May. For particularly accessible and attractive sites, backpackers must get their requests in early. Backpackers in Yellowstone may reserve campsites beginning on April 1 for that calendar year.

To plan your visit, read the following sections and decide when, how, and where you want to go. For the most complete and up-to-date information on both parks, consult their websites at *www.nps.gov/yell* (Yellowstone) and *www.nps.gov/grte* (Grand Teton). You can also write or call both parks to request maps and information. Contact the park concessionaires for information on lodging and activities. Request information from outfitters if you're interested in specialty trips, such as kayaking or horseback-riding overnights. Call for catalogs about organized backpacking trips, nature classes, or children's science camps. If you're planning to fly, contact airlines early to secure the dates you want. Flights are especially limited to Jackson, so reservations must be made far in advance.

If all this planning is distasteful, it is, of course, still possible to arrive at a park entrance gate with only a packed car and an open mind. Several good campgrounds are still first-come, first-served, and there are often cancellations at park lodging. This approach can work if you have a lot of time to explore the region and are highly flexible. My recommendation, however, is to plan at least part of your stay so that you will not be shut out of an area you really want to see.

Prepping the Kids

Before you head for the park, get the kids *psyched*. To jump-start your trip, visit Yellowstone's interactive website for children at *www.nps.gov/yell/kidstuff/index.htm*. Yellowstone's Kidsite offers activities for children of all ages, including match games, online coloring books, an animal alphabet book (with sound effects), and, for older children, quizzes, puzzles, scavenger hunts, and electronic "field trips" (Windows into Wonderland). It's a fabulous site that provides a fun and educational introduction. Grand Teton has a good but less-elaborate website for kids and parents at *www.nps.gov/grte/educ/educ.htm*. Another way to ready the kids is to order ahead some games and guidebooks. Log on to the websites for the Yellowstone Association *(www.yellowstoneassociation.org)* or the Grand Teton Natural History Association *(www.grandtetonpark.org)* to find age-appropriate books, games, and even CDs for traveling. Be creative; try wilderness survival-skills knowledge cards or animal track cards. Lastly, most kids will enjoy packing a light backpack with hiking "essentials." Load the backpack with a compass; camera; sketchbook; magnifying glass; child's field guide to trees, flowers, birds, or animals (or even scat!); snacks; water bottle; and binoculars. When the children earn their Junior Ranger badges, they can proudly display them on their packs.

IMPORTANT CONTACT INFORMATION

Yellowstone National Park Visitor Information
  (307) 344-7381; *www.nps.gov/yell*
Yellowstone Lodging and Activities Information
  (307) 344-7311; *www.travelyellowstone.com*
Yellostone Campground Information
  (307) 344-7311; *www.nps.gov/yell/planvisit/services/campgrnd.htm*
Grand Teton National Park Visitor Information
  (307) 739-3600; *www.nps.gov/grte*
Grand Teton Lodging and Activities Information
  (307) 543-2811; *www.gtlc.com*
Grand Teton Campground Information
  (307) 739-3603; *www.nps.gov/grte*

HOW TO GET THERE

By car: Yellowstone National Park has five entrances. The North Entrance is reached via US 89 from Gardiner, MT (165 miles from Billings and 79 miles from Bozeman, MT); the Northeast Entrance is reached via US 212 from Silver Gate and Cooke City (127 miles from Billings, MT; 68 miles from Cody, WY); the East Entrance is accessed via US 14-16-20 (53 miles from Cody, WY); the South Entrance is reached via US 89-191-287 from Flagg Ranch, WY (56 miles from Jackson, WY); and the West Entrance is reached via US 20 from West Yellowstone, MT (90 miles from Bozeman, MT). In winter, only the North Entrance is open to automobile use. Because of snow, the other four entrances are closed to automobile traffic from October 31 to May 1.

Grand Teton National Park can be reached from the north by traveling south 8 miles on US 89-191-287 from Yellowstone's South Entrance. Its East Entrance at Moran Junction is reached by driving west approximately 60 miles on US 26/287 from Dubois, WY. Its South Entrance at Moose Junction (Park Headquarters) is reached by driving north 12 miles from Jackson, WY, on US 89-191-287.

By air: If your initial destination is Yellowstone National Park, daily air service is available to the following cities: Bozeman, MT (79 miles from the North Entrance); Billings, MT (127 miles from the Northeast Entrance); and Cody, WY (53 miles from the East Entrance). Limited summer air service is also available to West Yellowstone, MT, just outside the West Entrance. If your destination is Grand Teton National Park, daily air service is available to Jackson Hole Airport, located within Grand Teton National Park, 10 miles north of the town of Jackson, WY. Service is also available to Idaho Falls on the west slope of the Tetons, about 100 miles from Grand Teton's Park Headquarters in Moose, WY.

By bus: Greyhound Lines service Bozeman, Livingston, and West Yellowstone, MT. From these cities, Karst Stage offers connecting service to Yellowstone's North and West Entrances. Powder River Transportation offers service to the East Entrance from Cody, WY. Gray Line Tours services Yellowstone's South Entrance and Grand Teton National Park from Jackson, WY, (307) 733-4325. Yellowstone Park Co. also services Livingston and Cooke City, MT, and Grand Teton National Park. Xanterra Parks and Resorts offers bus tours of Yellowstone National Park from locations within the park, (307) 344-7311. Buffalo Bus Lines offers tours from West Yellowstone, (800) 742-0665.

Rental cars: Rental cars are available at airports and in major towns near both parks.

WHEN TO GO

Spring (April through June): Spring visitors experience cool, sometimes cold, wet, and always unpredictable weather. Heavy snows can occur even in May and early June. Although the weather may be less than ideal, spring is a time to experience the parks' beauty in relative solitude. Runoff dramatically

Mount Moran above Colter Bay, Grand Teton National Park

swells rivers and waterfalls. Wildlife viewing is prime: large mammals are in the valleys, migratory birds are just returning, bears are foraging, and mule deer, elk, pronghorn, and bison are bearing their young. In spring, you have the best chance of sighting wolves and grizzly bears in Yellowstone's Lamar Valley. In both parks, baby bison and elk are plentiful and easily seen. In spring, the animals are more visible during daylight hours as they spend their days attempting to regain the weight lost over the long winter. In Grand Teton, bird-watchers can watch the male sage grouse perform its spectacular courtship dance in sagebrush meadows. Spring is also the prime time to fish for mackinaw at Jackson Lake. In June at lower elevations, flowers bloom gloriously.

In very early spring (mid-March through the third week in April), most Yellowstone roads are completely closed. However, the park does allow nonmotorized traffic between the West Entrance in West Yellowstone and Mammoth Hot Springs. Thus, there is a window of opportunity to enjoy biking on a road free of all traffic (except for the occasional park vehicle). If you plan to take advantage of this unique opportunity, verify these weather-dependent road openings by calling (307) 344-2109 or (307) 344-7381. Early season bike riding is also available in Grand Teton National Park. By March the park clears the snow from the road from Moose Junction to Jenny Lake. Weather-permitting, this is an exquisite ride, free of all car traffic in the month of April.

Because of persistent snow and/or soggy trails, spring hiking is generally limited to trails at lower elevations. The trails around Mammoth Hot Springs are the most accessible. Winter conditions prevail above 6,500 feet through May and persist above 8,500 feet through June. Daytime temperatures average in the 50s to 60s at lower elevations, with nighttime lows in the 30s. Campers should not be surprised to see a dusting of snow on the ground and frost on their cars in the morning. Periods of heavy rain are likely.

Summer (July through August): This is the tourist season, and visitors must be prepared to share the parks' treasures. Hiking begins in earnest, along with peak mosquito season. Elk and moose retreat to forests and higher ground to escape the heat, bugs, and tourists. A profusion of flowers graces the meadows.

In July, daytime high temperatures reach the 70s, although nights are still cold (15 to 40 degrees F), especially at higher elevations. Daytime temperatures in the valleys and in Jackson may climb into the 80s on sunny summer days. Mornings are often brilliant, with clear, bright blue skies. While thunderstorms threaten most afternoons, the sky generally clears after an hour or so. In early July, meadows and trails may still be wet.

In August, hiking is prime. The biting bugs retreat noticeably. Days are warm (65 to 80 degrees F), and nights are comfortably brisk, though sometimes cold (25 to 40 degrees F). Afternoon thunderstorms persist. Trails are drier in August than in July and are usually free of snow. Wildflowers bloom in alpine areas, and berries ripen throughout the parks.

It is important to remember that cold, wet weather can persist into July and August. While some park summers are dry and sunny, in other years, "summer" fails to arrive. The rule is to be prepared for severe conditions in any season.

Fall (September through October): Early autumn is exquisite, with excellent hiking conditions. Summer crowds are gone, and wildlife viewing peaks. Large animals return en masse to the valleys. In mid- to late September, elk are in their splendor performing their fascinating mating rituals. Valleys in Yellowstone are filled with bucks gathering their harems, jousting, bugling, and fighting. Ducks and geese fill the ponds. Aspen flash their gold, particularly in the Tetons. Fall may be the best time to view wildlife. The animals tend to be more active during the day as they work hard to fatten up before the arrival of winter. Days are often crisp and bright (40 to 45 degrees F), but noticeably shorter and cooler. Nights are cold (15 to 35 degrees F in September, 0 to 35 degrees F in October). Heavy snows are possible beginning in September, but more likely in October. Rain is common in both months. All roads in Yellowstone, except the North Entrance, generally close to all vehicular traffic the first week in November.

The Greater Yellowstone Ecosystem in Winter (December to mid-March)

Yellowstone National Park is pure magic in winter. Bison outnumber tourists, waterfalls are frozen in time, and geysers erupt in white steam against deep blue sky. Visitors disappear in warm sulfurous clouds of vapors only to reemerge moments later in the coldest, freshest, lung-stinging air they've ever breathed. It's a different park in winter and completely worth the difficult journey to get there. For hardy families who enjoy cross-country skiing or snowshoeing, this is the trip of a lifetime.

It is not, however, easy or inexpensive to enjoy Yellowstone in winter. The season runs roughly from early December to mid-March. There are two lodges open in the park, the Old Faithful Snow Lodge and the historic Mammoth Hot Springs Hotel. Visitors can drive to Mammoth via the North and Northeast Entrances, but the Old Faithful Snow Lodge is accessible only via snowcoach from Flagg Ranch (an hour ride), West Yellowstone, or Mammoth (at least three hours from each location) and by snowmobile. At Mammoth, the historic lodge offers hot tubs, ice skating, and a pianist in the elegant lobby. Temperatures are milder at Mammoth, and elk are plentiful. At the modern Old Faithful Snow Lodge, temperatures are lower due to the higher elevation and snow is more plentiful (averaging seventy-five inches). Most large ungulates have moved out of the area to lower elevations. The focus at the Snow Lodge is on skiing, snowshoeing, and snowmobiling. Trails through the Old Faithful Geyser Basin are out your front door, and wildlife viewing is superb. Despite snowmobile noise, the overwhelming beauty and unconquerable vastness and tranquility of this region clearly prevails. Both locations offer ranger walks and lectures. In addition, naturalist-led tours, including half-day wildlife tours, are available.

Those staying at the Old Faithful Snow Lodge have many great options for cross-country skiing: from the short Fern Cascades Trail (3 miles round trip) to the thrilling all-day, bison-filled tour of the Old Faithful Geyser Basin on the Upper Geyser Basin and Biscuit Basin Trail (6.8 miles round trip, Trip 27). Two trails a short distance from the Snow Lodge, Lone Star Geyser (4.6 miles round trip, Trip 28) and Fairy Falls (11 miles round trip, Trip 24), are also highly recommended. From the Snow Lodge, you can take a snowcoach to these and other trailheads for skiing and snowshoeing.

Winter visitors to Yellowstone must also experience Grand Teton National Park, for it is unforgettable as well. It is more accessible than Yellowstone, and visitors can easily drive from Jackson to the Grand Teton National Park ranger station at Moose and to nearby trailheads. Phenomenal cross-country skiing and snowshoeing awaits, absent the drone of the snowmobiles and with the addition of the occasional moose. Ranger-led hikes and programs are offered at the Moose Visitor Center. An average of four feet of snow covers the park each winter, opening up nearly endless terrain for skiing and snowshoeing. You can't beat the alpine scenery on the trail around Jenny Lake (5 to 8 miles round trip), and the rolling Taggart Lake Trail (5 miles round trip) offers pretty vistas amid tracks of snowshoe hare, moose, and coyote. Information on the park's winter activities, including ranger-led outings, can be obtained by calling (307) 739-3600. Cross-country skiers seeking groomed trails near Grand Teton National Park can find excellent trails at the Teton Pines Country Club, at Teton Village near the Granite Canyon Entrance Station, and at the Spring Creek Nordic Center just northwest of Jackson.

A winter trip to Yellowstone and Grand Teton can be as rugged or as pampered as you choose. The lodges in Yellowstone and in Jackson range from basic to downright luxurious. For very hardy souls, one campground is open in winter at Mammoth Hot Springs. For backpacking families, backcountry permits are required and may be obtained at ranger stations. Many businesses offer a variety of services, including snowcoach tours into Yellowstone and guided ski tours. Find a list at *www.nps.gov/yell/planvisit/services/wintbusn.htm*.

The controversy over snowmobile use in the parks is not over. The Park Service is still struggling with how to manage their use and balance the interests of wildlife and tourism. In 2004, the park implemented a three-year temporary plan. The plan allows 720 snowmobiles per day in Yellowstone and 140 snowmobiles per day in Grand Teton National Park and the John D. Rockefeller Jr. Memorial Parkway. The big change is that all snowmobiles must be commercially guided, and with minor exceptions, all snowmobiles are required to meet NPS "best available technology" requirements. For updates concerning this temporary plan, consult the Park Service website at *www.nps.gov /yell/planvisit/winteruse/index.htm*.

For families, there are other thrilling winter activities in the area, as well, and many are offered in the Jackson area. These include a horse-drawn sleigh ride through the National Elk Refuge, where 7,500 elk from the GYE spend the winter. In addition, there are opportunities to try dogsledding, an experience your family will never forget. For information on one-day and multiday trips, contact Jackson Hole Iditarod, (307) 733-7388; Jackson Hole's Continental Dogsled Adventures, (800) 531-MUSH; *www.dogsledadventures.com;* or Saddlehorn Activity Center Dogsledding, (307) 739-2710. The drawback is the high price of the experience. Finally, of course, there is world-class downhill skiing at the Jackson Hole and Grand Targhee Ski Resorts.

Any way you do it, you must be aware of the serious dangers inherent in a winter visit to the parks. Visitors may encounter severe cold, blizzards, and avalanches. At Old Faithful, the average temperature in January is 12 degrees F, and it has been as low as -66 degrees F. Awareness and education are the keys to a safe trip. Skiers and snowshoers must give bison wide berth, keep a healthy distance from thermal features, prepare for weather extremes, and exercise great caution when traversing frozen water (thermal features thin the ice unevenly). Read up on winter hazards, particularly avalanches and hypothermia before your trip. Lastly, before departing on any excursion, be sure to inform someone where you are going and your estimated time of return.

Yellowstone winters are even more dangerous for wildlife. No animal should be made to waste precious energy avoiding humans, particularly in winter. If you cause an animal to flee, that animal burns calories that might mean the balance between life and death. Check at park visitor centers for information about winter closures to protect critical winter wildlife habitat. Closures are most likely at Grand Teton National Park to protect moose.

Several good books on winter in the Greater Yellowstone Region are listed in Appendix A. These will fill you with inspiration for your winter visit.

WHERE TO STAY

From rustic cabins to spas, there are a multitude of options for lodging in and around the parks.

Park Lodging

There are many advantages to staying within the parks. Driving time is reduced and park programs, campfire talks, and ranger-led hikes are easily attended. Wildlife viewing is more fruitful, since dawn and dusk are the most rewarding viewing times. Park sunrises and sunsets are spectacular, whether on Jackson Lake, atop Signal Mountain, on the rim of the Grand Canyon, or on magnificent Yellowstone Lake.

Within the parks, accommodations of all kinds are available, from suites at historic inns to bare-bones tent shelters. Cabins may be rented at several locations. Cabins offer a rustic, historic, inexpensive, and yet comfortable experience for noncamping families and are especially enjoyed by children. Both Roosevelt Lodge Cabins in Yellowstone and Colter Bay Cabins in Grand Teton are located in particularly fine settings.

Yellowstone National Park

Yellowstone accommodations run the gamut from elegant to rustic. Consider your needs, pocketbook, and locational preference. For all accommodations, it is necessary to reserve well in advance by contacting Xanterra Parks and Resorts, Yellowstone National Park, WY 82190, (307) 344-7311, or *www.travelyellowstone.com.*

Lodging is available at all locations from mid-June until Labor Day. In spring and fall, the selection is more limited. In winter, only the Mammoth Hot Springs Hotel and Old Faithful Snow Lodge are open.

North Yellowstone

- **Mammoth Hot Springs Hotel and Cabins:** Modern hotel and cabins located at very busy Mammoth Hot Springs near Park Headquarters, Albright Visitor Center, and numerous stores and restaurants. Corral and guided trail rides nearby. NPS programs at Albright Visitor Center and Mammoth Campground as well as at Tower Campground, 18 miles to the east.
- **Roosevelt Lodge Cabins:** Rustic cabins (wood-burning stoves, no bath) located in quiet, historic setting near Tower Fall and the Lamar Valley. Small store and dining room. Corral with guided trail and stagecoach rides. NPS programs at nearby Tower and Mammoth Campgrounds. Excellent choice in spring and early summer when snow persists at higher elevations. Opportunities for observing wildlife (including wolves) are superb in the beautiful Lamar Valley.

Central Yellowstone

- **Canyon Lodge and Cabins:** Modern lodge and cabins located at scenic north rim of the Grand Canyon of the Yellowstone. Busy and congested complex includes stores, cafeteria, restaurants, post office, and Canyon Visitor Center. Located near wildlife-filled Hayden Valley. Corral with guided trail rides nearby. NPS programs at adjacent Canyon Campground and visitor center. Twelve miles from Norris Geyser Basin. Excellent hiking trails nearby.

South Yellowstone

- **Lake Yellowstone Hotel and Cabins and Lake Lodge Cabins:** Located on the scenic shore of Yellowstone Lake. Choose from elegant, historic Lake Yellowstone Hotel or rustic cabins adjacent to the hotel and lodge. Hotel offers formal dining room and snack bar; lodge provides a cafeteria. Near stores and visitor center at Fishing Bridge. Boat rentals and tours at nearby Bridge Bay Marina. NPS programs at Fishing Bridge Visitor Center and Bridge Bay Campground. Good fishing and superb hiking trails nearby.
- **Grant Village Motel:** Modern motel located on Yellowstone Lake. Sprawling complex includes Grant Village Visitor Center, stores, and restaurants. NPS programs at adjacent Grant Village Campground. Near West Thumb Geyser Basin. Good fishing nearby.
- **Old Faithful Inn, Old Faithful Lodge Cabins, and Old Faithful Snow Lodge:** Very busy complex located at Old Faithful (Upper Geyser Basin) includes Old Faithful Visitor Center, numerous stores, restaurants, and cafeteria. Accommodations range from the impressive, historic Old Faithful Inn to the Snow Lodge (renovated in 1999) and Cabins. Area is very congested in summer. NPS programs at Old Faithful Visitor Center and Madison Campground (16 miles north). Near Midway and Lower Geyser Basins and Firehole Canyon Drive swimming hole.

Grand Teton National Park

Grand Teton National Park also hosts a wide variety of accommodations. Beginning at the northern tip of the park just south of Yellowstone's South Entrance, find the newly constructed Flagg Ranch Resort offering lodge rooms, cabins, and a corral, open June to mid-October. Situated on the Snake River north of Jackson Lake, Flagg Ranch lacks the alpine scenery and proximity to excellent hiking that other locations offer. NPS programs are held at the Flagg Ranch Campground. For reservations, call (800) 443-2311, *www.flaggranch.com*.

For more classic Teton scenery, try beautiful Colter Bay located about 15 miles south of Flagg Ranch. Directly across Jackson Lake from magnificent Mount Moran, find the well-appointed Colter Bay Cabins near a marina, corral, and fine hiking trails. Cabins are open mid-May to late September. More rustic are the Colter Bay Tent Cabins, open early June to early September. These canvas-sided "cabins" have bunk beds, woodstoves, grills, and picnic tables. NPS programs are held at the adjacent Colter Bay Campground and Visitor Center as well as at the Indian Arts Museum. A few miles south, Jackson Lake Lodge offers top motel accommodations with a swimming pool, scenic views, good wildlife viewing, and restaurants, open late May to early October. Find NPS programs at nearby Colter Bay. Those staying at the Colter Bay Cabins and Tent Cabins also have use of the swimming pool at Jackson Lake Lodge. For reservations for all of the above, contact the Grand Teton Lodge Company, Grand Teton National Park, P.O. Box 240, Moran, WY 83013, (800) 628-9988 or (307) 543-2855; www.gtlc.com.

Signal Mountain Lodge is scenically located just south of Jackson Lake Lodge on Jackson Lake, about 15 miles north of park headquarters in Moose. The lodge offers motel accommodations, a restaurant, and a marina. NPS programs are held at the adjacent Signal Mountain Campground. Contact Signal Mountain Lodge at P.O. Box 50, Moran, WY, (307) 543-2831. Farther south, in an exclusive setting near world-renowned Jenny Lake, the Jenny Lake Lodge offers rustic elegance in elaborate cabins with formal dining, as well as a private corral. Open late May to early October. NPS programs at nearby Jenny Lake Campground. Call (800) 628-9988 for reservations. Lastly, just steps from Park Headquarters in Moose and a short drive away from superb trails, find Dornan's Spur Ranch Cabins set along the Snake River, near a small cluster of stores and restaurants, open year-round (www.dornans.com). NPS programs are at Moose Visitor Center and nearby Jenny Lake Campground. Call (307) 733-2522 for information.

CAMPGROUNDS

Camping in the parks is one of the best options for visiting families. The campgrounds give children maximum exposure to the outdoors, offer nightly ranger programs (many of which are geared to children), and provide everyone with the chance to stargaze the phenomenal Wyoming night sky.

Yellowstone National Park

There are twelve campgrounds in Yellowstone National Park, ranging from the gargantuan (420 sites) to the relatively intimate (29 sites). Advance reservations may be made at the five campgrounds (Bridge Bay, Canyon, Grant Village,

Campfire, Yellowstone National Park

Madison and Fishing Bridge RV Park) operated by Xanterra Parks and Resorts. To make reservations, call (307) 344-7311; write Xanterra Parks and Resorts, P.O. Box 165, Yellowstone National Park, WY 82190; or go online at *www.travelyellowstone.com/camping.* Same-day reservations can be made by calling the above number or by checking at a campground registration desk. All other campgrounds are operated by the NPS on a first-come, first-served basis. For these campgrounds, it is necessary to arrive as early as possible on the day you plan to camp. In July and August, many campgrounds are filled to capacity by mid-morning. Between June 15 and September 15, camping is limited to a maximum of fourteen days at all campgrounds.

For information about NPS campgrounds, call (307) 344-7381 or write NPS, Visitor Services Office, Yellowstone National Park, WY 82190, or visit *www.nps.gov/yell/pphtml/camping.html.* Yellowstone campgrounds are indicated on the park map at the beginning of this book and are described in the chart on the next page.

Campground	No. of sites	Open	Toilet	Showers/ Laundry	Dump station	Comments
North Yellowstone						
Mammoth*	85	Year-round	Flush	No	No	Open setting, little privacy
Indian Creek*	75	Early June–mid-Sept.	Pit	No	No	Some nice sites near river
Pebble Creek*	36	Mid-June–early Sept.	Pit	No	No	Near Northeast Entrance
Slough Creek*	29	Late May–late Oct.	Pit	No	No	Pretty creekside setting
Tower Falls*	32	Late May–mid-Sept.	Pit	No	No	Limited privacy
Central Yellowstone						
Norris*	119	Mid-May–mid-Sept.	Flush	No	No	Pretty sites near Gibbon River
Canyon Village**	280	Early June–early Sept.	Flush	Yes	Yes	Forest setting
Bridge Bay**	420	Late May–late Sept.	Flush	Yes	Yes	Very congested, little privacy
Fishing Bridge RV**	345	Mid-May–mid-Sept.	Flush	Yes	Sewer hook-ups	Hard-sided campers only
Madison**	281	Early May–late Oct.	Flush	No	No	Little privacy
South Yellowstone						
Grant Village**	403	Late June–mid-Oct.	Flush	Yes	Yes	Huge campground on Yellowstone Lake
Lewis Lake*	85	Mid-June–late Oct.	Pit	No	No	Forested site on Lewis Lake

*First come/first served

**Reserve through Xanterra

GRAND TETON NATIONAL PARK

Five NPS campgrounds are located in Grand Teton National Park. All are oper-ated on a first-come, first-served basis; reservations are not accepted. In Grand Teton, it is imperative to arrive as early as possible at the campground of your choice. At Jenny Lake Campground in August, for example, all available sites are assigned *before* 8:00 A.M. To avoid disappointment, check at entrance sta-tions and visitor centers for current status of campgrounds and approximate filling times. See the park map at the beginning of this book.

Campgrounds are located in the following areas: *Lizard Creek* open mid-June to early September, 60 sites; *Colter Bay* open late May to late September, 310 sites, marina, corral, restaurant, museum, visitor center, scenic location near hiking trails; *Signal Mountain* open early May to mid-October, 86 sites, marina, restaurant, store, ranger station, located on Jackson Lake; *Jenny Lake* open late May to late September, 49 sites, tents only, near store and ranger station, scenic location near hiking trails; *Gros Ventre* open early May to early October, 360 sites. More information on these campgrounds can be found at *www.nps.gov/grte/pphtml/camping.html.*

Backpacking

Both Yellowstone and Grand Teton National Parks have designated campsite systems to prevent overuse of the backcountry. A permit is required for all overnight trips. For Yellowstone outings, permits must be obtained at a ranger station no more than forty-eight hours before the camping date. Advance reservations for some backcountry campsites may be made in writing or in person for a $20 fee. To obtain the necessary forms, write the Backcountry Office, P.O. Box 168, YNP, WY 82190; use the Online Backcountry Trip Planner at *www.nps .gov/yell;* or inquire at a ranger station. The maximum stay per campsite varies from one to three nights per trip. Only a portion of backcountry campsites will be available for advance reservations. Thus, you may choose to wait until you arrive in the park to reserve your site and obtain your permit. Questions may be directed to the Backcountry Office at (307) 344-2160.

For backcountry overnights in Grand Teton, obtain a permit at the Moose or Colter Bay Visitor Centers or the Jenny Lake Ranger Station. Your length of stay is restricted based upon the specific campsite. Backcountry campsites may also be reserved by mail or fax between January 1 and May 15 for a $15 fee by writing to Grand Teton National Park, P.O. Drawer 170, Moose, WY 83012 or by faxing (307) 739-3438. To obtain a reservation, submit your itinerary, including dates, camping zone selection for each night, and the number of people in your party. Include a second choice itinerary in case a campsite is filled. For help in preparing this request, call the Permit Office at (307) 739-3309. Reservations are also accepted by fax at (307) 739-3438.

There are several backcountry campsites in both parks just a few miles from park trailheads that present ideal family backpacking opportunities. These campsites are noted in the trail descriptions and are also highlighted in the Trip Finder at the front of the book for easy reference.

Backpacking in the GYE calls for extra precautions to prevent bear encounters. Backpackers should follow the safety measures set out in the Introduction. In addition, to protect your family, the bears, and the Yellowstone ecosystem, follow the guidelines in the Introduction.

Nearby Accommodations

A wide variety of lodging is available in the towns surrounding the parks. From luxurious Snake River Lodge and Spa at Teton Village to quiet Moulton Ranch cabins bordering the park, there are accommodations to fit all needs, but you must plan ahead. Dude ranches are especially popular; information can be found at *www.ranchweb.com*. For general lodging information, contact the Chambers of Commerce in the following towns, depending on where you want to make base camp: West Yellowstone, MT, (406) 646-7701, *www.westyellowstonechamber.com;* Cooke City–Silver Gate, MT, (406) 838-2495, *www.cookecitychamber.org;* Gardiner, MT, (406) 848-7971, *www.gardinerchamber.com;* Cody, WY, (307) 587-2297, *www.codychamber.org;* and Dubois, WY, (307) 455-2556, *www.duboiswyoming.org.* For information on lodging in Jackson, WY, call the Jackson Chamber of Commerce, (307) 733-3316, *www.jacksonholechamber.com,* or Jackson Hole Central Reservations at (888) 838-6606, *www.jacksonholewy.com,* or write P.O. Box 2618, Jackson, WY 83001.

EMERGENCY MEDICAL SERVICES

For medical emergencies in either park, dial 911. To see a medical professional within the parks, consult the following:

In Yellowstone National Park, Yellowstone Park Medical Services (YPMS) provides health and emergency care at three park locations. YPMS's Lake Clinic, Pharmacy, and Hospital offers outpatient services, a full-service hospital, 24-hour ambulance, and emergency care. Lake Clinic is located near the Lake Yellowstone Hotel and is open daily, 8:30 A.M. to 8:30 P.M, (307) 242-7242. YPMS also operates clinics at Old Faithful, (307) 545-7325, open daily from 8:30 A.M. to 5:00 P.M, and at Mammoth Hot Springs, (307) 344-7965, open year-round, October 1 through May 30, Monday through Friday, 8:30 A.M. to 5:00 P.M. (closed Wednesday afternoons); June 1 through September 30, open daily 8:30 to 5:30 P.M. In Grand Teton National Park, find the Grand Teton Medical Clinic, (307) 543-2514, near Jackson Lake Lodge. The clinic is open daily, 10:00 A.M. to 6:00 P.M. A full-service hospital, St. John's Hospital, is located in Jackson, WY, at 625 East Broadway, (307) 733-3636.

ACTIVITIES WITHIN THE PARKS AND NEARBY

Take advantage of the GYE's rich recreational and educational opportunities by sampling a variety of activities that bring you closer to the natural wonders of the parks.

Interpretive Programs

From Memorial Day through September, NPS ranger-naturalists run a fine program of guided walks, slide shows, museum tours, art classes, and even canoe trips. Most are offered free of charge and many are geared for children. For information, inquire at any visitor center. At Grand Teton, many of the park programs are listed in the free park newspaper, *Teewinot*. Both parks also offer junior ranger programs, a recommended activity for children over age seven. Inquire at a visitor center for more information.

Yellowstone National Park Visitor Centers and Museums

Yellowstone offers five visitor centers, located near lodging and major camp-grounds, where rangers dispense information on trail conditions, camping, and interpretive programs. Many centers also contain informational exhibits. In addition, at each location the Yellowstone Association sells an extensive array of maps, trail guides, and natural history books. The centers are also the nucleus for many ranger-led programs and guided walks. In addition to visitor centers, Yellowstone operates two museums and two information stations. In spring and fall, check for hours of operation. Admission is free to all visitor centers and museums.

Albright (Mammoth) Visitor Center at Mammoth Hot Springs provides exhibits on the natural and human history of the park. Visitors may also view a short film. Open daily, year-round, (307) 344-2263.

Canyon Visitor Center at Canyon Village hosts an extensive interpretive exhibit on the park's bison. Open daily, mid-May through Labor Day, (307) 242-2550.

Fishing Bridge Visitor Center houses an exhibit on the ecology of the lake region, including specimens of many Yellowstone birds. Open daily, mid-May through Labor Day, (307) 242-2450.

Grant Village Visitor Center provides exhibits on the 1988 fires and a short film, continuously shown. Open daily, mid-May through Labor Day, (307) 242-2650.

Old Faithful Visitor Center offers a short film on geothermal features and up-to-date information on geyser eruptions. Open daily, mid-April to October 31 and mid-December to mid-March, (307) 545-2750.

Norris Geyser Basin Museum provides exhibits on geothermal features. Open daily, mid-May through Labor Day, (307) 344-2812.

Museum of the National Park Ranger offers historical exhibits on the role and importance of park rangers. Located in the historic Norris Soldier Station, 21 miles south of Mammoth Hot Springs. Open daily, mid-May through Labor Day.

Madison Information Station is housed in a charming log cottage on the Madison River. Offers information and publications. Open daily, late May through Labor Day, (307) 344-2265.

West Thumb Information Station offers publications and information. Open daily, late May through Labor Day.

Grand Teton National Park Visitor Centers and Museum

Colter Bay Visitor Center and Indian Arts Museum houses an impressive collection of Indian artifacts, including shields, pipes, weapons, ceremonial and domestic items, and a tepee. The museum sponsors ranger-led tours and craft demonstrations. The visitor center sells a wide range of publications, posters, maps, and cards. Nature films are shown continuously. Ranger-led hikes and junior naturalist programs meet at the center. Open daily, late May to October, (307) 739-3594.

Moose Visitor Center offers an outstanding collection of maps and nature books for children and adults, as well as topographic and natural history displays. The center is also a meeting place for the park's junior naturalist program. Open daily, year-round, (307) 739-3399.

Flagg Ranch Information Station, 2.5 miles south of the Yellowstone boundary, offers books, maps, and park information, as well as exhibits on J. D. Rockefeller Jr. and the Greater Yellowstone area. Open daily, winter and summer.

Jenny Lake Visitor Center provides information on backcountry trips, hiking trails, and park interpretive programs. Also offers books and maps. Open daily, June to early September, (307) 739-3343.

Menor's Ferry Historic Site offers a cable ferry across the Snake River. Original ferry buildings house a collection of authentic implements and wagons used by homesteaders and an old-fashioned general store, now selling an assortment of "penny" candy. NPS brochure offers self-guided tour. Located just north of the Moose Entrance Station off Teton Park Road. Open daily in summer.

Learning about wolves, Yellowstone National Park

Cunningham Cabin Historic Site includes a partially restored cabin circa 1890. A NPS brochure provides a self-guided tour. Located off US 89, about 5.5 miles south of Moran Junction. Open daily.

Nearby Museums

Jackson Hole Museum contains small but rich exhibits of the Native American, fur-trade, and early settler eras of Jackson Hole. The museum is located at the corner of Glenwood and Deloney Streets in downtown Jackson behind the historic Wort Hotel. Open daily, Memorial Day through September, (307) 733-2414. Admission fee.

National Wildlife Art Museum offers an extensive collection of wildlife paintings, sculptures, and photographs, including a special hands-on gallery for children. The museum also offers children's programs, studio classes, and performances. Located on US 89 directly across from the National Elk Refuge. Open daily in summer, closed Mondays, October through May, (307) 733-5771. Admission fee.

National Fish Hatchery invites visitors to view the hatchery and learn about native trout. Located off US 89, just west of the National Elk Refuge, 1 mile north of Jackson. Open daily, 8 A.M. to 4 P.M. Free admission.

Museum of the Yellowstone provides fine exhibits of native animals, Indian artifacts, and relics of the region's early settlement. Its theater shows a variety of nature and historical videos. Also offers an impressive bookstore. Located in West Yellowstone, MT, at the Union Pacific Depot, just west of the park entrance. Open daily, May through October, (406) 646-7814. Admission fee.

Grizzly Discovery Center contains a small museum on bears and five live grizzlies, which can be viewed in a small enclosure. Located in Grizzly Park, adjacent to the park entrance in West Yellowstone, MT. Open daily, year-round, (406) 646-7001 and (800) 257-2570. Admission fee.

Nature Courses and Camps

The Yellowstone Institute offers year-round programs for children and adults on wildlife, history, culture, and the natural wonders of Yellowstone. Courses range from one-day children's programs to five-day backcountry pack trips. The offerings are impressive, and almost all involve hands-on field participation. For a catalog, contact the Yellowstone Institute, P.O. Box 117, Yellowstone National Park, WY 82190, (307) 344-2294.

Located just outside Grand Teton National Park, the Teton Science School offers a wide variety of high-quality field programs for children and adults. Programs for young students include residential courses offered year-round and summer day-camps. Contact the Teton Science School, P.O. Box 68, Kelly, WY 83011, (307) 733-4765, *www.tetonscience.org*.

Horseback Riding
Yellowstone and Grand Teton National Parks

Concessionaires in both parks offer trail rides. To ride, children must be eight years of age, at least four feet tall, and accompanied by an adult. In Yellowstone, three corrals (Mammoth, Roosevelt, and Canyon) offer one- and two-hour rides. For those with younger children, there are stagecoach rides or rides in a horsedrawn wagon to a Western cookout from Roosevelt Lodge. During the summer, reservations are required. Call Xanterra Parks and Resorts, (307) 344-7311. In Grand Teton National Park, take a one-, two-, three-hour, or a half-day trail ride from corrals at Jackson Lake or Colter Bay Village. Horsedrawn wagon rides are also available. Those staying at Jenny Lake Lodge can use the corral at Jenny Lake. For reservations, call (800) 628-9988 or (307) 543-2855.

Outside the Park

Numerous ranches outside the park offer family trail rides. For inexperienced children, try Spring Creek Ranch, scenically located just south of Jackson, WY. For reservations, call W. W. Guides, (307) 733-8833. Other outfitters in the Jackson area offering trail rides include the following: Bar T-5 Corral, (307) 733-3534; Jackson Hole Trail Rides at Teton Village, (307) 733-6992; A/OK Corral near Hoback Junction, (307) 733-6556; Mill Iron Ranch (two- to four-hour rides), (307) 733-6390; Bud Nelson Outfitters, (307) 733-2843; and Grand Targhee Resort, on the west slope of the Tetons, (800) 827-4433.

Rafting

Rafting the Snake River is an exciting and unforgettable family experience. Choose between a slow, scenic float trip or a wild whitewater excursion. If you opt for a scenic float, take the shorter, 5-mile trip when traveling with youngsters. Book your float trip for early morning or dusk for the greatest likelihood of seeing wildlife.

Children ages six and up are likely to prefer whitewater rafting. Rafting the rapids is like riding a roller coaster; the waves keep children wet, screaming, and thrilled. For maximum excitement, request a paddle boat (as opposed to an oar boat, in which only the guide controls the raft). Prior to booking your trip, ask about conditions and appropriateness for children. Early in the season, when the water is high, the river may be too scary or dangerous.

For whitewater rafting trips, contact O.A.R.S. (expert guides also offer two- and five-day trips, minimum age four years, scenic/whitewater combo available), (800) 345-6277, *www.oars.com;* Sands Wildwater River Trips ("U-paddle" rafts available), (307) 733-4410, (800) 358-8184; Jackson Hole Whitewater (307) 733-1007, (800) 648-2602; Dave Hansen Whitewater, (307) 733-6295, (800) 732-6295; Mad River Boat Trips, (children must be over six

Rafting the Snake River with O.A.R.S., Grand Teton National Park

years old), (800) 458-7238; Lewis and Clark Expeditions, (307) 733-4022, (800) 824-5375; Barker-Ewing River Trips, (307) 733-1800, (800) 365-1800; Mill Iron Ranch Rafting/Fishing Trips (not recommended for children under five years), (307) 733-6390.

The following outfitters offer scenic float trips: O.A.R.S. (outstanding options), (800) 346-6277, *www.oars.com;* Barker-Ewing Scenic Tours, (307) 733-1800, (800) 365-1800; Grand Teton Lodge Company (10-mile float only, no children under six), (307) 543-2811; Triangle X Float Trips (children must be four years old), (307) 733-2183, (800) 860-0065; National Park Float Trips (10-mile float only, children must be four years old), (307) 733-6445; Lewis and Clark Expeditions (12-mile float or scenic/whitewater combo), (307) 733-4022, (800) 824-5375; Solitude Float Trips, (307) 733-2871, (888) 704-2800.

For scenic floats and whitewater rafting in Yellowstone, contact Flying Pig Rafting Company in Gardiner, MT, at Yellowstone's North Entrance, offering half- and full-day trips, (406) 846-7510, (866) 807-0744.

Boating

In Yellowstone, boaters must obtain a boating permit for all boats. Permits can be purchased at all ranger stations and visitor centers. The park allows motorboats, canoes, rowboats, kayaks, and sailboats on Yellowstone and Lewis Lakes. On Shoshone Lake, only oar-powered boats are permitted. All other lakes and rivers in Yellowstone are closed to boating. While boating, watch weather conditions carefully and exercise great caution due to the extremely cold water. Human survival time is measured in minutes in Yellowstone Lake. For rentals on Yellowstone Lake, go to Bridge Bay Marina (rowboats and motorboats). Bridge Bay Marina also offers scenic cruises and guided fishing trips. Experienced kayakers can be towed to the soutern end of Yellowstone Lake to bring paddlers beyond "motorized" traffic for a stunning wilderness experience. For information on all services at the Marina, call (307) 344-7311. In Grand Teton, all privately owned vessels must also be registered. During the summer, purchase permits at the Moose and Colter Bay Visitor Centers and at the Signal Mountain, Buffalo, and John D. Rockefeller Jr. Memorial Parkway Ranger Stations. Motorized vessels are only allowed on Jackson, Jenny, and Phelps Lakes. To float the Snake River, you must register your boat with the NPS and obtain a permit at Moose or Colter Bay Visitor Centers. For boat rentals in Grand Teton, contact Signal Mountain Lodge (canoes and motorized boats), (307) 543-2831; Colter Bay Marina (canoes, rowboats, and motorboats), no advance reservations, (307) 543-2811; and Jenny Lake Company, Inc., at Jenny Lake (motorboats, canoes, kayaks), (307) 734-9227. Outside the park, call Leisure Sports of Jackson (rafts, canoes, touring, and inflatable kayaks), (307) 733-3040 and Adventure Sports at Dornan's in Moose, WY (canoes, kayaks), (307) 733-2522.

Guided Kayaking and Canoeing Trips

Paddling is one of the best ways for families to enjoy the spectacular lakes of Yellowstone and Grand Teton National Parks. To reach the backcountry and

Kayaking instruction on Jackson Lake, Grand Teton National Park

scenic waters of Yellowstone Lake, contact O.A.R.S. (offering half-day and multiday unique tours of the Yellowstone Lake and West Thumb Geyser Basin), (800) 346-6277, *www.oars.com* and Far and Away Adventures, (208) 726-8888. Families are welcome, and both children and adults are taught to kayak and fly-fish in a remote and beautiful setting. For an unforgettable overnight trip on Jackson Lake, including kayak instruction, guided tours, and moonlight paddling, contact O.A.R.S. (one- to three-day family trips), (800) 345-6277. One- and two-person kayaks offer sufficient stability, even for novices and children. For paddling instruction and Snake River excursions, call the Snake River Kayak and Canoe School in Jackson, WY, (307) 733-3127 or (800) 529-2501.

Fishing

Trout fishing is spectacular in the unspoiled waters of the GYE. Anglers in great numbers are lured to the parks by rainbow, brown, brook, and lake (Mackinaw) trout; Arctic grayling; and mountain whitefish. The GYE also supports one of the last wild inland populations of cutthroat trout.

Before fishing in either park, obtain a copy of the fishing regulations at a visitor center or ranger station and check for location-specific restrictions. These may include restrictive use of bait, catch-and-release-only areas, limits on number and size of catch, and area closures. Waterways may be closed to protect sensitive nesting birds and threatened and endangered species, or to provide scenic viewing areas.

In all waterways, the NPS encourages catch-and-release fishing to preserve fish populations. This is accomplished by fly-fishing with barbless hooks. Bait fishing is discouraged or prohibited, since studies show that a fish caught by bait and released has only a 52 percent survival rate. Release of fish hooked on lures and flies boasts a survival rate of 96 percent.

Yellowstone National Park operates a park-specific permit system for all anglers. Anglers sixteen years of age and older must purchase a Special Use Permit. Anglers twelve to fifteen years of age must obtain a nonfee permit. Children eleven and under may fish without a permit. Obtain permits at any ranger station or visitor center or at sporting goods stores in nearby communities. As discussed in the Introduction, Yellowstone prohibits the use of any fishing tackle containing lead. Fishing in Grand Teton National Park requires a Wyoming fishing license. Licenses may be purchased at the Moose Village Store, Signal Mountain Lodge, Colter Bay Marina, Flagg Ranch Village, and sporting goods stores.

Children under age fourteen may also fish in North Elk Park Pond, located between the National Elk Refuge and US 191 in Jackson, WY, 11 miles south of Grand Teton National Park. This stocked pond was set aside as a training ground for young anglers.

For quick reference to trails offering fishing opportunities, check the Trip Finder in at the front of the book.

Climbing

Grand Teton National Park is a mecca for mountain climbers. The Tetons' soaring peaks pose challenges for climbers of every ability. All climbers are required to register prior to a climb. Register and obtain current route information at the Jenny Lake Ranger Station, (307) 733-2880. For families seeking climbing instruction or guided climbs, contact Exum Mountain Guides or Jackson Hole Mountain Guides. The Exum school offers daily basic and intermediate instruction within the park throughout the summer and private guides year-round. For information, contact Exum Mountain Guides, P.O. Box 56, Moose, WY 83012, (307) 733-2297, *www.exumguides.com;* or Jackson Hole Mountain Guides, 165 North Glenwood (families and children welcome), Jackson, WY 83001, (307) 733-4979, *www.jhmg.com.*

Learning to rock climb, Teton Village

For additional climbing experience and expert instruction, particularly in inclement weather, visit the Teton Rock Gym, an indoor climbing facility. Artificial-rock climbing walls pose challenges for novices and experts of all ages. The Teton Rock Gym is located in Jackson at 1116 Maple Way, (307) 733-0707.

Climbing is dangerous in Yellowstone due to loose and crumbly rock formations. Rock climbing is not recommended in most areas and is illegal in the Grand Canyon of the Yellowstone.

Biking

There are important restrictions on bicycling in Yellowstone and Grand Teton National Parks. In both parks, bicycling is strictly prohibited on hiking trails. Riding off-trail in the backcountry is also strictly prohibited. Before riding, check at a ranger station or visitor center for routes open to cyclists.

Riders must proceed with caution on park roads. Most have only narrow shoulders, and some have none at all. In July and August, RV traffic is heavy. Also, major road repairs occur every summer and fall, so check with a visitor center for road closures and delays before proceeding. In addition, drivers are easily distracted by scenery and wildlife, so cyclists must ride defensively.

Bike rentals for Grand Teton National Park are conveniently located at Dornan's Adventure Sports in Moose (offering children's bikes and bike trailers), (307) 733-2522. Rentals are also available in Jackson Hole at Hoback Sports, 40 South Millward, (307) 733-5335; and at Gart Sports, 455 West Broadway, (307) 733-4449. During the summer, call ahead for reservations. Bike tours in both national parks are available from Teton Mountain Bike Tours, Jackson, WY, (307) 733-0712, (800) 733-0788, *www,tetonbike.com,* and from Fat Tire Tours, Jackson, WY 83001, (307) 733-5335. At Teton Village near the Granite Canyon Entrance to Grand Teton National Park, bike rentals are available at Wildernest Sports, Village Center Building, Teton Village, (307) 733-4297.

Rodeos

The Jackson Hole Rodeo offers family entertainment every Wednesday and Saturday at 8 P.M. from Memorial Day through Labor Day. For ticket information, call (307) 733-2805. In Cody, WY, the world-famous Cody Nite Rodeo performs nightly June through August, (307) 587-5155.

Rainy Day Recreation

In inclement weather, families can take cover in a variety of interesting places. Try the museums or park visitor centers listed in this chapter. To please active youngsters in Jackson, visit the Teton Rock Gym, (307) 733-7707, or Jackson's Recreation Center, which houses a gym and elaborate swimming facility, complete with hot tub and water slides. The Recreation Center is located at 155 East Gill Street, just a few blocks north of the town square.

WILDLIFE VIEWING

One of the prime reasons to visit the GYE is to view its magnificent animals. From trumpeter swans to bull moose, the thrills are there for those who know when, where, and how to find them. To see as many animals as possible, put the following principles of wildlife observation to work. For maximum success, use them in conjunction with the Wildlife Locator and sample "safaris" at the front of the book.

Where to Look

To find a particular animal, know its habitat. The more you know about an animal's habitat, the easier it will be to locate the animal. Within their habitats,

Bison, Grand Teton National Park

look for wildlife in "edge environments." Edge environments describe the areas where one habitat meets another, such as the transitional area between forest and meadow. Edge environments offer greater diversity of food and cover than either of the neighboring habitats. They therefore support greater numbers and kinds of animals. Areas that have a wealth of edge environments, like patchy forests broken by meadows or winding rivers with long shorelines, are productive areas for watching wildlife. Lush vegetation in these areas attracts large herbivores, such as deer and elk, and small mammals, such as rabbits and mice, which in turn attract predators such as hawks, weasels, and coyotes.

When to Look

Animals are diurnal (active during the day), nocturnal (active after dark), or crepuscular (active at sunrise and sunset). In general, the best time to view wildlife is shortly after dawn or at dusk when diurnal, nocturnal, and crepuscular animals mingle in a transitional time zone. In contrast, the least rewarding time is in the middle of the day. At high noon in the summer when human activity is at its peak, animals generally avoid heat and activity and rest in day beds, out of sight.

In Yellowstone, spring and fall are the best times of year to see large numbers of elk, bison, moose, deer, bighorn sheep, and waterbirds. In summer, a large number of Yellowstone animals escape the heat and crowds by retreating to the backcountry. Nevertheless, observant and knowledgeable summer visitors can still see many animals by venturing into the park at dawn and dusk.

How to Look

Anyone serious about viewing wildlife should invest in a pair of good binoculars. Decent binoculars are available for less than $100, although the finest cost several times that much. Binoculars enable you to observe an animal without disturbing it. The most dedicated wildlife observers invest in a spotting scope. Although these are quite costly, their clarity and high level of magnification is invaluable for watching large predators, such as bears and wolves.

When searching for animals, be alert to signs of their presence. If you can read animals' signs—tracks, scat, feeding debris, nests, and burrows—you can deduce their movements and activities without actually seeing them. With a little knowledge of droppings, for example, you can determine whether elk, moose, or deer favor the area. By noting the bark missing from a tree, you can tell whether bison or elk rubbed it or whether it was eaten by a porcupine. Sometimes seeing signs of an animal can be almost as exciting as seeing the animal itself. Fresh claw marks on a lodgepole, perhaps with some grizzly hair stuck to the oozing sap, is likely to impress most hikers.

Viewing Ethics

When you do find wildlife, observe unobtrusively *and from a distance*. An animal's survival may well depend on it. *If you cause an animal to move, you are too close*. Remember that animals usually feel anxious around humans. If an animal shows signs of agitation, leave immediately. Most animals live in a precarious balance between the demands of survival and the costs of obtaining enough food to survive. Even short interruptions of an animal's normal routine, when multiplied by a park full of curious visitors, can have deadly effects.

If you find young animals, leave them alone and do not linger. They were probably not abandoned. More likely, the mother is nearby. Your presence, however, may stop her from returning or may anger her enough to precipitate an attack. Fawns and elk calves are routinely left in the forest while their mothers feed. The odorless and camouflaged young usually go undetected by predators. If you happen to find one, or any other young animal, quickly leave the area.

Opposite: The Narrows of the Yellowstone River

CHAPTER 2

NORTH
YELLOWSTONE

The northern portion of Yellowstone National Park is quietly scenic and wonderfully less congested than the central and southern portions of the park. With the exception of bustling Mammoth Hot Springs, the roads and trails are generally uncrowded. Its lower elevation makes it an excellent choice for spring and fall visits when snow covers trails in higher elevations.

Early summer is also a magical time here, for wildlife and wildflowers abound in the gorgeous, green Lamar Valley. Wildlife sightings in the valley include the newly introduced wolves as well as grizzlies, black bears, and the ever-present pronghorn, elk, mule deer, and bison. Even bighorn sheep may be glimpsed on cliffs near the North Entrance and occasionally at Calcite Springs Overlook on the Mammoth–Tower Road. Early morning and dusk are always the best times for viewing.

This area offers a variety of hiking trails, from easy outings (Trips 1, 2, 3, 6, 9, 10, 11) to more challenging climbs and descents (Trips 4, 5, 8). For a summer hike with a warm soak included, try strolling to Boiling River (Trip 2). For superb fishing, try Trips 5, 9, or 10. To visit the largest standing petrified forest in North America, try Trip 8. Those with strollers or wheelchairs can utilize the Forces of the Nothern Range Self-Guiding Trail (Trip 6). Visitors seeking history as well as scenery should try Trip 7. Lastly, for great views of northern Yellowstone, climb Bunsen Peak (Trip 4). For information on current trail conditions, inquire at Albright Visitor Center in Mammoth or at Tower Ranger Station near Tower Junction.

If you have no time for hiking but want to make some roadside stops, try beautiful Undine Falls on the Mammoth–Tower Road; Tower Fall, just southeast of Tower Junction; and the Sheepeater Cliff Picnic Area on the Mammoth–Norris Road. The latter is one of the areas where the Sheepeater Indians resided before the creation of the park. Today it is a quietly beautiful area and a good place to find yellow-bellied marmots.

Camping families have several options in North Yellowstone. For a measure of beauty and solitude, try Slough Creek Campground near the Lamar Valley. Its sites are attractively set along pretty Slough Creek. Another fine drive-in campground is Indian Creek Campground on the Mammoth–Norris Road.

BEAVER PONDS LOOP

Difficulty: moderate
Distance: 5-mile loop
Usage: moderate
Starting elevation: 6,239 feet; elevation gain, 350 feet
Season: late May to early October
Map: USGS 7.5-minute Mammoth, WY-MT

Escape busy Mammoth Hot Springs for a walk through grassy meadows and Douglas-fir to a series of beaver ponds. You'll spy historic beaver dams and lodges, whose former inhabitants changed the landscape but have, most likely, moved on to new ponds. This trail is best hiked in spring or fall, when insects are minimal and wildlife is abundant. In midsummer the trail is likely to be sunny and hot, so bring plenty of water.

Drive to Mammoth Hot Springs, 5 miles south of Yellowstone's North Entrance. To reach the trailhead, turn northwest on the road just south of the Mammoth Hot Springs Hotel (between the hotel and the dining room). Then take the first right and the next left. Look for the beginning of the unpaved Old Gardiner Road (on the slope immediately to the west). After you've located the road, you'll see the sign for the Beaver Ponds Trailhead, just above the road. Park in the large parking area directly adjacent. Walk up the Old Gardiner Road to begin the hike.

Almost immediately the trail leaves the road and heads left up the slope. Rise moderately among an abundance of waist-high sagebrush, rabbitbrush, and sun-loving flowers. To the east are steep cliffs known as the McMinn Bench, part of the northern flank of Mount Everts (7,841 feet). In spring, bighorn-sheep ewes and their lambs nimbly negotiate the precipitous slopes. With binoculars, you may spot them.

Follow the trail northwest traversing the hill. Then descend and cross a stream in the shade of Douglas-fir. Soon pass under powerlines and climb again. In late summer enjoy fields of bright yellow Dalmatian toadflax, an exotic brought here from Eastern Europe. Exotics, or nonnative plants, are often unwelcome and tenacious guests in the GYE. Seeds of exotics land in Yellowstone by a variety of means, including transport via bird and animal feces and adhesion to clothing and hay brought for horses. (For this reason, national parks require horses be fed only pellets within the park.) Hardy exotics crowd out rarer and less competitive native flowers and grasses and

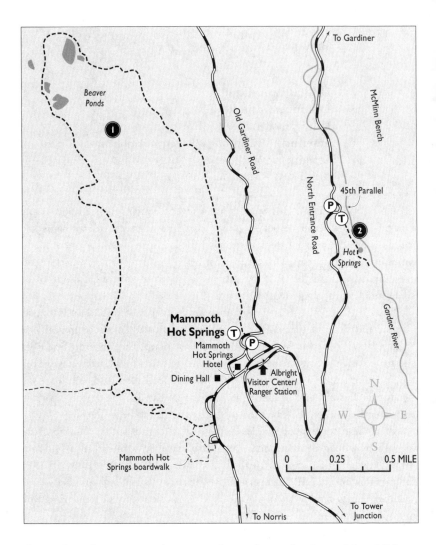

thus reduce the variety and amount of tasty forage for the park's wildlife.

Switchback up an open slope. To the left, note two small ponds that are prime watering holes for elk. At 2 miles from the trailhead, reach a bridge over the beaver pond's outlet creek. Shortly after, reach two ponds created by beaver dams. This is a good place to examine the work of these clever rodents or rest on the grassy shore and watch ducks cruise on the tranquil water.

The trail travels northwest around the pond past fields of flowers in late summer and early fall. Follow a creek bank covered with pink Canadian thistle and giant stalks of cow parsnip. Hardy cow parsnip can grow six feet tall. Its thick stalk is fuzzy, and its small white flowers are arranged in umbrella-shaped clusters. Today the park's wildlife enjoys this cousin of the carrot, but in earlier times, Native Americans also ate it (although it is reputed to be rather poor tasting). Find this remarkably large plant in wet areas throughout the park within the montane and subalpine zones.

At 2.5 miles, cross the stream and head south. In August, pass distinctive western coneflowers with their two-inch-high brown cones on green stalks up to five feet tall. Below the coneflowers, large, red-orange Indian paintbrush thrive. *The Legend of the Indian Paintbrush,* a Native American tale retold and illustrated by Tomie DePaola, delightfully describes the "origin" of these color-ful flowers (see Appendix A).

Cross a series of bridges over wet meadows. Plant life is much different on the latter half of this hike due to the abundance of moisture. Watch for the round-leaf harebell whose five-pet-aled purple flowers hang gracefully down like delicate bells.

Next pass aspen whose trunks have been grazed by elk to a height of seven to eight feet. In winter when forage is scarce, elk eat the inner bark, leav-ing the tree scarred with large black patches. If elk strip too much bark off the slender aspen, the trees will die. Some naturalists see the abundance of blackened aspen as evidence that the park's large herds exceed the natural carrying capacity of the land. The reintroduction of wolves in 1995, the elk's natural predator, is expected to bring about a reduction of the Yellowstone elk population.

Ahead lies a beautiful golden field with widely spaced aspen and layers of blue mountains on the horizon beyond. Cross a dry, open slope with improving vistas. At about 4 miles from the start of the trail, the steam from Mammoth Hot Springs is vis-ible. At 4.5 miles from the trailhead, its white terraces can be seen.

Pronghorn antelope, Old Gardiner Road, Yellowstone National Park

The Sepulcher Mountain Trail enters on the right and descends steeply, but continue left on the main trail. Shortly your trail also descends steeply in long switchbacks. Don't take shortcuts—this will only accelerate the erosion of the slope. After descending about 0.2 mile, reach a series of bridges and arrive at a rock chimney. Liberty Cap (the thumb-like, protruding rock formation) is visible to the east. A right turn will take you to the Mammoth Hot Springs boardwalk and paved trail. To return to your car, walk east out to the road, turn left, and follow the road just 0.25 mile back to the trailhead at the Old Gardiner Road.

2   BOILING RIVER   ◖◗

Difficulty: very easy
Distance: 0.5 mile one way
Usage: high
Starting elevation: 5,500 feet; no elevation gain
Season: mid-May to early October
Map: USGS 7.5-minute Mammoth, WY-MT

A short hike along the Gardner River takes visitors to Boiling River, where a hot spring mixes with the cool river to create a natural hot tub. The lure of this warm dip is incredibly strong, for Yellowstone's waters tend toward the frigid. Boiling River thus draws crowds of one hundred to two hundred people each summer day. For a bit of solitude, try this trail at dawn or in early autumn. In spring and early summer, the trail may be closed due to high water. It is critically important to follow all posted rules at Boiling River. The area has been significantly degraded due to high visitation; only your respect of its delicate beauty can hasten its restoration and preserve it for future generations. Also early in the season, be respectful of elk cows and calves who congregate along this section of the river.

The trailhead to Boiling River is located 2.6 miles south of Yellowstone's North Entrance and 2.2 miles north of Mammoth Hot Springs on the North Entrance Road. (See the trail map on page 82.) Look for signs indicating the 45th Parallel. Park in the lot on the east side of the road. Overflow parking is available on the road's west side.

The heavily traveled path to the "hot tub" parallels the Gardner River on its west bank. This river is a favorite for anglers. Its fast-flowing waters, gravelly bottom, and healthy vegetation supply an excellent habitat for varieties of trout.

Bathers in the Boiling River (Gardner River), Yellowstone National Park

The area through which you are walking, the northwest corner of Yellowstone, is the lowest and the driest in the park, receiving less snow than surrounding areas. Consequently thousands of elk, bison, mule deer, pronghorn antelope, and bighorn sheep winter here. In summer, only the pronghorn remain in large numbers, most of the other animals climb to higher ground.

Follow the trail south along the riverbank. Across the river the rocky slopes of the McMinn Bench rise steeply. The cliffs are a spring calving area for bighorn sheep. These amazing climbers deftly negotiate the sheer slopes, successfully evading most four-legged predators. Despite their uncanny skill on the cliffs, the park's bighorn sheep are in trouble. In the late 1800s, hunters decimated the herds, and they never recovered. Bighorn sheep are extremely vulnerable to habitat disturbances and stress. Furthermore, they compete poorly with more robust elk for forage. In recent decades, disease has also diminished their numbers. Yellowstone's northwest herd hovers around 325. Your best chance of seeing this remarkable animal is on the summit of Mount Washburn (Trips 12 and 13). Remember, if you are lucky enough to see one, do not approach it! Despite your peaceful intentions, a close encounter will cause it severe stress.

After only 0.5 mile of hiking, arrive at the famed Boiling River. Please respect the roped-off areas protecting the trampled vegetation. Watch children carefully. The currents of the Gardner River are strong and could easily overpower a child. This is not a safe swimming area. Furthermore, the NPS recommends that you keep your head above water at all times and do not allow the thermally heated water to enter your mouth or nose. The warm waters may contain bacteria that cause severe skin rashes or infectious or amoebic meningitis.

Without the crowds, the Boiling River is quite lovely and immensely enjoyable. From May through September, there are a variety of wildflowers. In any season, the glimpse of a bald eagle, hunting coyote, or graceful elk from the river completes a perfect picture.

3   MAMMOTH HOT SPRINGS LOWER TERRACES

Difficulty: very easy
Distance: 0.75 mile one way
Usage: high
Starting elevation: 6,239 feet; elevation gain, 175 feet
Season: mid-May through October
Map: USGS 7.5-minute Mammoth, WY-MT

Strolling the boardwalk of Mammoth Hot Springs Lower Terrace is a must for all visitors to the area. Join a ranger-led hike or take a self-guided tour with the aid of the Yellowstone Association's informative brochure (available at trailside dispensers). In spring and fall, hikers share the boardwalk with elk and often bison. This makes the walk especially delightful, but remember, do not approach closer than 25 yards under any circumstances. Also, never allow children to leave the boardwalk and risk injury on unstable ground.

Drive to Mammoth Hot Springs, 5 miles south of the North Entrance. The boardwalks of the Mammoth Hot Springs Lower Terraces are located just south of the Mammoth Hot Springs Hotel. At the beginning of the boardwalk, pick up the brochure describing the features of the terraces and the process by which they were created. In short, hot gases beneath the earth heat water (from rain and melted snow) that seeps through fissures in the ground. The heated water dissolves buried deposits of limestone, and then carries the dissolved minerals to the surface. When the hot water reaches the surface, some of the minerals it carries are precipitated out and deposited as ivory travertine. After years and

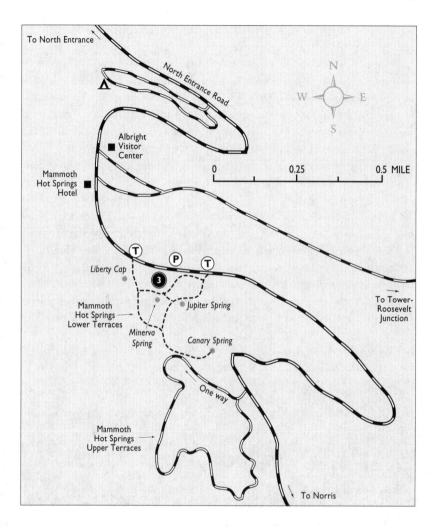

years of deposition, a travertine limestone "wedding cake" forms. In geologic time, this buildup is exceedingly rapid, averaging eight inches of deposited rock per year. Some years, up to twenty-two inches of rock are deposited at Mammoth, up to two tons of travertine per day!

Despite all the obvious thermal activity, visitors will find no geysers in the Mammoth area. This is because the water is not hot enough. The origin of Mammoth's hot springs is the Norris Geyser Basin, 21 miles away. Mammoth's distance from the source of heat at Norris is just enough to reduce the water temperature below the boiling point. In fact, none of the bubbling hot springs at Mammoth contain boiling water. The bubbling action that looks like boiling is caused by carbon dioxide gas expanding at the surface (like the bubbles in a glass of soda pop). This water, nevertheless, is still incredibly dangerous. It is easily hot enough to cause severe burns upon contact!

As hot springs flow over the white terraces, colorful bacteria and algae grow in the water, creating a fantastic spectrum of color. The temperature of the hot springs determines the particular type of bacteria that can survive in the water. Bacteria differ in color, so you can guess the temperature of the water with a fair degree of accuracy by looking at the color of its bacteria or algae. For example, yellow indicates water of about 167 degrees F, blue indicates a temperature of about 160 degrees F, and orange-brown indicates a temperature of 130 degrees F.

Around the hot springs, notice the many standing dead trees with white bases. These are "bobby-sock trees," actually tree skeletons cemented in place by the travertine. Bobby-sock trees were killed by the mineral-laden hot water. When the tree's roots drew up the water, the minerals solidified within the tree, eventually killing it by turning its inner workings to stone from the base up. Bobby-sock trees are a sure sign of past or present thermal activity.

One of the most amazing things about Mammoth Hot Springs is its never-ending evolution. Boardwalks frequently need to be removed or rerouted because of changes in thermal activity. A colorful pool this year may change the

Taking the temperature of thermal pool on a ranger-led hike. Never approach a pool without a ranger.

next year beyond recognition. Changes are caused by shifts in the underground plumbing, changes in water temperature, or blockage of water sources. Mild earthquakes common to the area can initiate the changes. Think of Mammoth Hot Springs as an artist's work in progress, and enjoy this living sculpture garden.

To see more fascinating hot springs and travertine formations, visit the Mammoth Hot Springs Upper Terraces that begin at the top of the Lower Terraces boardwalk. This is most easily done by vehicle via Upper Terrace Drive. The one-way road (1.5 miles) starts about 1 mile south of the Lower Terrace Parking Area on the road to Norris. For a more intimate view of Mammoth's Upper Terrace, take a guided walk with a ranger to view back-country thermal features seldom seen by the general public. Inquire at the Albright Visitor Center for a schedule of tours.

4 BUNSEN PEAK

Difficulty: strenuous
Distance: 2.2 miles one way
Usage: moderate
Starting elevation: 7,320 feet; elevation gain, 1,345 feet
Season: mid-June through September
Map: USGS 7.5-minute Mammoth, WY-MT

For the most commanding view in this region, climb Bunsen Peak. Its summit affords glorious views of the Yellowstone Valley, Mammoth Hot Springs, the mysterious Hoodoos, Swan Lake Flat, the Gallatins, and Mount Washburn. After the 1988 fires burned its slopes, these views were significantly improved. This hike is a tough family climb, but worth the effort, especially in the early morning. If you're hiking early in the season, use care crossing snow patches.

From Mammoth Hot Springs, drive about 5 miles south on the Mammoth–Norris Road. Just after passing the Golden Gate and Rustic Falls, look for a turnout on the left (east) side of the highway. Park, walk past the barricade, and hike on the closed road briefly until you see the Bunsen Peak Trail entering on the left.

The trail winds through burned lodgepole pine forest, soon climbing by switchbacks up the west slope of Bunsen Peak. You gain altitude swiftly, and with each footstep the views improve. Look west over Gardner's Hole, where fur trapper Johnson Gardner trapped extensively in the 1830s. In the Hole lies

Swan Lake, where trumpeter swans occasionally nest in the summer.

In the burned forest black sculptural forms stand. Beneath bare branches, newly enriched soil and the infusion of sunlight nourishes a variety of flowers. Look for red-orange Indian paintbrush and lavender lupine. Lupine was originally believed to be a noxious weed that stole valuable nutrients from the soil. For that reason, Europeans named the flower after the Latin word for wolf, *lupus,* for they considered the wolf also evil and destructive. We now know that both theories were far from the truth; lupine actually enriches poor soils, and wolves, of course, play an invaluable role in the ecosystem.

Soon a switchback brings you north to a dramatic overlook of Cathedral Rock, an impressive rock spire, and the Hoodoos, a jumble of travertine boulders. The Hoodoos are actually the ruins of an ancient terrace altered by hot springs. Below and beyond the Hoodoos lie Mammoth Hot Springs. Continue to rise and cross

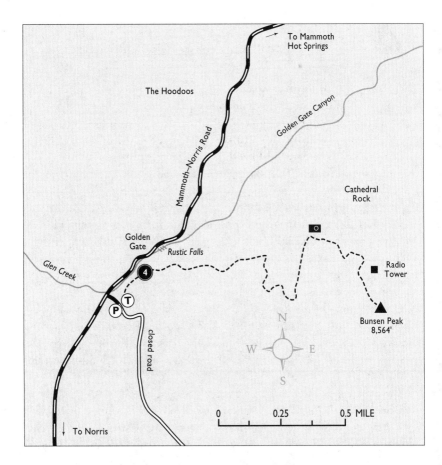

View west from Bunsen Peak, Yellowstone National Park

several talus slopes. Pass majestic Douglas-fir as great views open again to the southwest. Far to the west rise the peaks of the Gallatin Range.

Near the top the switchbacks steepen. Stay on the trail, for talus slopes and snow patches can be treacherous. (Near the top, find NPS radio relaying equipment. Please stay clear.) At the summit, look east for views of the Washburn Range, northwest for an impressive view of Electric Peak (named for its propensity to be struck by lightning), and south to the Tetons, which can be seen on a clear day.

Geologists believe Bunsen Peak is the cone of an ancient volcano. The peak was named for Robert Bunsen, the first scientist to conduct an in-depth study of the workings of geysers, and who also invented the Bunsen burner, a common piece of laboratory equipment. Lastly, look south to find the steam rising from Norris Geyser Basin. This is exactly how it was found by white men. In 1872, two expedition members climbed Bunsen Peak and "discovered" the immense and active basin.

Return carefully to the trailhead by retracing your steps. When you reach the bottom, look for bison that often travel the unpaved road.

5   BLACKTAIL DEER CREEK   🐾

Difficulty: strenuous
Distance: 3.7 miles one way
Usage: moderate
Starting elevation: 6,900 feet; elevation loss, 1,100 feet
Season: mid-May through early October
Map: USGS 7.5-minute Blacktail Deer Creek, WY

Brave a long descent along Blacktail Deer Creek to visit Yellowstone's magnificent Black Canyon. Along the way pass through gentle meadows, visit a small cascade, and try some fine fishing. Flower displays are excellent in July. Backpacking families can find a creekside campsite less than 2 fairly level miles from the trailhead. Hikers should bring plenty of water and save some energy for the arduous climb out.

Drive 6.5 miles west from Tower Junction on the Mammoth–Tower Road to a small parking area on the north side of the road (between Blacktail Pond and Blacktail Deer Creek) signed for the Blacktail Creek Trail. From Mammoth, drive 11.5 miles on the Mammoth–Tower Road east to find the trailhead.

The trail heads directly north past shallow ponds and climbs a gentle rise. Pass between two "exclosures," areas fenced by the NPS to study the impacts of grazing and browsing mammals such as elk, bison, deer, and moose. Where these animals are plentiful, young aspen are greedily munched before they have a chance to mature.

Just after the exclosures, descend to a trail junction with the Rescue Creek Trail on the left, 0.7 mile from the trailhead. Continue straight. A multitude of flowers adorn the rolling meadows. Look for lavender lupine, creamy buckwheat, and low-lying pink bitterroot, Montana's state flower. The roots of the bitterroot were an important source of food for Native Americans. The origin of this flower is explained by a Flathead Indian legend. It tells of an old woman whose family was starving to death. Seeing her crying, a spirit bird came to her rescue, and everywhere her tears fell, a nutritious bitterroot bloomed.

Also along the trail are plentiful Unita ground squirrels, which stand on their hind legs before diving into their burrows. Numerous, too, are the large elliptical holes dug by badgers. Badgers are far more secretive than the ubiquitous squirrels, so consider yourself lucky if the large, masked rodent shows its belligerent head.

The trail heads toward rushing Blacktail Deer Creek. The creek was named

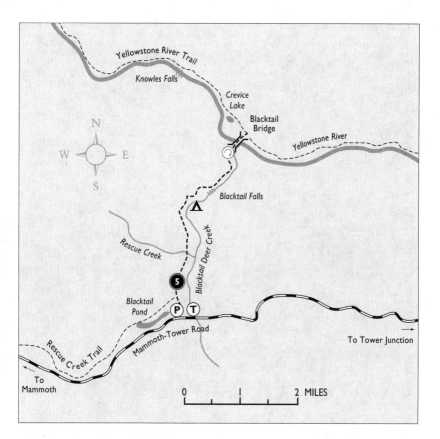

for the deer that frequent this section of the park. The park's deer, however, are actually Rocky Mountain mule deer and not true blacktail deer, which are found primarily on the West Coast. Look for the deer at dawn and dusk in edge environments, where the forest meets meadows or streams.

At approximately 1.75 miles from the trailhead, a spur trail leads down to a campsite by Blacktail Deer Creek. The main trail continues to descend, paralleling the creek. Anglers may be trying for brook and cutthroat trout along the banks, although the more coveted spots are closer to the creek's junction with the Yellowstone River. Just after the campsite watch for a second spur trail to Blacktail Falls, a nice cascade that provides a good spot to rest.

Evidence of the 1988 fire is apparent on the slopes above the creek. Walk through skeleton forests of Douglas-fir whose barkless snags raise bare, whitened branches. Across the creek, notice the pillarlike rock formation high above the water. This is an example of columnar basalt, a formation resulting from cooling lava flows.

Examining aspen bark eaten by elk

The descent becomes steeper as you approach the Yellowstone River and Black Canyon. The trail loses nearly 900 feet in the last 1.5 miles. Those who take the plunge are well-rewarded. The trail affords beautiful views of the powerful Yellowstone River and Black Canyon's magnificent rock walls. Bighorn sheep are occasionally spotted on the cliffs. A suspension bridge provides access across the river. For those with additional energy, Crevice Lake lies just 0.25 mile to the west on the Yellowstone River Trail and Knowles Falls is found just 1.25 miles beyond that. All others should retrace their steps to the trailhead, allowing plenty of time and water for the climb back.

6 — FORCES OF THE NORTHERN RANGE SELF-GUIDING TRAIL

Difficulty: very easy; handicapped accessible with assistance
Distance: 0.5-mile loop
Usage: low
Starting elevation: 800 feet; no elevation gain
Season: mid-May through early October
Map: USGS 7.5-minute Tower Junction, WY

This boardwalk provides visitors with expansive views of the Northern Range, coursing through a forest burned in Yellowstone's 1988 fires. Interpretive signs encourage visitors to explore the many forces of nature, including fire, that shape the landscape. While most children are familiar with Smokey Bear and the story of Bambi, few know the positive side of forest fires. Walking this boardwalk is a good introduction.

Drive 8.1 miles east of Mammoth Hot Springs or 9.9 miles west of Tower Junction on the Mammoth–Tower Road. Park in the turnout on the north side of the road. Begin on the boardwalk and walk clockwise.

Of the eight major fires that swept through Yellowstone in 1988, the one that burned the most acreage, including this area, was the North Fork Fire. From its discovery on July 22, 1988, until its smoldering demise two months later, the North Fork Fire consumed nearly 500,000 acres, more than half of the total acreage burned in Yellowstone that summer.

The North Fork Fire was started by a logger who discarded a lit cigarette just outside the park's southwest boundary. The National Park Service fought the fire immediately, but all attempts to subdue it were futile. Extreme drought conditions had so dried the forests that the trees lit up like matchsticks. High winds drove embers over natural and man-made firebreaks. Backfires and firelines were useless. In short, the North Fork Fire was uncontrollable.

Before the fires of 1988, much of Yellowstone was covered with dense stands of lodgepole pine. Unfortunately, many of these forests were not healthy. Years of fire suppression by the park service had created unnaturally old and

Forces of the Northern Range Self-Guiding Trail

uniformly aged stands. In the first hundred years of Yellowstone Park, the park's policy was to extinguish all fires quickly. The resulting densely packed trees were highly susceptible to disease and insect infestation. In the decades before the fire, pine beetles took great advantage of the weakened trees and killed a large percentage. Forests filled with standing dead and dying trees were ripe for burning when the North Fork Fire arrived.

Furthermore, historians claim that significant fires occur every 250 to 400 years in the Greater Yellowstone Ecosystem. Growth rings on the park's oldest trees revealed that a great fire had not swept the park since the early 1700s. Historically, Yellowstone was due for a fire.

The North Fork Fire was not an ecological catastrophe. As early as the spring of 1989, lush regrowth was already apparent. Along the boardwalk, notice the abundant pink fireweed and lavender lupine. Here and throughout the park, fireweed moved in rapidly to protect the soil from erosion. The vibrant pink flower takes its name from its swift invasion of fire-ravaged or disturbed areas. Lupine also came to the rescue by trapping nitrogen and returning it to the soil, thus aiding the growth of new plants. Look also for heart-leafed arnica, with its yellow daisylike flower. Arnica is another early pioneer that holds and enriches the soil.

A profusion of young lodgepole pine, now nearly ten feet tall, also grow along the boardwalk. These pines are specially adapted to fire. They bear serotinous cones that open and release their seeds only under conditions of extreme heat. The post-fire conditions of bare mineral soil and full sunlight are their prescription for rapid growth. The pines will rise quickly over the next thirty to eighty years. Children walking the boardwalk today who return with their own children will walk, twenty-five years hence, in the shade of a forest.

Wildlife, also, is faring well in post-fire Yellowstone. The dead trees that surround the boardwalk are a haven for insects. The insects attract birds such as woodpeckers and bluebirds, which make their homes in the standing snags. The young nutritious plants blanketing the ground attract marmots, mule deer, elk, and a host of small rodents. The rodents in turn are food for coyotes, hawks, and owls. Contrary to the message found in popular children's tales, most wildlife prospers from periodic forest fires. Their mobility saves them from harm during the actual burn.

Compared to the dense, dark forest that stood here before 1988, this area is filled with diversity, life, and potential. The burned area supplies food and homes to many more animals and opens up vistas that were blocked for hundreds of years. While it is natural to mourn destruction, it is wise to champion rebirth and understand the natural healing process already well underway in Yellowstone.

7 YELLOWSTONE RIVER OVERLOOK

Difficulty: easy
Distance: 2 miles one way
Usage: low
Starting elevation: 6,270 feet; elevation gain, 200 feet
Season: mid-May to early October
Maps: USGS 7.5-minute Tower Junction and Specimen Creek, WY

This short trail brings you to an impressive overlook of the Yellowstone River at the Grand Canyon's northern end. Walking along the canyon rim, 700 feet above the river, there is opportunity to see bighorn sheep on the cliffs, mule deer or elk in the meadows, and countless marmots on trailside rocks.

Drive 1.5 miles east from Tower Junction on the Tower–Northeast Entrance Road to the Yellowstone River Picnic Area on the right (south) side of the road. Park in the picnic area and look for the signed trail that heads southeast, ascending the hill behind the picnic area. (The trailhead sign indicates the junction with Specimen Ridge Trail in 2 miles.)

The trail climbs the grassy slope, thick with sagebrush and flowers in summer. Douglas-fir dot the hillside, easily recognized by their soft needles and distinctive cones with tiny trident-shaped bracts protruding from their scales. One Yellowstone ranger imaginatively likened the tridents to the backsides (two back legs and a tail) of tiny mice jumping into holes between the scales—an excellent description for children.

The trail quickly reaches the rim of the canyon. Below, to your right the Yellowstone River flows rapidly north. Walk east along the rim to enjoy the magnificent views. All around notice the glacial erratics (large boulders) dotting the hillsides and meadows. The erratics were dropped by the huge glaciers that shaped the valley. Note also that many erratics have a tree growing from their north sides. Boulders shelter seedlings from damaging winds, allowing them to flourish.

In early summer, arrowleaf balsamroot adorns the hillside. The large, yellow heads bloom in luxurious bunches. The flowers are easily identified by their arrowhead-shaped leaves. Young shoots are a favorite early summer treat of elk and deer. Native Americans also had many uses for this plant: a healing poultice was made from its leaves, its seeds and woody roots were roasted, and its ripe stem was peeled and eaten raw like celery. By July their bright heads shrivel to brown as these dry slopes welcome smaller and more subtle flowers.

Soon arrive at an area with an abundance of rocks and a large number of

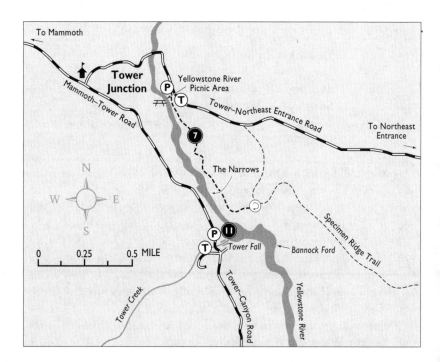

yellow-bellied marmots. Each morning, chunky marmots waddle from their rocky burrows to eat the nearby vegetation. By September their summer munching has added half an inch of fat all over their round bodies. Roly-poly marmots are a favorite prey of golden eagles.

The trail continues southeast along the canyon rim. Across the river the geothermal activity of Calcite Springs comes into view. This is an excellent place to see how heat and water dramatically change the appearance of rock. On cliffs opposite the springs, bighorn sheep can be seen in early summer and fall. As you walk, notice also the dark holes at the top of the cliffs, marked by white bird droppings. These are nests of ravens, the huge black birds seen throughout the park.

The trail approaches The Narrows, the narrowest section of the 14-mile-long Grand Canyon. Proceed to the junction with the Specimen Ridge Trail, 2 miles from the trailhead. Riverside at this point, you are directly opposite the Tower Fall parking lot. History enters here, just east (upstream) of Tower Creek's entrance into the Yellowstone River. There you'll find the site of the Bannock Ford.

From 1840 to 1878, at this relatively narrow and shallow section, Indians, including the Bannock, crossed the river to enter their summer hunting grounds. The scarcity of bison in the west drove the Bannock and neighboring tribes to seek bison herds in the east. The ford was part of the 200-mile trail across northern Yellowstone used by the Indians. The trail was only in use for about forty years, for by 1878, the government had forced the Bannock and other tribes onto reservations. Nevertheless, the trail is permanently a part of Yellowstone, for the present-day road from Mammoth to Cooke City closely follows the original Bannock Trail. The trail junction is a good place to turn around. Retrace your steps and enjoy the views as you head back to the trailhead.

8 PETRIFIED FOREST ◢◣

Difficulty: strenuous
Distance: 1.75 miles one way
Usage: low
Starting elevation: 6,200 feet; elevation gain, 1,150 feet
Season: late-May to mid-September
Map: USGS 7.5-minute Tower Junction, WY

High on an exposed ridge, reachable only by rugged, off-trail hiking, are some of the finest specimens of petrified trees on earth. Fifty-five million years ago, a tremendous rain of volcanic ash buried alive an immense standing deciduous forest. Beneath the ash, the trees absorbed silica and thus solidified in their original form. Some specimens stand fifteen feet high on the eroded slopes. Finding the trees in their remote and somewhat hidden location heightens the hiker's sense of mystery and discovery. In addition, numerous fascinating fossil imprints can be found on the surrounding volcanic rocks.

Finding the trees, however, requires a steep climb and some cross-country hiking. A steep, badly eroded trail leads straight up the ridge, but this is *not* the recommended route. Continued use will only make this trail more treacherous. Those interested in visiting the forest should stop at the nearby Ranger Station at Tower Junction, where the ranger will explain the best route to the forest and supply you with a map.

This area is well-frequented by bears, so take appropriate precautions. Lastly, remember, of course, that it is illegal to remove specimens from the park. Carrying away even a small fragment degrades the area and adversely affects scientific research there.

9   SLOUGH CREEK MEADOWS

Difficulty: easy
Distance: 2 miles one way
Usage: moderate
Starting elevation: 6,400 feet; elevation gain, 300 feet
Season: mid-May through late September
Map: USGS 7.5-minute Tower Junction, WY

The Slough Creek Meadows Trail provides access to a gentle and beautiful valley, much favored by fishermen. This easy hike offers flowers in summer, bright aspen in fall, and curvaceous, trout-filled Slough Creek and snowcapped Cutoff Mountain nearly year-round. Bring bug repellent in summer.

Drive east on the Tower–Northeast Entrance Road approximately 5.7 miles from Tower Junction to the dirt road leading to Slough Creek Campground. Turn north on this road and drive about 1.8 miles to the signed trailhead, located about 0.5 mile before the campground.

Ascend on the Douglas-fir-lined road, passing groves of blackened aspen whose inner bark has been eaten by elk. Creamy buckwheat, pink sticky geranium, lavender lupine, and bright yellow arrowleaf balsamroot decorate the meadows. Colorful butterflies also abound in summer. Yellowstone hosts at least

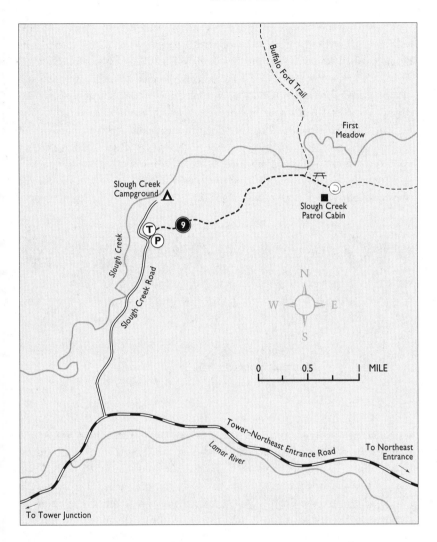

128 species of butterflies; this is a good hike for children to start counting.

Have children also look on the hillsides for "lollipop" trees, where elk have browsed so heavily on a tree's lower branches that the tree is shaped like a lollipop, with a bare trunk extending down from a roundish clump of vegetation. In winter, when food is scarce, elk will chew on nearly any plant.

After almost a mile, the trail levels, descends a bit, and bends north. Pass a very wet area to your right, perfect moose habitat, where there's likely to be at least one family of ducks. To the north, your first good view of Cutoff Mountain appears.

The trail next descends gently into a shady forest of fir and spruce, and then quickly reaches the First Meadow of Slough Creek. Explore the meadow by bearing right at the trail junction. The Buffalo Ford Trail heads left.

Slough Creek meadow is lovely and peaceful, framed by exquisite silhouettes of mountains to the north. On its green banks, anglers try for rainbow and cutthroat trout. You may also meet the stagecoach that works the wagon trail, bringing guests to the Silver Tip Ranch located just outside the park boundary.

Further exploration brings you to the Slough Creek Patrol Cabin. This is a good turnaround point for the youngest hikers. Those hungry for more meadows (or fishing) can follow the trail north over a 200-foot rise to the Second Meadow, another fine spot to fish or picnic.

10 TROUT LAKE 🐾

Difficulty: easy
Distance: 0.5 mile one way
Usage: high
Starting elevation: 6,800 feet; elevation gain, 150 feet
Season: early June to mid-September
Map: USGS 7.5-minute Mount Hornaday, WY

Trout Lake delivers a nice scenic punch. The perfectly round lake is gorgeously set beneath snowcapped peaks, amid gently sloping flowered meadows. Arrive when the trout are spawning and you can watch them lying in the outlet stream, flipping like pancakes. For those who have never seen multitudes of beautiful fish up close and wild, Trout Lake is a real treat. Be forewarned that Trout Lake is a popular fishing destination. You'll share the lake with numerous biting insects also, so be prepared.

Drive approximately 17.7 miles from Tower Junction on the Tower–Northeast Entrance Road to a pullout with a trailhead sign on the left side of the road. From the Northeast Entrance, the trailhead is about 1.5 miles south of the Pebble Creek Campground. Park in the small pullout and find the trail on the pullout's west side.

The trail climbs moderately amid flowers and mature Douglas-fir. Watch for pink sticky geranium, vivid blue forget-me-nots, and pastel pink phlox. Butterflies are especially attracted to the phlox's narrow tube where its nectar is stored. Sample the fragrance of this small, five-petaled flower. It is said to be particularly sweet at dusk.

A short climb quickly brings you over a small ridge to the lake. Trout Lake is scenically nestled amid the surrounding peaks of Druid Peak, Frederick Peak, and Mount Hornaday. Mount Hornaday was named for a naturalist instrumental in the fight to save the bison from extinction. A fine trail runs the perimeter of the lake, allowing for easy exploring.

The finest area for picnics is on the far side of the lake, where you have an impressive view of the Thunderer (10,243 feet). This formidable peak was named for its attraction of sensational lightning strikes. To reach the lake's opposite shore, turn right, avoiding the spillway that was built when this lake supported a hatchery. Along the way, pass the inlet creek, where just a bit upstream spawning rainbow trout can be seen in mid-June. Please don't unduly disturb the fish. This lake was once overfished and is now strictly catch-and-release. Its rainbows are quite hefty.

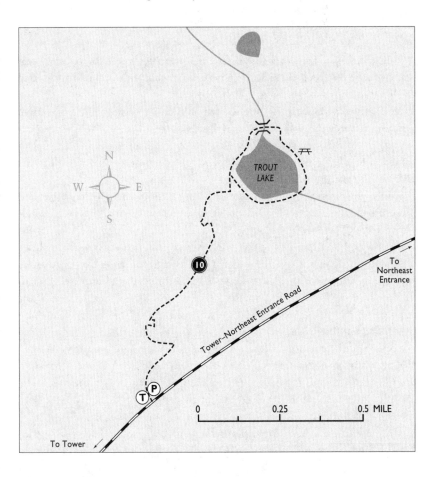

Families should venture all the way around the lake. Ducks, trout, and anglers may be all the wildlife visible at midday, but deer, elk, and bear may be present in the quiet hours. Hikers may also explore this beautiful area further by hiking off-trail in the surrounding meadows.

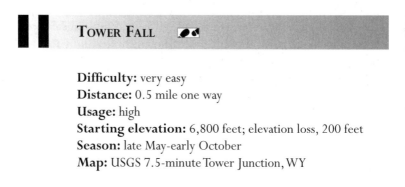

TOWER FALL

Difficulty: very easy
Distance: 0.5 mile one way
Usage: high
Starting elevation: 6,800 feet; elevation loss, 200 feet
Season: late May–early October
Map: USGS 7.5-minute Tower Junction, WY

A well-maintained trail leads to the base of Tower Fall, where torrents of water leap through tall, rock pinnacles. The best time to hike this trail is in spring and early summer, when the water is high, and in the early morning, when the sun casts a gorgeous rainbow. In summer, the only time to visit the falls is at dawn or dusk, for crowds easily overwhelm this short trail.

Drive to the Tower Fall Parking Area, located 2.5 miles southeast of Tower Junction on the Tower–Canyon Road. The trail starts on the paved path to the right of the Hamilton Store. (See the trail map on page 98.)

Walk down the path to the fall overlook, and then head to the right and descend on a staired trail. The trail is easy, but steep in places as it winds down through juniper and Douglas-fir. Arrive first at a bench overlooking the Yellowstone River. Across the river, the yellow rock cliffs of Specimen Ridge rise almost 700 feet above the water. Ocher sandstone cliffs like these along the lower reaches of the Yellowstone River inspired the Minnetaree Indians to call the river *Mi tsi a-da-zi*, or Rock Yellow River. The French recorded the name as *R. Des Roches Jaunes* (River of Yellow Rock). In 1798 the name was translated into English as Yellow Stone.

A short distance upstream lies the Bannock Ford, where between 1840 and 1878, Native American tribes crossed the Yellowstone River to visit their summer hunting grounds (Trip 7). It is also likely that John Colter, the first white man to enter Yellowstone, crossed the Yellowstone River at the Bannock Ford when he arrived in 1807.

To view Tower Fall, continue along the main trail (to the left). A few minutes' hiking upstream along Tower Creek brings you to the base of the fall.

Tower Fall

One hundred and thirty-two feet above you, water rushes between dark stone pillars. The eroding force of water and the differing resistance of the underlying rock created the falls and columns. The strangely eroded "towers" above the fall give the place a mystical feel. Around you, lush, green vegetation and colorful flowers are nurtured by the waterfall's spray. When sufficiently cooled by the spray, retrace your steps to return to the parking area.

Opposite: Yellowstone Lake, Yellowstone National Park

CHAPTER 3

CENTRAL YELLOWSTONE

The foremost attractions of Central Yellowstone are the magnificent Grand Canyon of the Yellowstone River, fascinating Norris Geyser Basin, and wildlife-filled Hayden Valley. This chapter describes many beautiful hikes in this region and one very challenging mountain bike route.

North of the Grand Canyon, on the Tower–Canyon Road, lie the trailheads for Mount Washburn, a popular and terrifically scenic destination. Summit climbers are rewarded with unparalled views of the park and surrounding mountain ranges. Try it by bike (Trip 13) or by foot (Trip 12) The meadows on the north side of Mount Washburn are excellent places to look for grizzly bears from the turnouts on the Tower–Canyon Road.

The Grand Canyon offers many trails around its rim, from the relatively easy (Trips 15, 16) to the moderately strenuous (Trips 17, 18) to the most challenging (Trip 14). If there is no time for hiking in this region, the most impressive canyon viewpoints are the north rim's Brink of Lower Falls Trail (Trip 16), which takes you to the dizzying edge of the magnificent Lower Falls, and the south rim's Artist Point overlook, where a panoramic view of

Norris Geyser Basin

the canyon and Lower Falls can be seen. Artist Point is especially breathtaking in early morning and at sunset.

Just south of Canyon Village, on the Canyon–Fishing Bridge Road, lies bison-filled Hayden Valley. This 9-mile-long valley hosts over one thousand bison, and numerous elk, grizzlies, and bald eagles from spring through the fall. During the bison's rut in August, driving is difficult, for the feisty bison often stubbornly occupy the roadway, generating "buffalo jams."

Just south of the Hayden Valley, Le Hardy Rapids deserves a short visit if you're touring the park during trout spawning season in early summer. At the height of the season, trout can be seen jumping the rapids three to four feet in the air, about every fifteen seconds. A boardwalk takes visitors to a beautiful viewpoint right above the rapids.

Norris Geyser Basin offers great opportunities to view geysers and colorful hot springs on an expansive system of boardwalks. Don't miss the eruption of Echinus Geyser, whose twenty-minute show rightfully draws substantial crowds. Check for predicted eruption times at the Norris Museum. To see fascinating geothermal features without the crowds, hike the Artist Paint Pots Trail (Trip 19). Camping families can find scenic riverside campsites at nearby Norris Campground.

Finally, those with strollers or wheelchairs can take the handicapped-accessible Two Ribbons Trail (Trip 20) and examine the jubilant rebirth of a burned forest along the beautiful Madison River.

12   MOUNT WASHBURN   ▰◣

> **Difficulty:** strenuous
> **Distance:** 3 miles one way
> **Usage:** high
> **Starting elevation:** 8,863 feet; elevation gain, 1,380 feet
> **Season:** late June to September
> **Map:** USGS 7.5-minute Mount Washburn, WY

This is a great climb for families. Strong youngsters can handle the grade, the views are fabulous, and an enclosed fire lookout on the summit shields you from the roaring winds. Hikers also have a good chance of seeing Yellowstone's elusive bighorn sheep—reason enough to climb 1,400 feet to the summit.

Drive to Dunraven Pass Picnic Area, located 5.6 miles north of Canyon Village and 13.4 miles south of Tower Junction on the Canyon–Tower Road.

Park in the lot on the east side of the road. In early summer, check for snow conditions prior to hiking. Even in midsummer, enough snow may linger for a few snowballs at the top.

This route to the summit follows an old road with a moderate grade. With each step, views improve and trailside flowers grow more abundant. Flower displays are quite grand in midsummer. Growing in profusion are red-orange Indian paintbrush, lavender lupine, and yellow windflowers. In early summer, pink shooting stars brighten the meadows.

Notice the abundance of whitebark pine lining the trail. Many were touched by the sweeping North Fork Fire in the summer of 1988. Recognize whitebark pine by its needles in bundles of five and its short, purplish cones. Whitebark pine seeds are an important food source for the park's grizzlies.

Two other woodland creatures, the red squirrel and Clark's nutcracker, also depend on the nutritious, high-fat seeds. Instead of competing, however, both of these creatures inadvertently assist the grizzly. First, in a good year, a red squirrel gathers and hides thousands of cones in middens (huge storage piles) in the whitebark forest. Bears have only to find these treasure troves to satisfy their voracious appetites. An indiscriminate (and ungrateful) bear will also dine on the red squirrel!

The Clark's nutcracker enters the picture by extracting thousands of pine seeds with its long, pointed beak. The bird then stores these seeds in underground caches. When the cone crop is good, a single Clark's nutcracker can remove over thirty thousand seeds! More importantly, the birds misplace half of the seeds they bury. Thus, many germinate, ensuring a continuing source of food. Many other forest animals enjoy the whitebark seeds, but none are so essential to the grizzly's survival as the industrious nutcracker and red squirrel.

The trail climbs steadily in long switchbacks up the ancient volcano. To the east, there are increasingly good views of the jagged Absaroka Range, named for the Crow Indians in their native language. On a clear day, look south for a distant view of the Grand Tetons. As you near the summit, scan the slopes for bighorn sheep. The sheep are frequently seen, often quite near the trail. If you encounter a herd, use binoculars and do not approach them. The animals are quite vulnerable to stress.

Regal bighorn rams can be recognized by their C-shaped headdress of horns. Bighorn sheep, both male and female, grow horns from birth, but only the males' horns reach majestic proportions. The oldest rams have nearly a full circle of horn, while young rams have short, straight horns. Young males, in fact, are easily mistaken for ewes (occasionally even by the other rams!).

In summer, the approach to the summit is bordered by ground-hugging, alpine flowers. Don't tread on these fragile beauties. In their extremely short

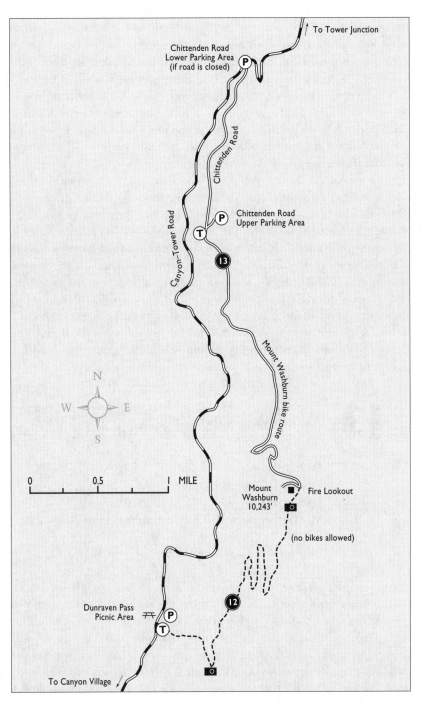

To Tower Junction

Chittenden Road Lower Parking Area (if road is closed)

Chittenden Road

Canyon–Tower Road

Chittenden Road Upper Parking Area

13

Mount Washburn bike route

N
W   E
S

0   0.5   1   MILE

Mount Washburn 10,243'

Fire Lookout

(no bikes allowed)

12

Dunraven Pass Picnic Area

To Canyon Village

growing season of just a few weeks, the flowers must grow, bloom, and set seed. Some of these tiny plants are actually decades old!

Finally, atop the summit, take in the fabulous view, and then duck out of the wind by visiting the fire lookout, open June through September. In the lookout's observation room are natural history displays and a powerful telescope. Be sure to bring a good map so you can locate landmarks from this central vantage point. To the east is the Grand Canyon of the Yellowstone, to the south Hayden Valley and Yellowstone Lake, and to the southwest Old Faithful and the Lower, Middle, and Upper Geyser Basins.

The summit of Mount Washburn is a great place to contemplate the Yellowstone caldera, for Mount Washburn sits on its northeast rim. Six hundred thousand years ago, an immense dome rose up and exploded in one of the greatest volcanic eruptions ever to occur on earth. Debris landed as far away as present-day Kansas. It is said that the volume of lava and ash hurled was ten thousand times greater than the 1980 eruption of Mount St. Helens. After the eruption, the dome collapsed, leaving a crater, or caldera, measuring nearly 50 miles across. This caldera was once thousands of feet deep, but subsequent lava flows and glacial sculpting have filled in most of the depression. Look south from the summit to the vast forested interior of Yellowstone and you'll be looking at the area encompassed by the immense crater. Retrace your steps to return to the trailhead and enjoy gorgeous views all the way down.

13 MOUNT WASHBURN

Difficulty: strenuous
Distance: 3 miles one way
Usage: high
Starting elevation: 8,840 feet; elevation gain, 1,440 feet
Season: late June to September
Map: USGS 7.5-minute Mount Washburn, WY

Strong mountain bikers can pedal to the finest lookout in Yellowstone via Mount Washburn's Chittenden Road. From the spectacular summit, take in the Absarokas, the Gallatins, and even the Tetons, and then prime yourself for a thrilling ride down, dropping 1,400 feet in 3 miles. Good brakes and self-control are essential on this busy trail. In early summer, cyclists should check road conditions before departing. This route is also recommended for hikers in early summer when the trail from Dunraven Pass (Trip 12) is impassable due

View south from Mount Washburn

to snowfields. Finally, don't forget to bring plenty of water, warm clothes, and raingear, in any season.

Drive to Chittenden Road, located on the Tower–Canyon Road about 5 miles north of Dunraven Pass (8.5 miles south of Tower Junction and 85 miles north of Canyon Village). Drive about 1.2 miles on the Chittenden Road to its upper parking area. Early in the season, this section of road may be closed and cyclists must park in the lower parking area, adding over 2 miles to the trip. (See the trail map on page 111.)

Tourists once drove to the top of Mount Washburn. Now, thankfully, only cyclists and hikers can use the Chittenden Road. This road was named for Hiram Chittenden, an innovative road engineer in Yellowstone and its first historian.

The road passes stretches of jubilantly flowered meadows. Standing snags welcome shockingly blue mountain bluebirds. Look for them among the bare, white branches. Long views from Chittenden Road reveal the mosaic pattern of the 1988 burns. Patches of meadows and new growth stand beside mature green stands. Shifting winds, differences in moisture levels, and variance in tree size and distribution all affected the path and severity of the burn.

Follow the road's long, loopy switchbacks. As you near the summit, watch for the mountain's small herd of bighorn sheep, present only during the summer. As described in Trip 12, a fire lookout station is located on the summit. Visitors can enter the lower level to escape the often bitter winds and inclement weather that frequents the 10,000-foot peak. For more detailed information on Mount Washburn and its incredible views, see Trip 12.

To return to the trailhead, cyclists must go back on the Chittenden Road. Do not take the road heading back to Dunraven Pass, as that is strictly for hikers.

14 SEVEN-MILE HOLE

> **Difficulty:** strenuous
> **Distance:** 5.5 miles one way
> **Usage:** moderate
> **Starting elevation:** 7,800 feet; elevation loss, 1,400 feet
> **Season:** late May through early October
> **Maps:** USGS 7.5-minute Mount Washburn and Canyon Village, WY

This difficult trail takes hikers to the bottom of Yellowstone's Grand Canyon, 7 miles downstream of the canyon's Lower Falls and a thousand feet beneath its gorgeous yellow cliffs. Be forewarned that climbing out of the canyon is very demanding, especially on a warm summer day. For those not up to this challenge, the trail's first 1.2 miles offer a shady, mostly level walk along the canyon's north rim, affording good views and an escape from crowded observation points.

The trail begins at a glacial boulder, a five-hundred-ton erratic dropped from a glacier moving through this area 15,000 years ago. (The gneiss is estimated to be more than 600 million years old.) To find the boulder, drive southeast from Canyon Village on the North Rim Drive (one way) about 0.75 mile, and then turn left on a two-way road heading east. Drive 0.5 mile and watch for the boulder on the left (north) side of the road. Park along the road next to the boulder.

The trail leads east through a lodgepole pine forest. The ground cover is thick with grouse whortleberry, a small, reddish purple berry with tiny elliptical leaves. The tasty berries provide hikers, birds, and bears with a delicious late summer snack.

The trail parallels the rim of the canyon. Short spur trails to the rim provide excellent views. While at the canyon's edge, scan the rock pinnacles for osprey nests, identifiable as large clumps of mud, sticks, and debris atop the columns. Osprey build nests as large as five feet in diameter. Sharp eyes might also spy the handsome brown and white hawks. The wings of an osprey are dark brown and its head white, with a distinctive black band across its eyes. Osprey can dive

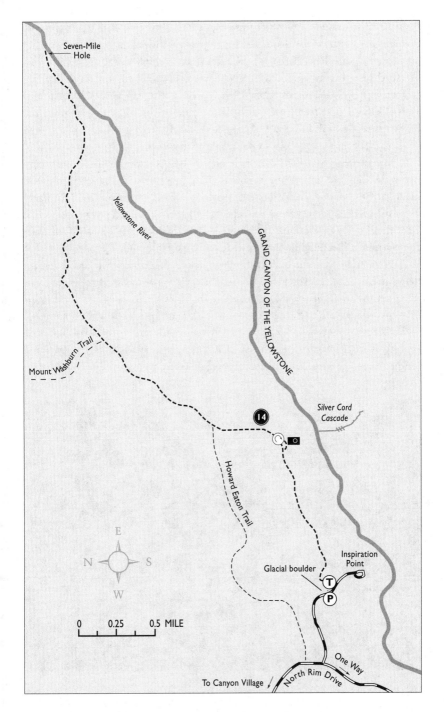

over 100 feet, plunging feet-first into the water, emerging with a fish securely clasped in its talons. The osprey always turns the fish to face forward, taking advantage of aerodynamics as it flies to its nest or perch to eat.

After only 1.2 miles, look for a well-trod spur trail to your right. Follow that trail to an overlook of Silver Cord Cascade. The cascade's thin ribbon of water drops 1,300 feet from the opposite side of the canyon, making it the highest cascade in Yellowstone. Those seeking only an easy walk should return to the main trail and go back to the trailhead at this point.

Those heading to Seven-Mile Hole continue northeast. The trail soon veers north, leaving the canyon rim. Arrive at a trail junction with the Howard Eaton Trail and stay right (north). Hike through lodgepole forest for approximately 1.3 miles. The trail begins to descend steeply. After crossing a bridge over a stream, arrive at a fork in the trail. To the left is the Mount Washburn Trail. Take the right fork (heading northeast) to Seven-Mile Hole.

The trail initially courses lazily through thick and peaceful forest and then suddenly arrives at the canyon rim. Dark pine boughs frame the immense orange and white canyon walls. Below, the green Yellowstone River runs white with frothy rapids. Steam rises from areas of thermal activity. The trail descends with seriousness.

Follow the steep switchbacks with care. Loose, gravelly soil provides poor footing. Pass steaming fumaroles, small meadows, and stands of low-lying juniper trees. Juniper trees are easily recognized by their hard, green berrylike

Falls of the Grand Canyon of the Yellowstone River

cones that are used as flavoring for gin. Crush one in your hand to detect its familiar scent. Native Americans ate juniper berries and, in times of scarcity, also consumed the tree's inner bark.

Pass signs for campsites and look for orange metal blazes marking the trail. The air becomes noticeably cooler and moister as you approach the river. Finally at the river's edge, at the bottom of the canyon, enjoy a well-deserved rest. Pull out a fishing pole, binoculars, or picnic and contemplate the peacefulness and wonder of this extraordinary space. To return, retrace your steps, allowing plenty of time for the tough trek up.

15 LOOKOUT POINT TO RED ROCK POINT

Difficulty: easy
Distance: 0.4 mile one way
Usage: high
Starting elevation: 7,840 feet; elevation loss, 500 feet
Season: late May to early October
Map: USGS 7.5-minute Canyon Village, WY

For fabulous views of Yellowstone Canyon's Lower Falls, hike down to Red Rock Point from Lookout Point. After several switchbacks, a wooden staircase leads hikers to a viewing platform overlooking the falls. It's an impressive reward for a short, albeit steep, walk.

From Canyon Junction, drive west 1.5 miles on the one-way North Rim Drive to Lookout Point and park in the well-marked parking area.

Before you descend to Red Rock Point, visit the Lookout Point viewing platform. As well as gaining an awesome view, sharp eyes can spy three osprey nests. Look for huge, bushel-shaped twig nests atop the rock pillars. From the viewpoint, look across the canyon to two pillars rising from the opposite side: one directly across, the other slightly to the left. A nest is also visible to the left of the viewpoint on the near side of the canyon. With binoculars, you may even see the birds or their young within the nests. Osprey mate for life and produce two or three offspring each year.

Next, descend on the steep path leading to Red Rock Point. The volume of water pouring through the narrow canyon is awesome. In spring, snowmelt swells its volume to 64,000 gallons per minute. At that rate, an Olympic-size swimming pool could be filled in a mere thirty seconds! This wild torrent of water continues to deepen the canyon by wearing away the soft volcanic rock. Since the last glaciers

Climbing the stairs from Red Rock Point, Yellowstone Canyon

moved through this area 10,000 years ago, the river has dropped 50 feet.

The Lower Falls is 308 feet high, about three times the height of Niagara Falls. It was Niagara's honky-tonk commercial development in the 1870s that prompted the awestruck members of Yellowstone's early expeditions to argue so persuasively for establishment of this park. Imagine, if you can, a power plant utilizing the immense hydropower of the Yellowstone River, accompanied by the smokestacks of factories using this electricity, joined by motels lining the North Rim Drive offering honeymoon suites, waterbeds, and cable TV. We must be thankful for the foresight of the early conservationists! The Yellowstone River remains the longest undammed river in the continental United States.

For an even more dramatic view of the Lower Falls, try the Brink of Lower Falls Trail (Trip 16).

16 BRINK OF LOWER FALLS TRAIL

Difficulty: easy
Distance: 0.75 mile one way
Usage: high
Starting elevation: 7,700 feet; elevation loss, 600 feet
Season: late May to early October
Map: USGS 7.5-minute Canyon Village, WY

The Brink of Lower Falls Trail drops quickly to a platform directly above the lip of the powerful 308-foot Lower Falls. Nowhere else can you feel the almost frightening, wild power of this great rushing waterfall. The raw immediacy of its racing water and the thunder of its falling torrents impresses even the weariest sightseer. If you have time for only one stop along the canyon, try this short hike.

From Canyon Junction, drive east and then south along the one-way North Rim Drive to a large, well-marked parking area located at its southern end. This is the last parking lot before the drive merges with the Canyon–Fishing Bridge Road. Don't mistake this trail for the Brink of Upper Falls Trail located farther south on the Canyon–Fishing Bridge Road. (See the trail map below.)

The trail switchbacks down steeply' losing 600 feet in only 0.75 mile. If hiking in spring or fall, watch for icy conditions that make this trail dangerous and slick. At the brink of the falls, keep a close eye on youngsters. The canyon has been the site of several tragic deaths.

Hikers should take their time on the return ascent, especially those not used to high-altitude hiking. If the kids are up for another close-up view of the falls, try Uncle Tom's Trail on the south rim (Trip 18).

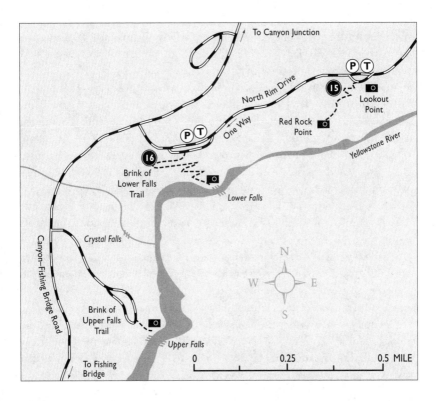

17 CLEAR LAKE LOOP

Difficulty: moderate
Distance: 3.75 miles round trip (add 3.1 miles for Ribbon Lake detour)
Usage: moderate
Starting elevation: 7,700 feet; elevation gain, 120 feet
Season: late May through early October
Map: USGS 7.5-minute Canyon Village, WY

Don't miss this easy, but extraordinary, gem of a hike. The trail offers awesome canyon views, a variety of thermal features, two lovely lakes, and meadows filled with flowers (and often wildlife). Early or late in the day, especially in the spring or fall, hikers may see elk, bison, or mule deer. Bears also frequent the area, particularly early and late in the season. For the most beautiful canyon views, hike this trail late in the afternoon.

Drive south from Canyon Junction 2.2 miles to the Chittenden Bridge. Turn left and drive over the bridge onto Artist Point Road. Drive approximately 0.5 mile to a large parking lot signed for Uncle Tom's Trail. As you enter the lot, note the trailhead for Clear Lake located on your right. Before setting out, pick up a NPS brochure describing the canyon area at a dispenser near the start of Uncle Tom's Trail.

The Clear Lake Trail immediately takes you south across Artist Point Road and into open meadows. Views to the north include Mount Washburn (10,243 feet). Watch for soaring red-tailed hawks hunting for meadow rodents. Throughout the meadow grows a scraggly shrub, called rabbitbrush, whose stems and leaves are covered with fine, whitish hairs. Wildlife, especially rabbits, enjoys its leaves and foliage. Small mammals also use the shrub for cover. Depending on the season, a variety of flowers graces the meadow. In early summer the display is at its finest. Watch for pink shooting stars, yellow arrowleaf balsamroot, and white sego lilies.

After 0.9 mile, arrive at a trail junction with the Wapiti Lake Trail. Take the left (northeast) fork. In 0.1 mile, arrive at Clear Lake. The large, beautiful green lake is a perfect place for a picnic, if the winds are cooperating. Thermal features on the north side of the lake emit a sulfurous odor that some may find objectionable.

The trail continues along the east side of Clear Lake. As you pass the lake, the odor of sulfur increases until you arrive at a particularly amusing mud pot. Stand back to avoid the splattering mud. Stay on the trail across a rocky area, a virtual garden of small thermal features. Look for bubbling hot springs, hissing steam vents covered with green and yellow algae, and more odorous mud pots. Do not approach any thermal feature, as the surrounding crust may be thin.

One-half mile from Clear Lake, arrive at a trail junction. Bear left for Lily Pad Lake. The trail to the right leads to Ribbon Lake in 1.3 miles. The trail to Ribbon Lake takes you through pleasant lodgepole forest to a series of lakes. If you choose to visit the Ribbon Lake area (the detour adds 3.1 miles to the hike), be sure to follow the Ribbon Lake Trail northeast to the lake's outlet. Cross the outlet and head north to the rim of the canyon. As well as gaining beautiful canyon views, you'll be at the head of Silver Cord Cascade, which plunges over 1,000 feet to the Yellowstone River. (For another view of the cascade, see Trip 14.) To return, retrace your steps along the Ribbon Lake Trail. Backpacking families will find a nice campsite at Ribbon Lake.

For those hiking the shorter loop, stay left to reach well-named Lily Pad Lake. The pond is covered with pond

Gently observing a nest. (Please do not remove natural objects.)

lilies, quite a pretty sight when the large yellow flowers are blooming. Native Americans enjoyed the seeds of the pond lily roasted, and they are reputed to taste like popcorn. Today they are relished by waterfowl. Watch also for muskrat who feed on the lily's submerged rootstalks.

The roar of the Yellowstone River is audible at Lily Pad Lake, for the canyon is only 0.1 mile to the north. Follow the trail along the west side of the lake via sandy switchbacks to the canyon rim. At the rim, the view is unequaled. The canyon's colors are almost shocking in their intensity, particularly late in the day. The intense pinks, oranges, and yellows of the canyon's walls were created when heat from thermal activity altered the normally brownish rhyolite rock.

Canyon enthusiasts can indulge in another detour by hiking 0.5 mile northeast along the rim to Point Sublime. The walk affords more magnificent canyon views, usually with few other hikers. The scenery is staggeringly beautiful. Pay attention

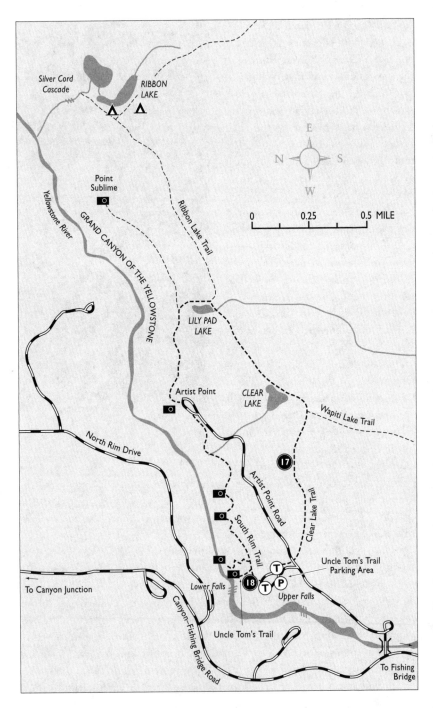

to youngsters on these stretches, as the trail drops off quite steeply in places.

To head back toward the trailhead, turn left toward Artist Point (0.5 mile to the southwest). The remainder of the hike follows the canyon's south rim. In the canyon, watch for brown-and-white osprey and jet black ravens. Osprey build huge nests atop the canyon's rock pinnacles. Two nests are visible from Artist Point Lookout. Ravens hide nests in holes in the canyon walls.

From Artist Point, the South Rim Trail continues southwest about 1 mile to Uncle Tom's Parking Area. The mostly paved path alternates between canyon views and shady lodgepole forest. Before you reach Uncle Tom's Parking Area, arrive at a trail junction with Uncle Tom's Trail. To view (and feel!) the Lower Falls from an observation platform dramatically constructed 500 feet below the canyon rim, turn right at the junction. (For a full description, see Trip 18.)

To return directly to the trailhead, keep left. At a second trail junction just 0.1 mile farther, again stay left to ascend to the parking area.

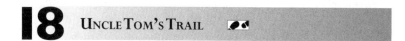

18 UNCLE TOM'S TRAIL

Difficulty: moderate
Distance: 0.25-mile trail, plus approximately 300 stairs
Usage: high
Starting elevation: 7,700 feet; elevation loss, 500 feet
Season: late May through early October
Map: USGS 7.5-minute Canyon Village, WY

A short but demanding hike on Uncle Tom's Trail leads to the brink of the Lower Falls for absolutely magnificent views. Hikers descend over 500 feet on steel platforms bolted to the canyon wall. This trail is often crowded, so arrive in the early morning for solitude. To view a rainbow in the spray, try late morning or early afternoon. Follow the directions in Trip 17 to reach Uncle Tom's Parking Area and Trailhead.

This trail was named for Tom Richardson, who, in 1903, built a "trail" at this location where hikers lowered themselves into the canyon on rope ladders. Today hikers descend on over three hundred steel stairs. Nevertheless, this trail can still be very dangerous. Be extremely careful when ice coats the stairs, as may occur in spring, fall, or early morning in any season.

Follow the clearly marked path from the parking lot. At the first junction, turn right. Shortly, arrive at a second junction and turn left. Immediately, meet another fork and stay right. To the left is a viewpoint over the Lower Falls; stay right to descend directly into the canyon.

Follow the stairs, descending along the moist canyon wall. At the bottom, the roar of the water is intense. In spring and early summer when the river is full of snowmelt, the platform is doused with spray. In spring, a glorious 64,000 gallons of water per second race over the falls. At times of low water, this volume is reduced to 5,000 gallons per second.

How were these awesome falls created? In simple terms, the Yellowstone River flows through an ancient geyser basin beginning at the Upper Falls. The river was able to erode this basin to a deep canyon because the hot, acidic water of thermal features weakened the underlying rock. Where the rock was thermally altered (and therefore softened), the river was able to carve it away. The Upper and Lower Falls developed in the transition zone where sections of underlying rock were not affected by thermal activity. These shelves of rock were stronger and therefore resistant to the eroding force of the flowing water. While the rock above and below it has fallen away, water tumbles over the enduring rock shelf of the Lower Falls.

If you think Uncle Tom's man-made stairway is too intrusive in a place of such natural grandeur, be thankful that commercial interests were prevented in the 1890s from installing an elevator at the Lower Falls! Owen Wister, author of *The Virginian,* wrote of the narrowly defeated elevator proposal, "Politics was behind it, as usual. To put a lot of machinery by those Falls at the head of the canyon, where the sublime merges with the exquisite, and which alone is worth crossing the continent to see, would have been an outrage more abominable than the dam at Jackson Lake."

If youngsters balk at climbing back up the gazillion stairs, try this: have each child guess how many steps there are, and then count them on the way back up. (The answer is 328; be prepared with suitable rewards!)

19   ARTIST PAINT POTS TRAIL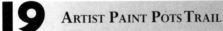

> **Difficulty:** very easy
> **Distance:** 0.5 mile one way
> **Usage:** moderate
> **Starting elevation:** 7,360 feet; elevation gain, 140 feet
> **Season:** late May through early October
> **Map:** USGS 7.5-minute Norris Junction, WY

Leave the crowds at Gibbon Meadows for a delightfully short hike to fascinating thermal features. Youngsters will be captivated by strange colored pools and a huge spitting, burping mud pot. In spring and fall, elk are plentiful along the trail.

From Norris, drive 4.2 miles south on the Norris–Madison Road to the trailhead on the road's east side, signed for Artist Paint Pots Trail. From Madison, drive 9.8 miles north on the Norris–Madison Road to the trailhead.

Most of the tourist activity in the area is directed toward Gibbon Meadows on the west side of the road, where elk and bison graze year-round along the Gibbon River. The number of animals visible in the meadow increases significantly from September through May. Gibbon Meadows and Elk Park (just a few miles north) are the wintering grounds for thousands of elk in Yellowstone's Gibbon-Madison-Firehole herd.

The trail to the paint pots begins on a boardwalk, then heads east (left) along the base of a charred hillside. This area was extensively burned in 1988 by the North Fork Fire, the largest fire of that extraordinary summer. Happily, regrowth is robust along the trail. Young lodgepoles reach nearly ten feet tall. Along the hillside in late summer, watch for grouse whortleberries, a delicious relative of the blueberry with very delicate, egg-shaped leaves.

Roiling mudpot on Artist Paint Pots Trail

These sweet, reddish purple berries were much enjoyed by Native Americans and today are relished by wildlife and hungry hikers. Hugging the ground also are small woodland strawberries, another particularly tasty treat. Above you, in the branches of the fir and lodgepole, hang bright green lichen. In the winter when forage is scarce, the lichen is a nutritious food for elk and mule deer.

As you walk among the lodgepole pine, notice the many slender trees whose bark has been scraped off. This is the work of bull elk that use the trees to remove velvet from their antlers. Fuzzy "velvet" covers the elk's fast-growing antlers throughout the summer. Blood vessels within the velvet nourish the growing antler bone. Elk antlers grow extremely fast, as much as an inch a day! Full-grown racks of a mature bull can reach five feet across and weigh forty pounds. When the antlers cease growing, the elk rubs off the velvet by using the sides of young lodgepoles. Observant visitors may spy a bull "jousting" with a lodgepole, his velvet hanging like a decrepit rag from beautiful, burnished antlers.

After 0.2 mile, reach a trail junction. Stay to the left and regain the boardwalk. The rumbling, steam, and smell of the thermal area are now evident. Pass the first of the "paint pots," a milky blue pool, followed by a chalky white pot. Iron-oxide minerals give the pools their unusual colors. Yellow, brown, and orange algae expand the palette.

Cross a bridge over a hot spring, and then rise with the trail as it loops back in a westerly direction. The views improve with the elevation gain. Below are pools of various colors, easily visible in the fire-cleared landscape. Beyond on the northern horizon are the Gallatin Mountains.

On the upper loop, mud pots and hot springs are plentiful. The trail's highlight for most children is the large mud pot at the west end of the upper loop. Behind a splattered wooden corral, a huge belching, spitting mud pot entertains noisily. Mud is routinely flung 10 feet in the air. On angry days, visitors must stand a few feet behind the railing. Mouths may fall open in wonder at the strange burping, but watch out. On our last visit, a high-flying gob of mud landed right *in* the mouth of a fascinated seven-year-old!

What is causing this strange phenomenon? Mud pots are hot springs with a limited water supply. Boiling water beneath the surface produces sulfuric acid. Because of the scarcity of water, the acid cannot be washed away. This acid dissolves some of the rock with which it comes in contact, creating a thick, sticky clay. The burping and bubbling of the mud pots is produced by steam and gas vapors rising and escaping through the mud.

From the mud pot, the trail reenters the lodgepole forest and heads downhill rather steeply. At the bottom of the hill, bear left to return to the trailhead.

20 TWO RIBBONS TRAIL

Difficulty: very easy; handicapped accessible according to federal standards
Distance: 0.75 mile round trip
Usage: low
Starting elevation: 6,700 feet; no elevation gain
Season: mid-May to early October
Map: USGS 7.5-minute West Yellowstone, WY

The Two Ribbons Trail provides a handicapped-accessible boardwalk over riverbank burned by the 1988 fire. Like the Forces of the Northern Range Trail (Trip 6), the Two Ribbons Trail is an intimate introduction to fire ecology. It is also a pleasant stroll among sculptural snags, vivid flowers, and the sparkling Madison River.

From Yellowstone's West Entrance, drive 3 miles east on the West Entrance–Madison Road to a turnout (11 miles west of Madison Junction) on the left (north) side of the road. There are two turnouts, so you may begin the hike at either end. The following description is written for those beginning at the easternmost turnout.

The boardwalk heads immediately to the edge of the Madison River. This river is one of the most highly prized trout streams in North America. Trout favor its clear waters and ample gravel spawning beds. But the real secret of the Madison is its temperature. Thermal runoff from nearby hot springs keeps the Madison relatively warm year-round. Hot springs also add minerals to the water, which promote the growth of aquatic plants that in turn attract insects (food for the trout).

In midsummer the flowers are striking along the boardwalk. Silver snags and young green lodgepole contrast pleasingly with the magenta fireweed. Fireweed (also called "blooming Sally") is one of the first plants to colonize burned areas. Its parachuting seeds (with long hairs that catch the wind) quickly spread the plants over wide areas. Fireweed helps hold and enrich scorched soil so that a variety of plants, shrubs, and trees can follow. Fireweed is also a valuable food source, especially for elk. Before the fireweed blooms, lavender lupine, buckwheat, and a variety of yellow composites add color to the area.

Already a great many young lodgepole are thriving along the boardwalk. Prior to 1988, this forest was not a healthy one. Many of its pines were killed by pine bark beetles. When the North Fork fire swept the area, these dead and dying trees, lacking the moisture of healthy pines, went up like matchsticks. Consequently, the fire actually hastened a rebirth. Without fire, a fallen lodgepole can take a century to decompose. After the fire, valuable soil nutrients were released from standing snags and downed trees in a fraction of the time.

As you continue west on the boardwalk, stay to the right and enter a stand of trees spared by the fire. This is characteristic of most of the burned areas of the park. Shifting winds and tree conditions caused the fire to burn in patches rather than wreaking total destruction.

Look down to find large, round patties by the boardwalk. These were left by bison, which are frequently seen in the meadows along the Madison River. The banks of the Madison also provide excellent year-round habitat for elk, trumpeter swans, and occasional moose.

From the boardwalk, there are good views of the Gallatin Range to the north and west. To the immediate southeast, Mount Haynes rises to 8,235 feet. Follow the boardwalk as it loops around closer to the road and returns you to the trailhead.

Opposite: Old Faithful from Observation Point

CHAPTER 4

SOUTH YELLOWSTONE

The southern half of Yellowstone National Park contains some of its most famous sights, including the Upper, Middle, and Lower Geyser Basins and lovely Yellowstone Lake. Visitors can find hiking trails rich in diversity, three fine biking trails, and a wealth of boardwalks from which to view fascinating thermal features.

To find beauty along the shore of Yellowstone Lake, hike the trails in Trips 21 and 22. For an impressive lake overlook, try Trip 23. A picnic on the beach behind the Fishing Bridge Visitor Center can also be quite relaxing and offers a 0.5-mile stretch of sandy beach on which to stroll or cast for fish. Those wanting to explore Yellowstone Lake by boat should inquire about guided tours or charter boats at Bridge Bay Marina (see Chapter 1).

Hikers seeking thermal features can explore Biscuit Basin and a lovely cascade on Trip 25, the Old Faithful Geyser Basin on Trip 26, or a unique backcountry geyser on Trip 28. Two pretty backcountry lakes are also easily accessible, Shoshone Lake (Trip 29) and Riddle Lake (Trip 30). Backpacking families can find good sites on Trips 28 and 29.

There are some good cycling opportunities in South Yellowstone also. Cyclists can ride the bike trail at the Upper Geyser Basin (Trip 27), ride the scenic Fountain Flat Drive (Trip 24), cycle the strange and interesting Firehole Lake Drive, or take their mountain bikes to a backcountry geyser (Trip 28).

Water adventures are available as well. Hot summer days bring carloads of swimmers to the swimming hole at the end of Firehole Canyon Drive. From wading to intrepid wave riding, youngsters of all ages enjoy the natural setting and thermally warmed waters of the Firehole River. It's also an immensely popular place to picnic. Swimmers should remember, however, that diving and jumping from cliffs is strictly prohibited and unconscionably dangerous.

Visitors to South Yellowstone should stop by the Grant Visitor Center to view its fascinating fire exhibit and films. For the many interpretive talks and walks offered by the park service in this area, inquire at park visitor centers or consult the park publication *Discover Yellowstone*.

21 | PELICAN CREEK LOOP

Difficulty: easy
Distance: 1-mile loop
Usage: low
Starting elevation: 7,760 feet; no elevation gain
Season: July through September
Map: USGS 7.5-minute Lake Butte, WY

On a hot summer day, Pelican Creek Loop is an excellent hike for young families. A short and shady path leads to a lovely sandy beach on Yellowstone Lake, where the water is shallow and temperate and magnificent scenery abounds. Pelican Valley, located just north of this trail, is prime grizzly habitat, so be sure to check with rangers before hiking. Closures or restrictions may apply.

Drive 0.9 mile east of the Fishing Bridge Visitor Center on the Fishing Bridge–East Entrance Road. Find the trailhead and parking pullout on the south side of the road, just west of the Pelican Creek Bridge.

Nearby Pelican Valley is one of Yellowstone's most important habitats for grizzlies. Since 1975, the grizzly has been listed as threatened under the Endangered Species Act. In fact, Yellowstone has one of only two viable grizzly populations south of Canada. Where 100,000 grizzlies once roamed from Mexico to the Arctic in the 1800s, now only 1,000 (at best) inhabit islands of protected habitat in Wyoming and Montana. Currently the park estimates that there are about 250 grizzlies left in Yellowstone, owing to encroachments upon their habitat by development and recreational use. Consequently, hiking in Pelican Valley is restricted to day use between 9 A.M. and 7 P.M. to minimize human contact with the bears.

Follow the trail into a lush forest where it immediately forks. Head right and enter gardens of lavender lupine, magenta fireweed, white buckwheat and yarrow, blue phlox, and numerous yellow composites. Watch for mule deer sampling this colorful buffet. In late summer, you may taste too; try the wild strawberries and sweet, blue huckleberries.

In the rich, moist soil near the lake, forest succession is taking place. The older lodgepole pines are giving way to spruce and fir. The sun-loving lodgepole was the pioneer. Its dense canopy provided the shade essential to spruce and fir seedlings. When the spruce and fir mature, their branches will shut off the sun and ensure that future generations of their seedlings will thrive. Lodgepole will not return until fire, insect infestation, landslide, or other natural disturbance clears the trees and opens the land once again to the sun.

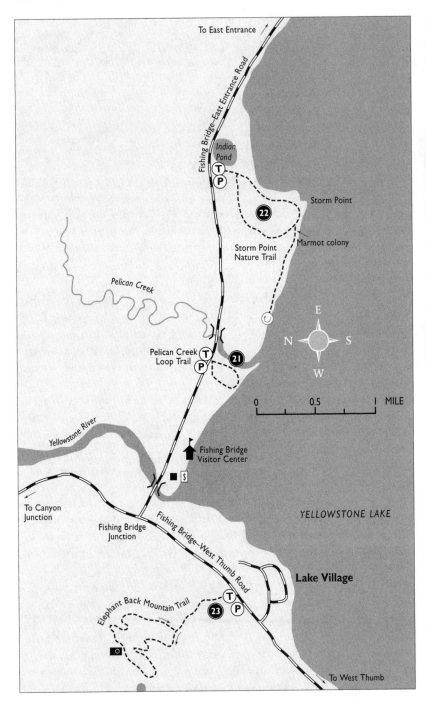

Hikers making strides along Yellowstone Lake

The trail soon arrives at the sandy beach. Strip off your boots and wade in the shallow water. Most of Yellowstone Lake is frigid, making swimming impossible. Most summers the water here warms to tolerable levels because of the shallowness of this section of the lake.

On nearby rocky islands, watch for the American white pelican. White pelicans are quite large and beautiful, with snow-white feathers and a long, bright orange beak. The white pelican lives exclusively on lakes of the American West. Unfortunately, its population has suffered in recent years due to habitat loss and the thinning of its eggs from pesticide poisoning. Enjoy watching these magnificent birds, but never approach too closely. You may inadvertently drive a bird from its nest and cause it to abandon its eggs or even its young.

The trail travels a few yards to the left (west) along the beach, and then turns back into the woods. A scenic spur trail on your right brings you to the bank of Pelican Creek.

To return to the trailhead, regain the main trail and follow it to the fork in the forest, traversing first a set of boardwalks over a wet meadow. When you arrive at the junction, bear right to reach your car.

22 STORM POINT NATURE TRAIL LOOP

Difficulty: moderate
Distance: 3- to 5-mile loop
Usage: moderate
Starting elevation: 7,800 feet; elevation gain, 50 feet
Season: July through September (check for trail closings)
Map: USGS 7.5-minute Lake Butte, WY

The trail to Storm Point is especially delightful. It covers beautiful and varied terrain, visiting meadows, forests, ponds, and a stunning beach. It also provides excellent opportunities to see wildlife. This hike traverses prime grizzly territory, so hikers must check with rangers for closures or restrictions prior to departure. Because of bear activity, it is recommended that the trail be used by parties of four or more.

From Fishing Bridge Junction, drive east 3 miles on the Fishing Bridge–East Entrance Road to the Storm Point Trailhead on the right (south) side of the road. (See the trail map on page 132.)

Yellowstone Lake, near Storm Point

The trail begins in a pretty meadow west of Indian Pond, a favorite camping site for Native Americans. In 1880 numerous stone tools, brush horse corrals, and human shelters were found near the pond. Recently a perfectly preserved tepee ring was also discovered nearby. Indian Pond lies in an ancient volcanic crater created by a steam explosion. Its circular shape and high embankments are clues to its violent origin. In the pond, there's a small population of cutthroat trout. Watch also for Canada geese and Barrow's goldeneye ducks. The male goldeneye has a purple head, black-and-white body, white crescents in front of its eyes, and bright orange feet.

The trail continues south past the pond. At the first fork, stay left, continuing south. As you pass mature lodgepole pines, check for signs of bear. Grizzlies rub their massive backs against the trees and often leave bits of fur in the bark or on the exposed sap. Further up the trunk look for narrow, vertical cuts. These were likely made by a grizzly's long, curved claws. Grizzly claws were prized by Native Americans and were worn as a sign of bravery. Awesome specimens can be seen at the Indian Museum in Colter Bay and at the Jackson Hole Museum in Jackson.

Bison also leave their mark on mature lodgepole. They rub their massive heads and horns against the trees, removing large patches of bark. You may also find their hair matted in the sap of the debarked trees. Both males and females have horns that are never shed and are composed of tightly compacted hair over a core of bone. Another sign of bison is a "wallow," a shallow depression in the ground where a bison has rolled around on its back.

Follow the trail to the beautiful and dramatically sculptured shore of Yellowstone Lake. There is plenty of beach to explore and rocks to climb. At the beach, look for tracks in the sand. Grizzly bear tracks can be identified by their large size (their hind feet may be a foot long!) and the claw marks in front of each toe.

Storm Point was named for the tremendous waves and winds that regularly batter the point. The prevailing winds on Yellowstone Lake blow from the southwest, bringing with them severe weather. The winds tend to build in the afternoon, so plan your outing accordingly. While at the lake, watch for graceful white pelicans, goldeneye ducks, and osprey.

The trail heads west above the lakeshore. In this area, watch for yellow-bellied marmots. On clear days, they are likely to be sunning themselves on the rock outcroppings. Marmots, a relative of the eastern woodchuck, spend their summer days lazily munching the park's greenery. They must build up a thick layer of fat to last them through their long winter hibernation. Please do not feed these roly-poly beggars; nature supplies them nutritionally with all that they need.

After a short stroll along the lake, the trail turns north (right) into the forest. Before entering the woods, take a short and beautiful side trip farther west along the lakeshore. Just continue along the shore for more views of striking

Storm Point and a variety of waterfowl. Watch for moose in the wetlands to the right of the trail. To return to the Storm Point Trail, just retrace your steps to the point where the trail turns into the forest.

Enter the dense lodgepole forest. This type of lodgepole stand is called a "doghair" forest, for the trees are "as thick as the hair on a dog's back." Another way to explain this to youngsters is to ask them to imagine how fur looks to a flea on a dog. A doghair forest is created when trees grow so close together that the sun is unable to reach a tree's lower branches. Consequently, the lower branches lose their needles, die, and fall off, leaving a forest of bare trunks. Make a lot of noise as you hike, for bears often retreat to the forest during the day to rest. If a bear should hear you, it is likely to move away to avoid an encounter. In August, don't miss the plentiful whortleberries and wild strawberries growing on the forest floor.

Finally the trail leaves the woods, crosses a creek, and arrives in an open meadow. In the meadow grows yampah, or squaw potato, a plant whose plump roots are much loved by grizzlies. The grizzlies dig them up with their long claws, which they can move independently like fingers. Yampah tastes a little like carrot and was a staple of Native Americans and mountain men. Yampah sports clusters of small, white, five-petaled flowers arranged in umbels and has slender, fernlike leaves. It grows one to three feet tall and blooms in July and August.

The trail loops back to a junction near Indian Pond. At the junction, head left (north) to return to the trailhead.

23 ELEPHANT BACK MOUNTAIN LOOP

Difficulty: moderate
Distance: 3.5-mile loop
Usage: moderate
Starting elevation: 7,800 feet; elevation gain, 750 feet
Season: late June through September
Map: USGS 7.5-minute Lake Butte, WY

This steep trail climbs through dense forest to an excellent view of Yellowstone Lake. Youngsters may, however, find the trail tough and a bit monotonous. Also, those seeking a pristine view will be disappointed to see the park's development so obvious along the lakeshore. Despite these drawbacks, the vista from the summit is still gorgeous. This trail is not recommended for spring hiking, since grizzlies are frequently sighted in the area in May and June.

Drive about 1 mile south from the Fishing Bridge Junction on the Fishing Bridge–West Thumb Road. The trailhead is on the west side of the road. (See the trail map on page 132.) Park along the roadside.

The trail parallels the road briefly, and then turns westward to head into lodgepole forest. The forest is pleasant, with a green undergrowth of grass and flowers. For a refreshing treat, look for tiny wild strawberries in late summer. The trail soon climbs moderately. At a fork in the trail, take the left path and switchback up, sometimes steeply, to the top of the mountain.

At the top there are excellent picnic spots with panoramic views. Below you is magnificent Yellowstone Lake, measuring 20 by 14 miles, with islands, beautiful bays, and a gorgeous undulating shoreline. Don't miss viewing the lake at sunrise and sunset when the water's still surface shares the brilliant colors of the sky and mountains.

At the summit, a young hiking companion asked, upon seeing the sprawling hotel/hospital/lodge complex below, "When are we going back to the park?" His idea of Yellowstone was forests, not parking lots; bears, not buildings. I directed his gaze south to the Red Mountains and east to the snowcapped Absarokas, but deep down, I felt his question was wise and telling.

To return to the trailhead, follow the loop trail northeast. The trail descends via switchbacks, and then swings southwest to meet the main trail. At the junction, keep left to reach the trailhead.

24 FOUNTAIN FLAT ROAD AND FAIRY FALLS

Difficulty: easy
Distance: 5 miles one way via bike (plus 1.6 miles one-way hike)
Usage: moderate
Starting elevation: 7,200 feet; elevation gain, 50 feet
Season: mid-May to early October
Map: USGS 7.5-minute Lower Geyser Basin, WY

Cyclists will enjoy riding through open meadows and forest along the scenic Firehole River to Midway Geyser Basin. The first 1.6 miles are on paved road, but car traffic is thankfully prohibited. At about 4 miles from the trailhead, cyclists can leave their bikes and take a short hike (1.6 miles) to pretty Fairy Falls. To have the road to yourself, begin this ride early in the day.

To reach Fountain Flat Road, drive 10 miles north of Old Faithful on the

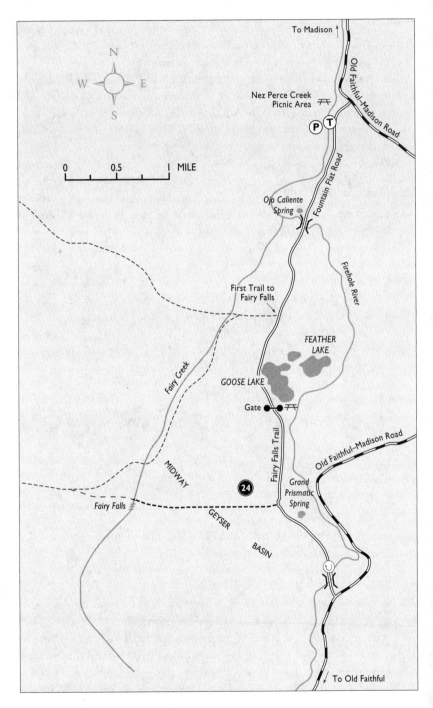

To Madison ↑

Nez Perce Creek
Picnic Area

P T

Old Faithful–Madison Road

Fountain Flat Road

Ojo Caliente
Spring

Firehole River

First Trail to
Fairy Falls

FEATHER
LAKE

GOOSE LAKE

Fairy Creek

Gate

Fairy Falls Trail

MIDWAY

24

Grand
Prismatic
Spring

Old Faithful–Madison Road

Fairy Falls

GEYSER

BASIN

To Old Faithful ↙

N
W E
S

0   0.5   1 MILE

Arrowleaf balsamroot

Old Faithful–Madison Road or drive 6 miles south of Madison. Turn southwest onto Fountain Flat Road. There is parking just across the bridge at the Nez Perce Creek Picnic Area.

From the Nez Perce Creek Picnic Area, ride south along the Firehole River. The meadows flanking the river are home to elk, bison, coyote, and sandhill cranes. The warmth of the river keeps the mammals here year-round. In 1850, mountain man and raconteur Jim Bridger reported that the Firehole River "flowed so fast down the side of the hill that the friction of the water against the rocks, heated the rocks." Though this is obviously a tall tale, hot springs beneath the riverbed do heat the river bottom in many places. For example, at 1 mile, pass Ojo Caliente Spring, a fine, crested hot spring just west of the road. Hot springs like Ojo Caliente can raise the river temperature a toasty 20 degrees. Cross the river on a narrow bridge. The waters are rich with cunning brown, rainbow, and brook trout.

After the bridge, the Firehole slips out of sight, and you proceed through an area burned by the 1988 North Fork Fire. It was this blaze that swept voraciously southeast to nearly consume the historic Old Faithful Inn. Miraculously, winds shifted just in time to save the magnificent structure.

At 1.6 miles, the dirt road begins. Pass the junction with the first trail to Fairy Falls and a lake on your left. At a little over 3 miles, arrive at Goose and Feather Lakes and the end of the old automobile road. This is an excellent place for a rest stop. The Firehole River winds scenically below you. The water here is fairly warm, so you may want to soothe your feet at the river's edge. Swimming in the river, however, is discouraged by the NPS.

Resume your ride on the road beyond the gate, traveling south. After 0.6 mile, the level road brings you to the junction with the second trail to Fairy Falls. If time allows, hike the 1.6-mile trail to the 200-foot-high falls (about one hour round-trip, no bicycles allowed). The easy, mostly level trail travels west through rebounding forest to the high, feathery falls. In midsummer, the forest is colorful with flowers and the occasional mountain bluebird. Imperial Geyser, just 0.7 mile farther on the well-marked trail, has unfortunately ceased erupting.

From the Fairy Falls Trailhead, the road continues south, and then curves southeast along the edge of the Midway Geyser Basin. At the steel bridge across the Firehole River, turn around and ride back to your car.

25 MYSTIC FALLS LOOP

Difficulty: moderate
Distance: 3.2-mile loop
Usage: moderate
Starting elevation: 7,274 feet; elevation gain, 420 feet
Season: late May to early October
Map: USGS 7.5-minute Old Faithful, WY

Hike a diverse and pleasant trail to 70-foot Mystic Falls. Enjoy fine forest walking, a clear rushing stream, some boulder-hopping, cascade viewing, and a superb overlook of the Upper Geyser Basin. In spring and fall, you may encounter bison, elk, and even moose along the trail. For a special treat, leave the trailhead forty-five to sixty minutes before the estimated eruption of Old Faithful or Castle Geysers, and you'll have a fabulous view from the scenic overlook (about 1.7 miles from the trailhead).

Drive to Biscuit Basin, located 2 miles north of the Old Faithful cloverleaf on the West Thumb–Madison Road and park in Biscuit Basin's large parking lot. Before you leave the parking lot, take note of the steam rising from vents in the asphalt. You are standing in the crater of an immense volcano, created by an eruption 600,000 years ago. The volcano's fiery remains still smolder beneath your feet. Its thermal power fuels the largest collection of hot springs, geysers, and mud pots known on earth.

Cross the Firehole River (trout are often visible from the bridge) and walk

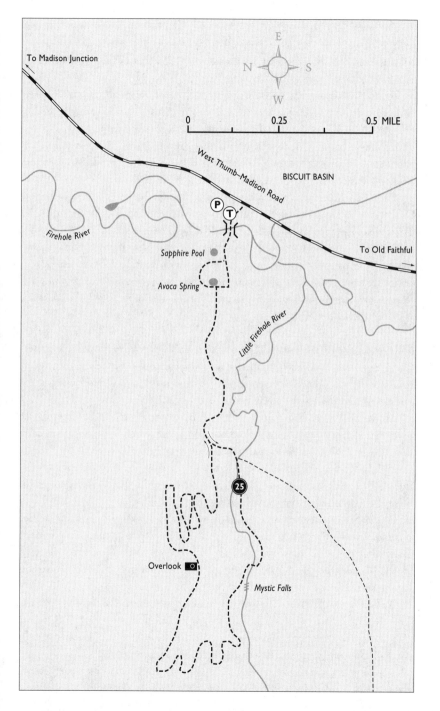

on the boardwalk to beautiful Sapphire Pool. Billowing clouds of steam waft from its jewel blue depths. Sapphire Pool was once edged with biscuit-shaped rock formations, but a major earthquake in 1959 caused the pool to erupt violently, knocking off all the "biscuits."

To find the trailhead, continue west to the end of the boardwalk. Across from tumultuous Avoca Spring, the trail begins. This area was badly burned by the 1988 North Fork Fire. In the forest today, regrowth is evident everywhere, with abundant young lodgepole, bright pink fireweed, and lavender lupine. The abundance of snags (standing dead trees) is good news for bluebirds, woodpeckers, and other insect-loving, cavity-nesting birds.

After 0.6 mile, arrive at a trail junction with the trail to the overlook. Descend to the left. In just 0.1 mile, arrive at a junction with the Summit Lake Trail. Head right for Mystic Falls. As the trail approaches the falls, it follows the Little Firehole River. The moisture of the vegetation near the riverbanks spared most of the trees from the fire, though you have only to look on the river's opposite bank to see the devastation. Relish the green garden of pines and flowers growing lushly along this stretch of trail, accompanied by the sparkling water of the Little Firehole.

Prominent among the many flowers is the beautiful fringed gentian, Yellowstone's official flower. The gentian is easily recognized by its deep purple, fringed petals. In early summer these slopes are also covered by arrowleaf balsamroot, a bright yellow composite whose leaves are shaped like arrowheads. Elk and mule deer enjoy the balsamroot's tender shoots.

Arrive at Mystic Falls, just 1 mile from the trailhead. The small, tiered cascade is delightfully situated for exploration. For good views, descend (carefully) to the river. Watch for hot springs feeding into the river at the base of the falls. To observe from above, follow the switchbacks. A steep spur trail to the left descends dramatically to the lip of the falls. This maneuver requires the utmost care, and children should be watched diligently.

In the rocky area around the falls, watch and listen for yellow-bellied marmots, also called "whistle pigs" for the high-pitched sound they emit as a warning to fellow marmots. Marmots resemble rotund groundhogs, with small, fur-covered ears, golden bellies, and reddish brown backs. Marmots can be seen in rocky areas from June to September.

At the top of the falls, climb briefly on switchbacks to the top of the ridge. Then head north (right) to return to Biscuit Basin via the overlook (1.7 miles). You are now traversing the edge of the Madison Plateau. Look carefully through the forest to the left for elk and possibly moose.

Arrive at the overlook and enjoy panoramic views to the east over Biscuit Basin, Black Sand Basin, and the Upper Geyser Basin, including Old Faithful. In the Upper Geyser Basin alone, there are 140 geysers within 1 square mile, nearly 20 percent of the entire earth's geysers. Add the Lower Geyser Basin, and there are more than 300 geysers and about 10,000 thermal features, more than exist in all the rest of the world combined. You can easily pick out Old Faithful in the Upper Geyser Basin by identifying the wooden buildings surrounding it.

From the overlook, the effects of the 1988 fire are dramatic. Fallen trees lie like toothpicks on the hillsides. Islands of trees relatively untouched by the fire illustrate the mosaic pattern of the burn. To return to Biscuit Basin, follow the switchbacks down the steep slope. At the trail junction at the bottom of the hill, stay left and continue east to reach the basin boardwalk.

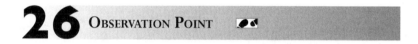

26 OBSERVATION POINT

Difficulty: easy
Distance: 1.9 miles one way
Usage: high
Starting elevation: 7,340 feet; elevation gain, 260 feet
Season: late May through early October
Map: USGS 7.5-minute Old Faithful, WY

The trail to Observation Point climbs quickly to a wonderful view of the entire Upper Geyser Basin. Before you begin, stop by the visitor center to check for predicted eruptions and pick up the Yellowstone Association's *Upper Geyser Basin Guide* available from dispensers outside the center. For optimum enjoyment, combine this short hike with the eruption of Old Faithful. The view is particularly splendid at sunset.

Drive to Old Faithful, located on the West Thumb–Madison Road 17 miles north of West Thumb and 16 miles south of Madison. Follow signs for the Old Faithful Visitor Center and park in any of the large lots surrounding the complex.

From the visitor center, walk toward Old Faithful, and then head east on the paved path keeping Old Faithful on your left. Soon pass the Old Faithful Lodge and Cafeteria. Under the boardwalk in front of the lodge, you are likely to see yellow-bellied marmots. The marmots congregate here for the handouts doled out each day by hundreds of tourists. Please do not feed or touch these appealing beggars. It is harmful to the health of the marmots and can be dangerous for you (see the Introduction). After the lodge, the trail forks; stay right and cross the Firehole River. Just after crossing the river, the trail forks again. Take the unpaved trail to the right that ascends a forested slope.

The trail switchbacks up the slope, bringing you quickly to an impressive viewing perch complete with safety rail and tree-stump seats. After you've taken in the view, and hopefully an eruption, continue north 0.3 mile to view Solitary Geyser before you head back to Old Faithful. From Solitary Geyser the trail heads south to Geyser Hill, where an assortment of pools and geysers await. At the junction with the paved trail, turn left. Pass beautiful blue Doublet Pool, and

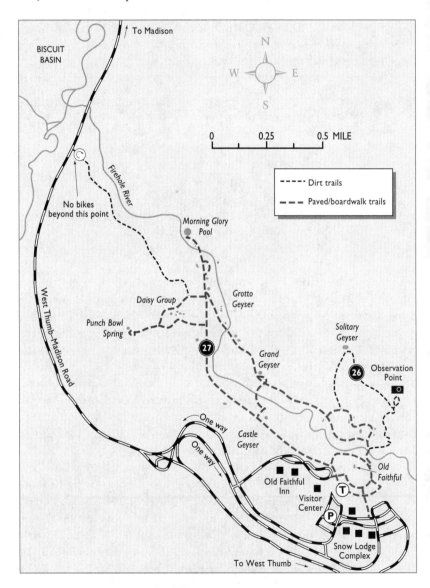

Eruption of Old Faithful

then Giantess Geyser. If you're really lucky, you'll witness one of its dramatic, but infrequent, eruptions. Giantess erupts only two to six times a year, with pre-eruption ground shaking and plumes of water shooting 100 to 200 feet. When Giantess is active, eruptions occur once or twice each hour. After Giantess, continue to the bridge over the Firehole River, and then head back to Old Faithful.

If you want to continue exploring the fascinating Upper Geyser Basin, do not recross the Firehole River. Instead, turn right on the paved trail or boardwalk just before the bridge and head northwest to see Beehive Geyser, the Lion Group, and 0.3 mile farther, Grand Geyser. To return to the parking lot from Grand Geyser, just retrace your steps about 200 feet to the trail junction. Then head west across the Firehole River and turn left at the next junction. Pass Castle Geyser and return to Old Faithful via the paved path. This worthwhile tour adds 0.9 mile to your hike.

For additional hiking suggestions in the Upper Geyser Basin, consult the *Upper Geyser Basin Guide*. Remember, while at the basin, watch your children carefully and never leave the boardwalk or paved trail. In addition, do not throw any object, even a coin, into any thermal feature. Even small objects can cause severe and irreparable damage.

27 UPPER GEYSER BASIN ⌒

Difficulty: easy
Distance: 1.5 miles one way to Morning Glory Pool; 1.9 miles one way additional to Biscuit Basin
Usage: high
Starting elevation: 7,340 feet; no elevation gain
Season: late May to early October
Map: USGS 7.5-minute Old Faithful, WY

This effortless bike ride tours the fascinating Upper Geyser Basin. Because of the crowds, this ride is best done in the early morning. The level terrain and good surfaces make this an excellent trip for young children. Before you depart, check at the visitor center for predicted eruption times, particularly of Castle, Riverside, and Daisy Geysers. Start at the Old Faithful Visitor Center as described in Trip 26.

Begin your ride by heading northwest (left) along the paved walkway. Pass the Old Faithful Inn on your left and ride toward Castle Geyser, about 0.7 mile. Castle Geyser was named for the cone's resemblance to a ruined castle. It is an especially fine geyser to watch, having a long and powerful eruption. Across the boardwalk from the bike path is Grand Geyser and several smaller thermal features. To visit this group, you must leave your bike; riding is prohibited on the boardwalks.

Next ride north along the Firehole River to the intersection with the boardwalk to the Giant-Grotto Group. Ride past Grotto Geyser and cross the bridge over the river to visit Morning Glory Pool. On the way you'll pass Riverside Geyser, whose frequent eruptions arch impressively over the Firehole River.

Backtrack on the bike path to see Grotto Geyser. If you want to extend your ride, turn right on the paved path just after Grotto Geyser that leads to the Daisy Geyser Group. (Those who want to return should continue riding south on the path back to the visitor center.) Before you reach Daisy Geyser, turn right on the dirt path that runs north alongside the Firehole River. Take this gentle path for 1.9 miles until its intersection with the Grand Loop Road. At this junction, you may either proceed on foot to Biscuit Basin (no bikes allowed) or ride back via the bike path to the visitor center.

28 LONE STAR GEYSER

Difficulty: moderate
Distance: 2.3 miles one way
Usage: moderate
Starting elevation: 7,580 feet; elevation gain 160 feet
Season: late May through early October
Map: USGS 7.5-minute Old Faithful, WY

Hike or bike a lovely old road along the Firehole River to the active and impressive Lone Star Geyser. Check at the Old Faithful Visitor Center for the geyser's last recorded eruption and its current eruption interval (historically about three hours). Good planning brings rich rewards at the end of this delightful trail. Try to visit in the afternoon when a rainbow may be visible in the geyser's spray. For backpackers, a fine campsite is located just 0.4 mile past the geyser.

Drive 2.7 miles southeast on the Old Faithful–West Thumb Road from the Old Faithful Overpass to reach the turnoff for the Lone Star Geyser Trailhead. The small parking area is located adjacent to Kepler Cascades. From West Thumb, drive about 14.3 miles northwest on the Old Faithful–West Thumb Road. Find the trail (an old road) at the south end of the parking area.

The road courses through forest untouched by the 1988 fires. Mostly level and with some paving still intact, the road provides an excellent surface for young hikers and mountain bikers. Along both sides of the narrow road, lodgepole pines stand straight and tall. Lewis and Clark named the pine for its use as the supporting element in tepees. Each spring, Native American women cut down young lodgepole, stripped their bark, and allowed them to dry. By fall, the two- to three-inch-diameter poles weighed only seven pounds but retained their strength. To construct a tepee, fifteen poles were bound at one end, spread at the base, and then covered with buffalo hides. Lodgepole pine is easily recognized by its needles, in bundles of two, and by its tall, straight trunk. (It is said to resemble a Christmas tree atop a telephone pole.)

The road soon crosses the Firehole River. Flowers grace the riverbank, including purple harebells and red-orange Indian paintbrush. At the intersection with the Spring Creek Trail, stay (right) on the road. At 1.9 miles from the trailhead, the road meets a service road; stay left. One-tenth of a mile farther, pass a pretty meadow on the left. Watch for grazing elk in the meadow, especially early or late in the day. Just 0.5 mile after the junction with the service road, arrive at Lone Star Geyser.

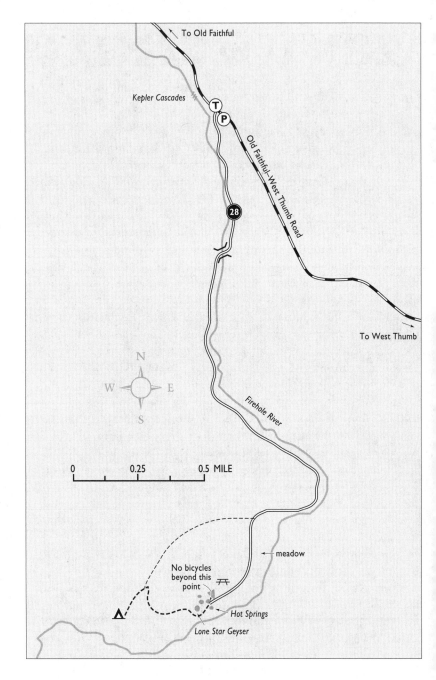

Lone Star's impressive twelve-foot-high calcite cone was formed by the continuous deposition of sinter. The process began when hot water dissolved rock (silica) deep beneath the earth. When the hot water rose to the surface, it carried dissolved minerals which precipitated out as the water cooled, leaving a coating on the cone. Lone Star Geyser splashes much of the time, so its cone continues to grow with each dousing of mineral-laden water.

To determine when the geyser will erupt, observe what is happening at the cone. (But do not approach it!) Beginning approximately one hour before an eruption, Lone Star spurts water from its cone. After an eruption, the geyser boisterously releases steam. During an eruption, water and steam shoot 25 to 40 feet into the air for about fifteen to twenty minutes. (To estimate the time of the next eruption, you can also check the logbook for the most recent entry, and then assume eruptions at three-hour intervals.)

Geyser viewing in the unspoiled backcountry is a whole different experience than in the developed basins. The event is both wonderful and bizarre, especially at Lone Star Geyser. When viewed from the north, the cone resembles the head

Lone Star Geyser, Yellowstone National Park

of a lion. Shrouded in steam during an eruption, the image is awesome and unforgettable.

Even without an eruption, Lone Star Geyser's location by the scenic Firehole River provides a fine destination and superb picnic spot. Cyclists must turn around here, for bicycles are not allowed in the backcountry beyond this point. Backcountry campers can continue to their campsite; they'll be hearing the eruptions throughout the night.

To return to the trailhead (record your eruption first!), just retrace your steps. Back at the trailhead, be sure to take a short walk north to impressive Kepler Cascades, where the Firehole River tumbles 125 feet down a series of rocky tiers through a narrow canyon. Finally, if you're returning to Old Faithful, drop by the visitor center to tell the ranger the time of the eruption you witnessed.

To reach Lone Star's backcountry campsite, continue south past the geyser, and then follow the trail west for 0.2 mile. The trail turns briefly north and reaches a trail junction in 0.1 mile. Bear left and walk southwest just 0.1 mile to the campsite.

29　SHOSHONE LAKE

Difficulty: moderate
Distance: 3 miles one way
Usage: moderate
Starting elevation: 7,920 feet; elevation loss, 120 feet
Season: mid-June through September
Map: USGS 7.5-minute Craig Pass, WY

A pleasant, nearly level hike through meadows and lodgepole forest brings you to the shore of beautiful Shoshone Lake, the second-largest lake in the park. Hike early or late in the day, especially in spring and fall, and you have a good chance of seeing moose in the open meadows north of the lake. There are good campsites for backpackers at the lake.

To reach the Delacy Creek Trailhead, drive 8 miles east of Old Faithful or 9 miles west of West Thumb on the Madison–West Thumb Road. Park in the pullout on the north side of the road. The trail begins on the road's south side.

From the roadside, the trail descends through forest into grassy meadows and follows slow-flowing Delacy Creek. A wide variety of flowers—lavender lupine, creamy yarrow, red-orange Indian paintbrush, and purple aster—adorns

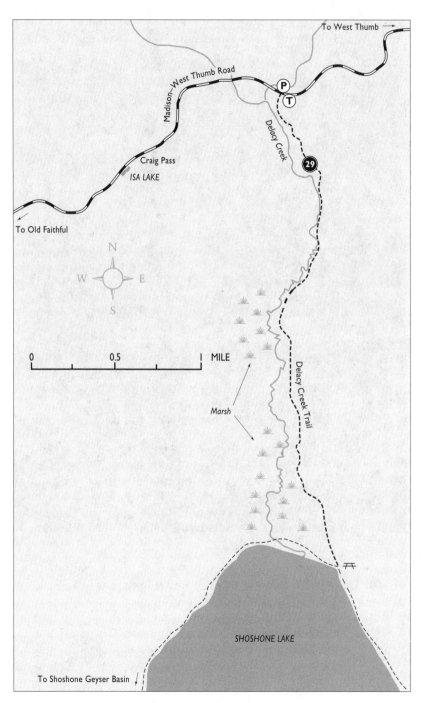

Doghair lodgepole pine forest

the trail. Look also for purple monkshood, a tall flower whose petals resemble the robes and hood of a monk. Monkshood blooms throughout the summer in wet meadows and along streambanks.

Follow the rolling trail as it crosses and recrosses the lazy Delacy. Come upon an open meadow giving you a glimpse of Shoshone Lake in the distance. In the meadows, watch carefully for moose and coyote. Bull moose can reach seven feet at the shoulder, and their antlers can spread over four feet. Each year a bull sprouts this headgear at the rate of up to an inch a day. Bulls shed their antlers each fall, and, as soon as they hit the ground, small mammals greedily consume them for the calcium. The whole rack may disappear overnight.

Despite a moose's somewhat comic appearance, they can be dangerous. Bulls have been known to "tree" hikers during their rut, and cows will aggressively defend their young. It is said that before a cow charges, she sticks out her tongue. Never approach close enough to find out!

Along the trail, look for droppings that resemble chocolate Easter eggs. These are moose droppings. Throughout the winter, moose feed on the tender ends of branches. Their woody diet (the Indian word for moose means "twig eater") produces scat that is remarkably like compressed sawdust. Native Americans and early settlers used moose scat for fuel. It is known for its pleasant piney aroma.

Watch also for waterfowl along Delacy Creek. Look in particular for the regal sandhill crane. This impressive bird stands almost four feet tall and has a wing span of six to seven feet. Adults are brown, with long legs and necks, white markings on the face, and an unmistakable red cap. Cranes like to hunt for insects, seeds, roots, and small rodents in the wet meadows along the creek. If you're incredibly lucky, you might happen upon the courtship dance of two smitten cranes. The huge birds use their long, spindly legs to leap 6 to 15 feet into the air. The dramatic leap is followed by several graceful bows to their partners. Unfortunately, the sandhill crane population has been declining dramatically in the last fifty years as nesting sites are lost to development.

As you approach the lake, the trail once again enters the lodgepole forest. Note the shiny black gravel on the trail. These are pieces of obsidian, a volcanic glass formed when lava flows ran into glacial ice about 75,000 years ago. Obsidian was very valuable to Native Americans, who fashioned it into razor-sharp arrowheads. Obsidian arrowheads from Yellowstone have been found as far away as the Ohio River Valley. Today, obsidian is crafted into high-tech blades used in the most delicate surgery. Far north of this trail, on the Norris–Mammoth Road, you can visit Obsidian Cliff, where a large deposit of obsidian remains to this day.

Finally, the trail leaves the forest to arrive at Shoshone Lake. The lake was named for the tribe of Native Americans originally residing southwest of Yellowstone. Shoshone Lake is said to be the largest lake in the country with no roads leading to it. The lake hosts a healthy population of water birds and brown, brook, and lake trout. On its western shore is an impressive geyser basin with a few active geysers. The geyser basin is about 6 miles away via the lake's north shore trail. Easier exploring is immediately accessible by strolling the beach in any direction. To return to the trailhead, simply retrace your steps.

30 RIDDLE LAKE

Difficulty: moderate
Distance: 2.5 miles one way
Usage: low
Starting elevation: 7,988 feet; no elevation gain
Season: mid-June through September
Map: USGS 7.5-minute Mount Sheridan, WY

The trail to Riddle Lake is pleasant and tranquil. Meadows near the lake provide good opportunities to see moose and waterfowl. Since the trail traverses grizzly habitat, check with a ranger at the Grant Visitor Center for closures or restrictions prior to hiking, especially in spring and early summer. This trail is best hiked in late summer when the meadows have dried and biting insects decrease. Here is a riddle for Riddle Lake: Who was richer, the famous naturalist John Muir or railroad magnate Averell Harriman? The answer is found below.

The Riddle Lake Trailhead is located about 3 miles south of the Grant Village intersection on the east side of the West Thumb–South Entrance Road.

The trail begins at the northeast end of the parking area. Follow the trail northeast through fire-touched woods. Forest regrowth is striking in vibrant greens and pink. Watch for elk enjoying the bright fireweed. Almost immediately

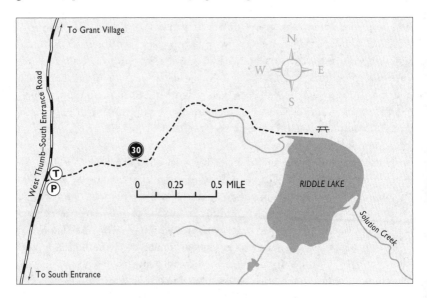

Girl launching a homemade boat

the trail crosses the Continental Divide. You are unlikely to notice, however, since there is nearly no elevation change. Snaking across Yellowstone, but lacking a precipitous crest, the Continental Divide passes through the park with little drama. Its significance, nevertheless, is profound. All water to the east (or north) of the divide eventually flows to the Atlantic Ocean via the Missouri and Mississippi Rivers. All water to the west (or south) of the divide flows into the Snake and Columbia Rivers and eventually to the Pacific Ocean.

The question of water flow is the real riddle behind the name of the lake. Early explorers believed that this lake drained to both sides of the Continental Divide, until the discovery of its outlet stream, Solution Creek. Riddle Lake, in fact, drains to the Atlantic.

Proceed through the forest amid seasonal wildflowers, including yarrow, asters, and lupine. Watch for wildlife as you pass small meadows. Arrive at a large marshy area just before reaching the lake. Then follow the trail east to reach the north shore of Riddle Lake. Pond lilies cover much of the lake's surface. This is prime moose habitat. The north side of the lake is also a prime picnic spot as the view to the south encompasses Mount Sheridan and the Red

Mountains. Watch also for waterfowl, including white pelicans, goldeneye ducks, and Canada geese.

The burn still visible on the southeast side of the lake was a hot spot of the Snake River Complex fire that burned much of the forest from West Thumb to the South Entrance. In July of 1988, the Snake River Complex forced the evacuation of tourists from Grant Village. Although a few buildings were touched, Grant Village was largely spared. Today the Grant Visitor Center has an excellent exhibit describing the fires of 1988.

While picnicking by the lake, you may recognize a particularly familiar and pleasant scent. It comes from the field mint that grows profusely along the lakeshore. Plants in the mint family can be easily recognized by their square stems, opposite leaves, and irregular flowers. Aromatic oils of the mint have long been used as medicines and as food and beverage flavorings by Native Americans and Europeans.

To return to the trailhead, simply retrace your steps. Before you head back, you've learned the answer to the riddle: The wise conservationist John Muir once said about Averell Harriman, "I'm richer than he is. I have all the money I want, and he doesn't."

Opposite: Mount Moran and Jackson Lake

CHAPTER 5

NORTH GRAND TETON

The northern portion of Grand Teton National Park offers spectacular mountain scenery, dominated by majestic Mount Moran. Beautiful Jackson Lake and the scenic Snake River provide plentiful water recreation. The area boasts several gentle hiking trails, excellent backcountry sites for camping, and two easy canoe/kayaking trips.

This relatively small area sees quite a bit of visitation from those staying at nearby campgrounds (Lizard Creek, Colter Bay, Signal Mountain), lodges (Jackson Lake, Signal Mountain), and cabins (Colter Bay, Jackson Lake). Boating and horseback riding are immensely popular. The NPS also offers numerous worthwhile programs. Take advantage of the many lectures, campfire programs, and guided hikes and boat trips offered by rangers at Colter Bay and Signal Mountain.

Set off on your own to find terrifically scenic lakes and wildlife (including trumpeter swans) by hiking in the Colter Bay area (Trips 32 and 33). A superb lakeside campsite can be found just off the latter trail. Canoeists can try the often gentle waters of sheltered Colter Bay (Trip 34) or float a fairly quiet section of the Snake River (Trip 35). There are also two very short walks that offer good views and possibly moose (Trip 36) or scenic river habitat and possibly beaver (Trip 37). Finally, hikers and backpackers can drive out to Togwotee Pass to find a hike and campsite in a strikingly different setting with the possibility of a little more solitude (Trip 31).

Lastly, for a magnificent view at sunset, drive to the top of Signal Mountain, just south of the Jackson Lake Dam. The 7,593-foot summit gives you expansive views of Jackson Hole and the surrounding ranges.

31 JADE LAKES 🐾

Difficulty: easy
Distance: 2 miles one way to Upper Jade Lake; 2.5 miles one way to Lower Jade Lake
Usage: low
Starting elevation: 9,100 feet; elevation gain, 432 feet
Season: mid-June through September
Map: USGS 7.5-minute Togwotee Pass, WY

Set high in the Absarokas, the lovely Jade Lakes lie under dramatically eroded breccia cliffs. Although nearly an hour's drive from Moran Junction, this trail's dramatic setting and relative isolation is well worth the effort. Visit in August

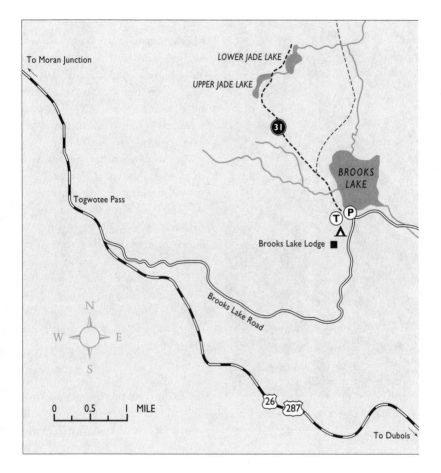

when glorious wildflowers are at their peak. For backpacking families, this short trail leads to superb lakeshore campsites at Upper Jade Lake, only 2 miles from the trailhead.

From Moran Junction, drive east toward Dubois on US 26-287 for about 32 miles to Brooks Lake Road, an unpaved road on the left leading to Brooks Lake Recreation Area (Road 515), 7.8 miles east of Togwotee Pass. Follow Brooks Lake Road about 5.2 miles to Brooks Lake Campground, but do not enter the campground. Turn left (northwest) toward the campground, but stay west to reach a parking area at the south end of Brooks Lake, where you'll find the trailhead.

Head northwest on the wide trail running alongside Brooks Lake, marked for Brooks Lake/Cub Pass. To the east, stratified cliffs rise thousands of feet above the lake. Thirty-eight million to 50 million years ago, Absaroka volcanoes

Making a wish—but do not pick wild plants within the parks!

poured layers of volcanic ash and lava over the range. This mixture of rock, ash, and mud hardened into a rock called breccia. Wind, water, and ice sculpted the breccia into shear cliffs and dramatic pinnacles. Its volcanic layers are visible today in handsome bands of purple, red, and brown.

The Absaroka Range (pronounced Ab-sar-O-ka) was named for the Crow Indians. In their native language, *absaroka* meant "people of the great winged bird." The Crow inhabited lands to the north along the Yellowstone River. Originally farmers in North Dakota, the Crow migrated to the plains when they acquired horses in the mid-1700s. Known as superb horsemen, the Crow adapted rapidly to a nomadic plains culture that revolved around bison hunting.

After just 0.5 mile, the trail forks. Stay to the left (northwest) for Jade Lakes and follow several parallel paths up a steep, open hillside for 0.5 mile. At the top of the rise, the trail forks again. Take the left fork along the forested ridge. The trail levels off and provides good views of Brooks Lake and its magnificent cliffs.

The trail travels west briefly through lodgepole forest and then swings northwest by a meadow that blooms profusely in mid- to late summer. Reenter a mixed forest of pine and fir, and then approach a small pond on the right. Stop a moment to check for tracks in the mud at the pond's edge. You are likely to see the three-inch heart-shaped prints of mule deer. Closer inspection of the murky pond might reveal tiger salamanders and spotted, boreal, and chorus frogs.

Travel through another meadow bursting with bright flowers, and then arrive at Upper Jade Lake. Once again the magnificent banded cliffs rise spectacularly thousands of feet above the water. Come early in the morning to see a perfect reflection on the still, green lake. The trail along the east side of the lake allows for easy exploring.

To find excellent campsites, continue north on the trail along the lakeshore.

(Fine sites are also found on its southwestern shore.) To continue on to Lower Jade Lake, follow the trail another 0.5 mile northeast. Cross the outlet creek at Upper Jade Lake's northern end, and then descend somewhat steeply to the east. Although Lower Jade Lake lacks the dramatic cliffs of Upper Jade, it receives fewer visitors and offers additional fishing opportunities. To return to the trailhead, retrace your steps.

As you drive back to Moran Junction, observe herds of cattle grazing in the Teton National Forest. Livestock grazing on public land takes its toll on the ecosystem. Native wildlife must compete with cattle for limited forage. Ranchers must divert rivers and streams to irrigate fields to produce hay to feed livestock. This diversion of water hurts local fish populations. Furthermore, cattle trample streambanks and hasten erosion near water sources. This leads to sedimentation of streams, which further damages fish habitat. Finally, the protection of grazing livestock leads to the need for predator control. This endangers native species such as bears, coyotes, mountain lions, eagles, and wolves. All activities permitted in the national forests of the GYE, including ranching, mining, logging, and recreation, should be evaluated for their potential negative impacts on the greater ecosystem.

32 SWAN LAKE AND HERON POND LOOP ⬛◀

Difficulty: easy
Distance: 3-mile loop
Usage: high
Starting elevation: 6,780 feet; elevation gain, 80 feet
Season: late May through early October
Map: USGS 7.5-minute Colter Bay, WY
Note: In 2004, the NPS was in the process of redirecting trails in this area. Please check with a ranger to obtain the most up-to-date trail map.

The walk to Swan Lake and Heron Pond is one of the finest family hikes in Grand Teton National Park. The terrain is gentle and the scenery glorious. Go in early morning or evening for the best chance of seeing moose and trumpeter swans. Also highly recommended are the ranger-led hikes to Swan Lake conducted daily from the Colter Bay Visitor Center. For a longer hike, combine this outing with the trail to Hermitage Point, described in Trip 33.

From Jackson Lake Junction, drive north 5.5 miles on US 89-191-287 to

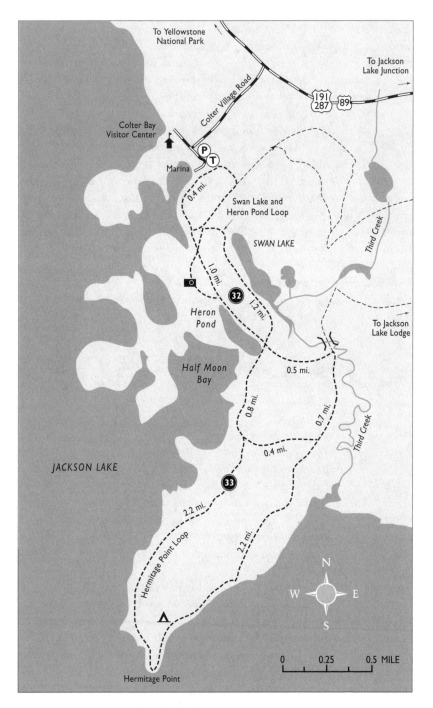

Colter Bay Village. Turn left and follow the Colter Village Road to the parking lot at its western end. Drive to the south end of the parking lot, near the marina. At the lot's south end, look for the Hermitage Point Trailhead sign at the start of an old service road.

Begin walking southwest on the service road where beautiful views of Colter Bay are framed by lodgepole pine. At 26,000 acres, Jackson Lake is the largest lake in Grand Teton. In its natural state, the glacier-carved lake was only 17,000 acres, but in 1905 a dam was built at its outlet, financed by drought-prone Idaho farmers. The dam raised the level of the lake 39 feet, and today Idaho agribusiness controls the water level. Consequently, in late summer when farmers need water, the lake falls considerably, forcing closure of marinas and wreaking havoc on tiny amphibians.

Across the lake, Mount Moran (12,605 feet), the fourth-tallest peak in the Teton Range, dominates the horizon. On its face hangs Skillet Glacier, named for its frying-pan shape. Mount Moran has a distinctive flat top and a black stripe of volcanic rock that runs clear to Idaho. The mountain was named for Thomas Moran, a landscape painter and member of the 1870 Yellowstone Expedition. Moran's monumental paintings helped convince Congress to establish Yellowstone as the world's first national park.

At 0.4 mile, arrive at a junction and bear right. Look for subalpine fir, an evergreen whose needles are short and flat and whose cones stand erect. In winter, moose and deer browse all reachable needles and twigs of the fir. Since deep snow covers the lowest branches, the animals browse only the center of the tree. The moose and deer thus create a "skirted" shape, seen commonly on firs throughout the park.

Less than 0.1 mile farther, come to a second trail junction and again keep right. Immediately following is a third junction. The left fork leads directly to Heron Pond on a level trail. The right fork also leads to Heron Pond but on the way rises 80 feet to a lookout over Jackson Lake. The view of the Tetons is beautiful from the rise.

Take either trail for 0.6 mile until they join again near the north end of Heron Pond. (Those on the overlook trail should bear right at the junction.) Travel briefly through a dense forest of lodgepole pine. Look on trunks for large bare patches, a sign that porcupine have eaten the pine's inner bark. Although porcupines waddle awkwardly on the ground, they climb trees with surprising speed and agility, using long curved claws and their stout tails like a fifth foot. Even so, wildlife biologists claim that, not infrequently, porcupines fall out of trees. Heads up!

Watch for more evidence of wildlife in the lodgepole forest. Bark removed from trunks of younger pines is a likely sign of deer, elk, or moose. These creatures choose small and flexible trees to rub the velvet off their antlers.

Shortly, arrive at Heron Pond (just 1 mile from the trailhead). The pond is covered with pond lilies, an important source of food for wildlife. Ducks eat its large seeds and muskrats gather its rootstalks. Native Americans also enjoyed eating the thick stalks. Indian women waded into the water to cut the rootstalks, or they raided the caches of muskrats. In Scandinavia, they tell of a troll, Näck, who waits at the bottom of ponds, fishing for people to eat. His bait is the yellow pond lily and his line is the rootstalk. The pond lily in Scandinavia is called the Näck rose.

Pond lilies are considered successional plants, for after they have grown in a pond for a long time, plant material and silt build up, filling in the pond and hastening its transition to meadow. Over the years, shallow Heron Pond will continue to shrink and silt up, eventually forming a moist, flower-filled meadow.

The trail continues along the flowered east shore of Heron Pond. The view west of the Teton Range is magnificent. Visible are Mount Moran and the peaks of the Grand, Middle, and South Tetons. The Shoshone aptly called this range *Teewinot*, meaning "many pinnacles." Look to the far side of Heron Pond to locate the remnants of an old beaver lodge.

At the south end of Heron Pond, arrive at a three-way trail junction. The trail to the right heads to Hermitage Point (Trip 33). Continuing straight (east) will

Hikers near Heron Pond

lead to Third Creek and Jackson Lake Lodge. Take the trail to the left (north) that leads to Swan Lake in 0.3 mile. Swan Lake's shallow waters and green vegetation provide prime habitat for moose, which frequently feed there. In the middle of the lake, a beaver lodge sits on a small island. The island also provides nesting grounds for a pair of rare and beautiful trumpeter swans. The huge, snow-white birds are America's largest waterfowl, having wingspans of up to 7 feet. Once hunted for their glorious plumage, the swans were driven to near extinction early in this century. Because of conservation efforts in Yellowstone and a nearby wildlife refuge, the swans have made a tenuous comeback. To give the swans the greatest chance of producing cygnets, never approach them or their nests. Bring binoculars and consider yourself very fortunate to hear the distinctive "koh-ho, koh-ho, koh-ho" of the trumpeters. Continue briefly along Swan Lake's west shore, traveling north. The trail veers away from the lakeshore to pass through forest, protecting the shy swans from their many admirers.

In late summer, hikers can sample the sweet whortleberries covering the forest floor. Just north of the lake, meet a three-way trail junction. Take the trail to the right, the shortest route back to the trailhead. Ascend a small hill, then descend to the last trail junction and stay left. From this junction, it is only 0.1 mile to the trailhead. For further exploring in the area and the opportunity for backcountry camping, take the 8.8-mile Hermitage Point Loop (Trip 33).

33 HERMITAGE POINT LOOP

Difficulty: strenuous
Distance: 8.8-mile loop
Usage: low
Starting elevation: 6,780 feet; elevation gain, 160 feet
Season: late May through early October
Map: USGS 7.5-minute Colter Bay, Two Ocean Lake, WY
Note: In 2004, the NPS was in the process of redirecting trails in this area. Please check with a ranger to obtain the most up-to-date trail map.

This lengthy trail takes hikers to the flowered meadows and forests of Hermitage Point where terrific views of the Tetons abound. For backpackers, there is a stunning lakeside campsite 4.7 miles from the trailhead. This is an excellent hike for wildlife: look for mule deer, moose, elk, coyote, sandhill cranes, great

Campsite, Hermitage Point

blue herons, porcupine, and beaver. Be aware that bears also inhabit the area and take appropriate precautions.

Start at the Hermitage Point Trailhead, as described in Trip 32. Follow Trail 32 to the southeast end of Heron Pond. (See the map on page 162.) At the trail junction for Swan Lake, head south (right) for Hermitage Point.

Enter dense forest and walk south through mixed stands of lodgepole, spruce, and fir. In August, tiny purple grouse whortleberries sweeten this section of trail. Pass a small meadow with superb views of Mount Moran.

Travel about 2 miles farther until the forest finally gives way to sage-covered meadows and dazzling views of the Teton Range. Sun-kissed hills of flowers climb from the water's edge. Purple larkspur and lupine, vanilla buckwheat, and bright red skyrocket gilia light up the grasses. Relatively few hikers make the long trek to Hermitage Point, so you'll have this magical place mostly to yourself.

From the point, there's a good view of all the major peaks of the range. The closest mountain, Mount Moran (12,605 feet), dominates, although the Grand at 13,770 feet is actually taller. The Grand's Matterhorn-like peak (the second highest in Wyoming) is a magnet for climbers worldwide. The grueling climb is often made immensely difficult by sudden strong and frigid storms, even in summer. In midsummer 1985, three experienced climbers froze to death on the Grand when blinding snow and hurricane-force winds swept the summit.

Next, climb a small hill and round the point to head north. The glorious hiking continues across meadows dotted with large Douglas-firs. At 4.7 miles from the trailhead, pass a campsite with tremendous views of both the Gros Ventre Range to the southeast and the Tetons to the west. Prominent on the eastern horizon is Sleeping Indian, a Gros Ventre peak that resembles the reclining figure of a chief with headdress. This is truly a heavenly place to camp and a fabulous place to watch the sunset.

After hiking about a mile along the lakeshore, the trail bends back into the forest. After another mile, arrive at a fork. Stay right to hike along winding Third Creek. Skirt the edge of the wet meadows, thick with willows by the creek. This is superb moose habitat. You may also see the rare trumpeter swan in the creek's waters and ponds. In the drier areas of meadow look for hunting coyote.

Seven-tenths of a mile from the trail junction, arrive at another fork. This time take the left fork to head toward the south end of Heron Pond. After 0.5 mile, reach the pond and another trail junction. At this junction, take the trail to the right, heading north to Swan Lake. From Swan Lake, follow the directions found in Trip 32 to return to the trailhead.

34 COLTER BAY

> **Difficulty:** moderate
> **Distance:** 2 miles one way to Half Moon Bay
> **Usage:** high
> **Starting elevation:** 6,780 feet
> **Season:** late May to late September
> **Map:** USGS 7.5-minute Colter Bay, WY

For a wonderful day's outing, paddle beneath towering Mount Moran among Jackson Lake's terrifically scenic islands and bays. Bring a fishing rod, picnic, and binoculars for watching bald eagles and the occasional moose. From the Colter Bay marina, it's only a 2-mile paddle to gentle Half Moon Bay. Although the bay is often calm, sudden storms and high winds can develop at any time. For your safety, check water conditions and weather reports before you depart, don't venture too far from shore, and always wear life vests. In addition, the water level of Jackson Lake fluctuates by about 10 feet, being lowest in early fall. Consequently, boaters may have to portage in August and September. Check at the marina for current conditions. And don't forget to bring a map!

Drive to the Colter Bay Marina as described in Trip 32. If you're carrying your own boat, find the launch just left of the marina store. Canoe rentals are

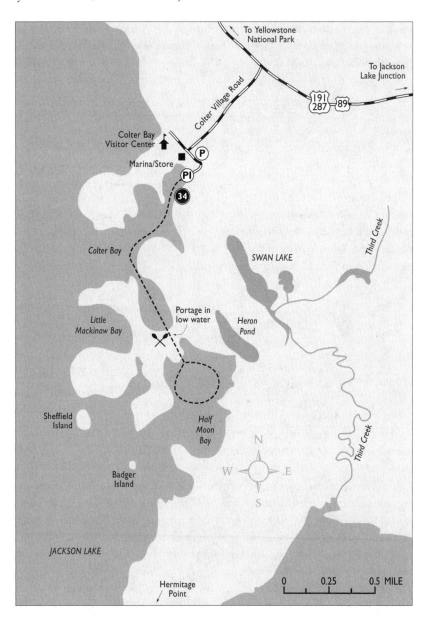

Canoeing on Colter Bay, Grand Teton National Park

available at the marina. The route described below (4 miles round trip) is easily accomplished by canoe in two hours (without stops) with one child and one adult paddling.

From the marina, paddle southwest through the narrow channel. Once beyond the protected waters, continue southwest about a half mile to the end of the land mass to the south. Turn between the mainland and an unnamed island to the west. As you glide through the channel, watch the forests and meadows for elk and deer. In early summer, you may see both with their spotted young. At any point along the trip, feel free to beach your vessel and explore.

After another 0.5 mile, slip through a second narrow channel (you may have to portage here) to enter the northern reaches of Half Moon Bay. In front of you is another small unnamed island. Bird life is plentiful here. You can't miss the abundant California gulls that migrate from the Pacific Coast to summer in the Tetons. Watch also for osprey and the American white pelican. The white pelican is awkward on land, but graceful in flight. Unlike its cousin, the brown pelican, the white does not dive for its dinner. With its oversized yellow bill, it scoops up two-foot trout, suckers, minnows, and occasionally salamanders while cruising across the water. Pelicans seen in Colter Bay come from a protected nesting colony on the Molly Islands in Yellowstone Lake.

Paddle around the island, and then head back to the marina by the same route you came. For a longer paddle, continue southwest, and then northwest to pass Sheffield Island, returning to the marina via Little Mackinaw Bay. The extra touring will add about 1 mile to your trip.

35   SNAKE RIVER FLOAT (JACKSON LAKE DAM TO PACIFIC CREEK LANDING)

Difficulty: moderate
Distance: 5 to 6 miles one way (trip is one-way only)
Usage: moderate
Starting elevation: 6,800 feet
Season: late May to late September
Map: USGS 7.5-minute Moran, WY

This serenely beautiful float trip is especially memorable in the early morning when there are good chances of seeing moose, great blue herons, beaver, osprey, and bald eagles. While this trip is fine for novices, all paddlers must be prepared to make a strong and timely exit at Pacific Creek Landing. After Pacific Creek, the Snake River's current increases substantially, generating dangerous conditions for novices. Before departing, obtain a boat permit, secure life vests for all passengers, and inquire about river flow. Allow a few hours for the float.

Drive to Pacific Creek Landing, 3.4 miles southeast of Jackson Lake Junction on US 89–287. Take a good look at the landing and observe how Pacific Creek enters the Snake River to the north. Boaters need to paddle across swift current

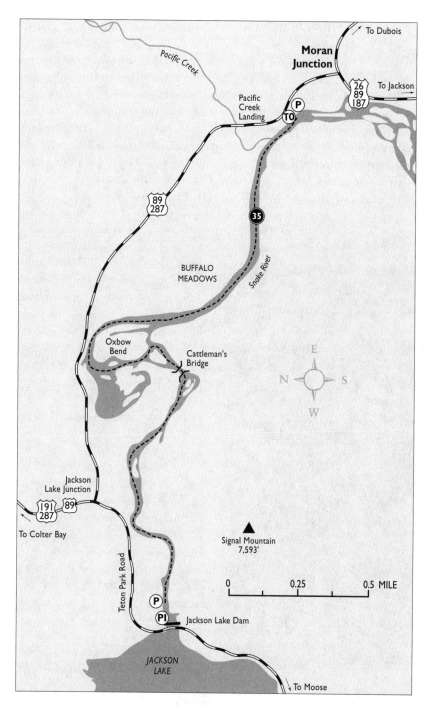

just after the entry of Pacific Creek to reach the landing safely. Observe land-marks and signage in this area to ensure that you will recognize the landing in time. If you have two cars, leave one in the lot, and drive northwest 4.4 miles to the last turnout before Jackson Lake Dam. The put-in is directly below the dam.

Begin your trip by launching downstream and floating with the current. It is said that the best fishing in the Snake River is in this spot directly below the dam. American white pelicans seem to agree, judging by the crowd usually congregated at the foot of the dam. Anglers and pelicans, as well as eagles and osprey, fish for the Snake's cutthroat, rainbow, and brook trout. Pass under Cattleman's Bridge, originally used for driving cattle across the river. The bridge now provides access to the east side of Signal Mountain.

Just after the bridge, float down to Oxbow Bend on your left for a paddling detour in its calm waters. Look along the willow-choked banks for moose, otter, beaver, and muskrat. Don't be surprised to see a moose partially or wholly submerged in the river. Moose love the soggy aquatic plants growing on the river bottom and will readily dive for them (as deep as 25 feet). Moose are well-adapted for swimming. Their coats are water resistant, keeping them comfortably warm in the cold water, and one layer of their hair is hollow, giving them great buoyancy.

The Oxbow Bend is superb bird habitat. Watch for Canada geese, bald eagles, trumpeter swans, numerous songbirds, and great blue herons. The four-foot-tall herons have a grace-ful, smoky blue body, long neck, and endless, sticklike legs. They stalk fish, insects, and frogs along the water's edge. Cruise this area quietly. Herons are particularly vulnerable to human disturbance.

Bald eagles are also very vulnera-ble. When rangers discover an eagle's nest in Grand Teton National Park, they limit human activity in the area

Getting ready to float the Snake River

to allow the eagles to breed. Mature bald eagles of both sexes (four to five years old) have black wings, snow-white head and tail, and bright yellow beak and eyes. Immature bald eagles are brown and are often mistaken for golden eagles and osprey. Look for bald eagles in tall trees above the river. After exploring the Oxbow Bend, paddle back out into the current to continue your float. Pass Buffalo Meadows, where moose and abundant bird life can also be seen. The confluence of Pacific Creek is about 1.75 miles downstream of Oxbow Bend. Paddlers should watch for the creek well in advance.

The safest way to reach Pacific Creek Landing is to stay close to the Snake River's left bank. After the entrance of Pacific Creek, paddle hard to cross its current and exit the river on the left bank, at the landing just downstream.

For a truly magical trip, experienced boaters should make this trip under a full moon.

36 WILLOW FLATS OVERLOOK

Difficulty: very easy
Distance: 0.5 mile one way
Usage: high
Starting elevation: 6,840 feet; elevation gain, 80 feet
Season: late May through early October
Map: USGS 7.5-minute Two Ocean Lake, WY

This very easy hike ascends tiny Lunchtree Hill for views of Willow Flats, the Tetons, and Jackson Lake. Lunchtree Hill is a convenient picnic spot for those staying at or near Jackson Lake Lodge. Come at dusk or dawn for striking views of sunlit mountains, and bring your binoculars to search the flats for moose. The hike is not recommended for midday in summer, for the shadeless trail can grow quite hot. Try it in fall for views of brilliant red-gold foliage.

Drive to Jackson Lake Lodge, located just off US 89-191-297, 1 mile north of Jackson Lake Junction. Enter the lodge, walk through the lobby, and exit the building on its west side. Find the paved trail to the right of the building.

Begin on the paved trail and climb to the top of Lunchtree Hill through the sagebrush community. Crush a few leaves of this pervasive shrub and smell the pungent aroma to see how it got its name. Sagebrush is critical winter food for pronghorn antelope, and it provides food and shelter for a variety of smaller creatures as well, such as the snowshoe hare, least chipmunk, Unita ground squirrel, and sage grouse. Colorful flowers grow among the sage-brush, including red-orange Indian paintbrush, yellow arrowleaf balsamroot, and blue harebell.

Once on top of the hill, visit the monument commemorating the historic meeting in 1926 of John D. Rockefeller and family and Horace Albright, super-intendent of Yellowstone National Park. At this site, above beautiful Jackson Lake and under towering Mount Moran, the group discussed the inclusion of the Tetons into the national park system. The dream was finally realized twenty-six years later, after years of controversy and through generous land donations from the Rockefeller family.

Scan the willow-filled wetland to the west for moose. Moose love the soggy area, filled with tasty willow for them to eat. In summer, they frequently stand knee-deep in mud, lazily pulling up soggy green plants (dubbed "moose muck") and munching them contentedly. Visitors, in fact, rarely see a moose's full body, for its legs are either underwater or obscured by thick underbrush. Their thin, gangly legs are specially jointed to allow them to walk easily in deep snow or mud. A moose can lift its leg out of the same hole in which it was placed, so that it doesn't waste energy unnecessarily.

To hike north of Lunchtree Hill, follow informal trails through the sage-brush. Explore the level bluff, heading north until the trail becomes indistinct and begins to descend into trees. At that point, about a half mile from Jackson Lake Lodge, turn around and return to the lodge.

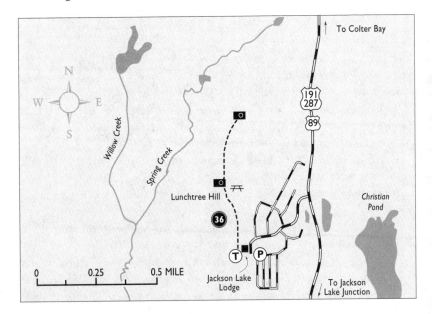

Moose in Grand Teton National Park

37 SCHWABACHER'S LANDING

> **Difficulty:** very easy
> **Distance:** 0.5 mile one way
> **Usage:** moderate
> **Starting elevation:** 6,420 feet; elevation gain, 20 feet
> **Season:** late May through mid-October
> **Map:** USGS 7.5-minute Moose, WY

Stroll along an incredibly scenic tributary of the Snake River to explore beaver dams, flowers, and waterfowl. Arrive at sunset for the chance to see elk, moose, coyote, and bison under a sky framed by the Teton's most majestic peaks. Bring a fishing rod to try for trout in this angler's paradise. This trail makes a superb and effortless late-afternoon outing.

From Moose Junction, drive north 4.5 miles on US 191-89-26 to the turnoff for Schwabacher's Landing on the left. From Moran Junction, drive 13.5 miles

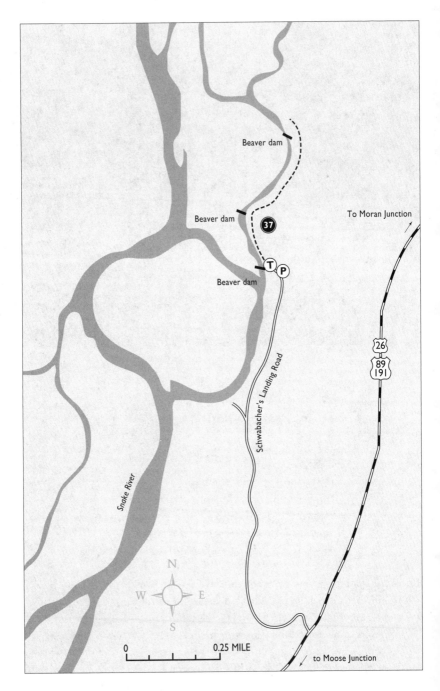

Beaver dam

Beaver dam

To Moran Junction

Beaver dam

Schwabacher's Landing Road

Snake River

N
W · E
S

0   0.25 MILE

to Moose Junction

south on US 191–89–26 to the turnoff. Turn west onto the dirt road and drive 1.1 miles to a small parking area. The informal trail begins near the river.

Head north (right) on the narrow trail. Above the swift river soars the spectacular Cathedral Group (the trio of Grand Teton, Mount Owen, and Teewinot). Almost immediately, find the first of three beaver dams. Beavers build dams to provide quiet water for food gathering and a safe haven for their lodges. A pair of beavers can build an average-sized dam, two feet high by twelve feet long, in just *two* nights.

Beavers are nocturnal; their activity usually begins at dusk. Beavers were originally diurnal (active during the day), but intensive trapping in the early 1800s changed their habits. In those days, men's stovepipe hats, constructed of fine felt from beaver pelts, were the rage. After trappers nearly exterminated the beaver east of the Mississippi, mountain men came to the Rockies seeking the luxurious chestnut fur, nicknamed "soft gold." They might have wiped out the western beaver also, but men's fashion fortunately turned to silk, and North America's largest rodent was saved.

Your best chance of seeing beaver is in the fall. Beavers do not hibernate, so they must stockpile a large reserve of food for the winter. On autumn days, beavers can be seen cutting and dragging aspen branches to their underwater cache beneath their lodge. A family of nine beavers gathers literally a ton of bark to carry it through until spring.

Look and listen for signs of beaver. A domed lodge, constructed of sticks and mud, is the most obvious. Look also for conical tree stumps with teeth marks, peeled limbs where beaver chewed off the bark, and scent mounds (hills of mud and sticks about one foot high by three feet wide) that mark a beaver's territory. Listen for the resounding slap of a beaver's flat, hairless tail on the water. It sounds the family alarm, warning others of your presence.

Follow the narrow trail upstream along the grassy bank. Flat, Frisbee-sized patties—"buffalo chips"—often litter the path. These were left by the small herd of bison that inhabits the park. Native Americans and settlers burned the chips as fuel.

In the early 1800s, forty million to sixty million bison roamed the western plains. Beginning in the mid-1800s, settlers shot the herds wholesale to attain hides and to deprive the Plains Indians of their means of survival. Tribes depended upon bison for their food, shelter, tools, weaponry, warm clothing, and bedding. Indians used nearly every part of the animal. Visitors can view fascinating bison artifacts from this era at Colter Bay's Indian Art Museum.

By 1889 bison were nearly extinct; less than one hundred survived in a remote part of Yellowstone National Park. All bison in the parks today are descendants of those last few. Currently the GYE bison population hovers around four thousand,

Grand Teton National Park

but fluctuates based on weather, which affects the viability of food, and on the tolerance of communities bordering the park to wintering bison.

Serious threats to bison still exist. Bison carry brucellosis, a disease that causes miscarriage in domestic cattle. Even though there has *never* been a documented case of bison passing the disease to cattle (and experts believe it would be highly unlikely), ranchers, particularly in Montana near Yellowstone's northern border, fear the presence of free-ranging bison. Consequently, there is great pressure to reduce the size of Yellowstone's herd.

Continue to walk north along the creek. Arrive at a second, much older beaver dam. Check for waterfowl, most likely mallards, Barrow's goldeneye, and red-breasted mergansers. Be alert also for a small, beaverlike creature, the muskrat. (Watch for its long, thin tail.) The muskrat builds a smaller domed lodge, constructed from cattails, reeds, and mud. Look also for the playful river otter in these environs.

Just 0.25 mile farther, arrive at the third dam. Beyond the dam, the trail fades. This is a good turnaround point. On your return, scan tall trees for the osprey and bald eagles that frequent the Snake River bottomlands. Look down also, in the grass beside the creek, for green garter snakes or the rare rubber boa, both harmless.

Opposite: The Snake River at Schwabachen's Landing, Grand Teton National Park

CHAPTER 6

SOUTH
GRAND TETON

The southern portion of Grand Teton National Park offers the most breathtaking scenery in the region. Its massive sweep of jagged peaks displays a soaring handsomeness that lifts the spirit. To enter this wilderness is the ultimate adventure. Whether by bike, canoe, or your own two feet, check out the following excursions.

There are several short and easy hikes to beautiful lakes (Trips 38, 39, 40, and 46) and longer, challenging climbs to steep-walled canyons (Trips 43, 45, 48, and 49). Three bike rides offer spectacular scenery with relatively little effort (Trips 47, 51, and 52). Paddle a canoe or kayak to two beautiful lakes (Trips 38, 44) or take a ferry across one of the park's finest (Trips 41, 42, and 43). Lastly, ride an aerial tram to visit the alpine environment (Trip 50).

Other family activities in the park include several self-guided trails. Try Menor's Ferry, where children can be "ferried" across the river in a re-creation of a circa 1890s contraption. Children can also participate in the NPS junior ranger program. Rangers lead children-only adventures weekday afternoons from the visitor centers. In summer, a family picnic and swim at warm and scenic String Lake is the perfect park outing.

There are also family activities offered in and around the nearby town of Jackson. Whitewater rafting on the Snake River is perhaps the most popular. Horseback riding in the park and in the nearby national forests is also much in demand. For rainy days, Jackson offers several museums as well as an indoor recreation center and climbing gym.

The region also offers rich evening activites. Early evening is one of the best times to see the numerous deer and elk that inhabit the south park. A quiet moonlight paddle is also highly recommended (Trips 38, 44). For those seeking more structure, the NPS offers numerous evening programs and guided walks. And for a different kind of fun, Jackson hosts biweekly rodeos.

38 LEIGH AND BEARPAW LAKES

Difficulty: moderate
Distance: 2.3 miles one way to Leigh Lake Beach; 3.7 miles one way to Bearpaw Lake
Usage: high
Starting elevation: 6,870 feet; elevation gain, 30 feet
Season: late May through early October
Map: USGS 7.5-minute Jenny Lake, WY

Leigh Lake is a fabulous family destination. Paddle 3 miles to the north end of Leigh Lake or hike the short, scenic trail for incomparable views of Mount Moran's hanging glaciers and steep-walled canyons. After 2.3 miles, hikers and paddlers are treated to Leigh's postcard-perfect white sand beach where picnics and bathing suits are a must. For backpacking families, there are excellent lakeside campsites. Further exploring in the area brings hikers to pretty Bearpaw Lake. There are only two drawbacks: carry insect repellent and expect company on this gem of a trail.

Begin at the String Lake Picnic Area, located at the north end of the String Lake Parking Area. To find the parking area, drive north 10 miles on the Teton Park Road from the Moose Entrance Station to the turnoff for String Lake, signed North Jenny Lake Junction. Turn west at the junction and drive 1.5 miles to the String Lake Parking Area. The parking area is 0.4-mile long, with the picnic area at its north end.

To reach the trailhead, hikers and paddlers must pass the most scenic and warmest swimming hole in Grand Teton, located adjacent to the picnic area. Swimmers should bring a float and wear foot protection, for the bottom is studded with old logs. Boats (oar-powered only) can enter the water at the picnic area or at the canoe launch immediately south of the picnic area.

Find the Leigh Lake Trailhead just north of the picnic area. Head north on the wide trail paralleling the shore. (Paddlers should follow narrow String Lake to its northern end.) Travel 0.9 mile under the shade of lodgepole pine, subalpine fir, and Englemann spruce. In late summer, enjoy tiny grouse whortleberry and sumptuous wild huckleberry growing along the trail. The woods are also sprinkled with delicate, blue harebells (bluebells) that hang gracefully downward and bloom from June through September. Deer, elk, pika, marmot, bear, and snowshoe hare, of course, enjoy eating the harebells.

At the north end of String Lake, arrive at a junction. The left fork heads

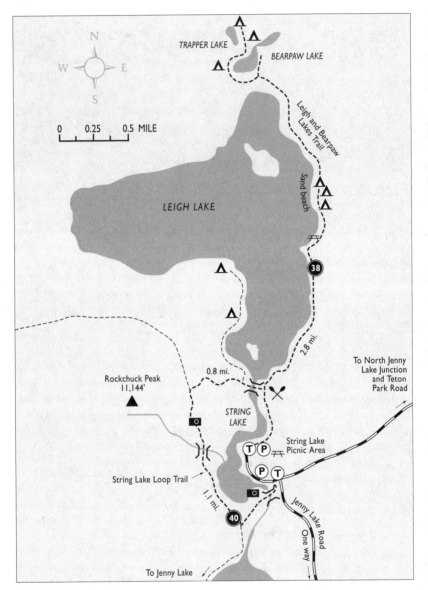

over Leigh Lake's outlet bridge to Paintbrush Canyon and provides access to Leigh Lake's west shore campsites. Backpackers (sites 13 and 15) should cross the bridge and then turn right onto the unimproved path that follows Leigh Lake's west shore. The campsites are about 1 and 1.5 miles from the bridge, respectively. Campsite 13 is spectacular, having its own sandy beach and grand views of the lake and the Gros Ventre Range.

Hikers take the right fork to Leigh Lake and immediately come upon another junction. Again bear right. (The left fork is for canoe portages.) Enter forest; then climb 20 feet up the sandy slope of Leigh Lake's terminal moraine. The 2-mile-long lake is the third largest in the park and one of the deepest at 250 feet. Continue north on a trail paralleling the lakeshore. (There are minor trails in this area; choose the well-defined trail closest to the shore.)

Paddlers should take their vessels out of the water on String Lake's northeast shore, just before the Leigh Lake outlet bridge. At this point, paddlers, carrying their vessels, pick up the Leigh Lake Trail. Take the first left for the short canoe portage to Leigh Lake. Upon reboarding, paddle along the east shore of Leigh Lake, staying east of the lake's small islands. Or, if wind is a factor, determine the wind direction (usually from the west) and hug the upwind shore for more sheltered paddling.

Meltwater from Falling Ice Glacier, wedged between the east and west summits of Mount Moran, gives Leigh Lake its greenish hue. The 100-foot-thick glacier sends milky glacial "flour" (finely ground rock) to the lake each spring. Falling Ice Glacier is a reminder of the mammoth forces that created Leigh Lake. Imagine colossal tongues of ice, 1,000 feet tall, pushing down Paintbrush and Leigh Canyons, located just south of Mount Moran. At the canyon mouths, the glaciers flowed together, fanned out, and then bulldozed their way east. As the two glaciers melted, the water was held by the moraine, or hill of soil and rock, that the glaciers pushed out in front of them. Hikers follow the moraine as the trail continues north along the lake. Spur trails on the left lead to the lakeshore. Continue north 1.3 miles through lush, dense forest to reach the lake's splendid sand beach. Winds blowing continuously (and sometimes ferociously) from Leigh and Paintbrush Canyons have battered the rocks on the east shore to fine white sand. On sunny summer days the water is filled with bathers. The lake is also popular with anglers trying for mackinaw and cutthroat trout. In this area, hikers also pass three superb group campsites for parties of seven or more.

Across the lake is majestic Mount Moran, its snowcapped peak rising almost 6,000 feet above the lake. The dark vertical stripe on its face is a 150-foot-wide column of black low-silica rock called "diabase." The diabase formed when molten rock flowed up into a fissure. The diabase extends 77 miles west to the other side of the mountain range. Imagine the heat and force that extruded this tremendous quantity of molten rock.

From Leigh Lake's sand beach, Bearpaw Lake lies 1.5 miles to the north. To reach Bearpaw, continue hiking (or paddling) north. Near the north end of Leigh Lake notice a rocky island with burned snags. In the 1980s, a fire on the island jumped across the water and burned the area north and east of Leigh Lake. Look for osprey atop the tall snags.

At the northernmost tip of Leigh Lake (3.4 miles from the trailhead), hikers arrive at a junction. Paddlers must leave their boats on the north shore to find this intersection. The junction's right fork leads to Bearpaw Lake in approximately 0.3 mile. Follow the trail across a meadow and arrive shortly at the small, quiet lake. The lovely lake is surrounded by pines, its grassy shore delicately flowered in purple and white. Bearpaw is a nice place to explore when Leigh Lake attracts too many visitors.

Energetic hikers may also want to visit tiny Trapper Lake, just 0.8 mile from the trail junction at the north end of Leigh Lake. To reach Trapper, backtrack to the junction and take the left fork. Fine campsites on the north end of Trapper Lake and the northwest side of Bearpaw Lake can be reached from this trail.

39　STRING LAKE TO JENNY LAKE'S WEST SHORE

Difficulty: easy
Distance: 1.7 miles one way
Usage: moderate
Starting elevation: 6,880 feet; elevation gain, 40 feet
Season: late May through early October
Map: USGS 7.5-minute Jenny Lake, WY

The lush and shady 1.7-mile trail from String Lake to the west shore of Jenny Lake is an excellent alternative to riding the busy Jenny Lake shuttle boat, especially at peak season. Once at Jenny Lake's west shore, hikers can access trails to Hidden Falls (Trip 41), Inspiration Point (Trip 42), and Cascade Canyon (Trip 43).

To find the String Lake Trailhead, follow the driving directions for Trip 38 to the String Lake Parking Area. Park at the south end where there's a sign for the String Lake Trailhead. Find the trail at the lake's edge and follow it south to the substantial bridge over the String Lake outlet. Views from the bridge of the Cathedral Group (Teewinot, Mount Owen, and the Grand) are breathtaking. Continue southwest as the trail cuts through dense thimbleberry bushes, cow parsnip, and purple monkshood. In late summer, when the thimbleberries are ripe, watch for black bears feeding in the brush. In areas of dense vegetation, hikers should make noise to avoid surprising a foraging bear. At 0.3 mile from the trailhead, arrive at a junction. The trail to the right travels along the west shore of String Lake (Trip 40). Take the trail to the left, which leads to Jenny Lake.

Head through a lush forest of Engelmann spruce and subalpine fir. Learning to recognize these trees is easy: just "shake hands" with the nearest evergreen, feeling its needles. If the needles are sharp to the touch and squarish, you have met a spruce. If the needles are flat, friendly, and soft (think "fur"), you are holding a fir. If you have encountered a tree with thin, longish needles (two to three inches long) in bundles of two, it is a lodgepole pine, for fir and spruce needles are never "bundled." This trail and the trail to Hidden Falls pass some of the oldest and most magnificent Engelmann spruce in the region; some are estimated to be over four hundred years old.

Proceed southwest past a variety of moisture-loving flowers, including purple

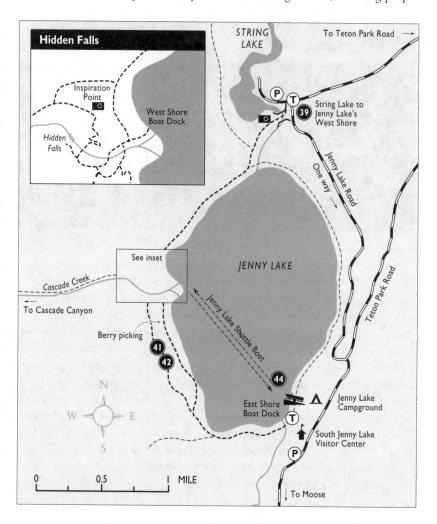

Bridge over String Lake Outlet, Grand Teton National Park

monkshood, coneflower, and giant white cow parsnip. The latter, a member of the parsley family, can grow to eight feet with umbels of tiny white flowers. Black bears and other large mammals enjoy its leaves and stem. In rocky areas, watch for yellow-bellied marmots. This handsome rodent (a western cousin of the wood-chuck) dens in rock piles and is frequently seen on summer days atop the rocks.

Next approach a series of wooden bridges. To the right, an unmarked path by a creek leads to Hanging Canyon, a very difficult 2,800-foot climb from Jenny Lake. Continue southwest over the bridges and, at 1.7 miles from the trailhead, arrive at the junction with the horse trail to Cascade Canyon on the right. Those headed for the canyon (bypassing Hidden Falls and Inspiration Point) should turn right here. The trail into the canyon is described in Trip 43.

For those wishing to visit Hidden Falls and Inspiration Point, continue on the main trail 0.3 mile to the junction with the well-worn trail from the West Shore

Boat Dock. Turn right at this junction and follow the trail as described in Trip 41.

It is possible to hike the circumference of Jenny Lake and return to String Lake via Jenny Lake's east shore (a 6.8-mile loop), but it is not recommended. Jenny Lake's east shore trail closely parallels the Jenny Lake Road, so traffic noise is intrusive. The superb trails to Hidden Falls (Trip 41), Cascade Canyon (Trip 43), and the west shore of String Lake (Trip 40) are far more enjoyable.

40 STRING LAKE LOOP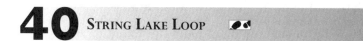

Difficulty: easy
Distance: 3.5 miles round trip
Usage: moderate
Starting elevation: 6,880 feet; elevation gain, 260 feet
Season: late May through early October
Map: USGS 7.5-minute Jenny Lake, WY

String Lake is a magical spot. Its shallow, swimmable waters and sublime mountain backdrop make it an absolute favorite for all ages. This trail is one of several options for hikers departing from String Lake. Less scenic than Trip 39, this trail is nevertheless enchanting in fall. Those planning to swim in String Lake should bring footwear, for the lake bottom is littered with logs.

Drive to the String Lake Trailhead, as described in Trip 38. Then follow Trip 39 south to its first trail junction 0.3 mile from the String Lake Trailhead. (See the trail map on page 182.)

Head right (northwest) at the junction. The trail soon leaves the forest to arrive at the dry and sunny west shore of String Lake. Rise gently and cross a burned slope, now populated by mountain ash and aspen, punctuated by colorful fireweed, aster, arrowleaf balsamroot, and Indian paintbrush. Mount St. John (11,430 feet) rises to the west.

Ascend through sagebrush and aspen as the trail heads north, gaining good views of the Gros Ventre Range to the east and String Lake below. In French, *gros ventre* means "big stomach," and the range was named for the Gros Ventre Indians. The tribe's name was the result of a miscommunication between French trappers and Shoshone Indians. When trappers asked the Shoshone about the tribe living in the neighboring mountain range, the Shoshone motioned to their stomachs to indicate that the tribe was always in a state of hunger. The French assumed that the Shoshone were describing a weight problem, and thus the Gros Ventre tribe was named.

At approximately 1.1 miles from the trailhead, cross a bridge over a stream originating on Rockchuck Peak above you to the west. As you cross the slope of Rockchuck, look below to a marshy area west of String Lake. These wetlands are prime moose habitat. Next, enter again the shade of Douglas-fir, mountain ash, and mountain maple, and climb to a junction with the Paintbrush Canyon Trail. At this junction, descend to the right into a dense forest of lodgepole pine.

Red squirrels are plentiful in this pine forest. Look for pinecones stripped of scales lying on the forest floor like discarded corncobs. Enter the squirrels' territory and they assault you with shrill chattering. Their scolding persists until you leave (unless, like a squirrel, you can answer back requesting temporary silence). Every red squirrel, both male and female, defends a territory of one to three acres, sometimes with physical combat. Only during mating does a female let down her guard and allow a suitor to enter. Look for the squirrels screaming from tree stumps or branches. If you can't locate the source (some seem to have the skill of ventriloquists), listen for the sound of claws scampering up bark.

You may spy the red squirrel's giant middens. A midden is both the squirrel's pantry and his garbage pile, composed of pine, fir, and spruce cones as well as their inedible remains. Buried in the large mound of scales are scores of freshly cut cones, stored for later consumption. Successive generations of squirrels often use the same midden, resulting in piles up to six to ten yards across and thirty inches deep.

Enjoying String Lake, Grand Teton National Park

Descend gently through the forest for about 0.8 mile to a bridge over the shallow stream connecting String and Leigh Lakes. Just before the bridge, find a house-sized boulder to the left of the trail. This is a glacial erratic, a rock carried miles by a descending glacier. The boulder illustrates the power of glaciers to tear, transport, and drop debris from mountaintop to valley. It also provides an irresistible climbing opportunity for youngsters.

Cross the bridge to reach the east shore of String Lake. Then turn right to walk south along the lakeshore. In early morning or at dusk, watch for mule deer. Their large ears give the deer extraordinary hearing. Each ear moves independently to pick up sounds of potential predators. If a sound is heard, the deer's tail rises to reveal a bright white underside, signaling others of danger. When alarmed, mule deer bound away with lightning speed and amazing grace—all four feet leaving the ground and then landing together—practically flying through dense forest.

From the bridge, it is 0.9 mile to the String Lake Picnic Area. Before leaving the area, let children sample String Lake's warm waters. With magnificent mountains rising from its western shore, this may be the prettiest swimming hole on earth. From the picnic area, follow a patchy trail, interrupted by parking lots and canoe launches, along the lakeshore for 0.3 mile to the start at String Lake Trailhead.

41   HIDDEN FALLS

Difficulty: easy
Distance: 0.5 mile one way via ferry; 2.2 miles one way from the String Lake Trailhead; 2.5 miles one way from the East Shore Boat Dock
Usage: very high
Starting elevation: 6,794 feet; elevation gain, 160 feet
Season: mid-May through early October
Map: USGS 7.5-minute Jenny Lake, WY

The trail to Hidden Falls is short and sweet. A boat at Jenny Lake ferries hikers across the lake, saving them 2 miles each way. Consequently, this trail attracts more hikers than any other in Grand Teton. To avoid crowds, take the first boat over. For your effort, you'll be rewarded with solitude and, in late summer, a tasty treat from the berry bushes lining the lake's west shore. Late risers should be prepared to wait at the dock as long as forty minutes in midsummer. Alternatively, start this hike at the String Lake Trailhead and travel a scenic 1.7

miles (one way) to the West Shore Boat Dock (Trip 39). Hikers can also start at the East Shore Boat Dock and walk around the southwest shore of Jenny Lake, adding 2 miles each way to the hike.

Those starting at Jenny Lake should enter the park via the Moose Entrance Station and drive north 6.7 miles on the Teton Park Road to the turnoff for South Jenny Lake. Turn left, drive toward the ranger station, and park in the large Jenny Lake parking lot. Find the boat dock at the southeast end of Jenny Lake. Round-trip fares are $4.00 per adult, $2.25 per child, and free for those under six. Boats leave every fifteen minutes from 8:00 A.M. to 6:00 P.M. For those starting at String Lake, follow the directions for Trip 39. (See the trail map on page 185)

If you're hiking from the East Shore Boat Dock, proceed west over the bridge on the clearly marked trail around the lake. This route is less scenic than the trail starting at String Lake, but it does give you the option of riding the boat on the way home. On the west side of the lake, watch for black bears and make noise when passing the dense berry bushes that line the trail.

After the Jenny Lake shuttle boat delivers you to the West Shore Boat Dock, turn immediately left (south). The trail soon swings west and arrives at a three-way junction (those hiking from the East Shore Boat Dock will arrive at this junction). Continue straight (west) for Hidden Falls. The trail to the right (north) leads to the String Lake Trailhead.

To sample berries before viewing the falls, turn left at the three-way junction and cross Cascade Creek. Continue south along the shore of Jenny Lake keeping left at the next trail junction. In late summer, you can't miss the breast-high bushes of sweet wild raspberries and bright red thimbleberries. When lifted from the plant, thimbleberries fit on the thumb just like a thimble! The park allows picking for personal consumption; just be considerate of the many hungry hikers and creatures following you. Watch for bears.

After berry picking, return to the first junction and then travel west, crossing Cascade Creek on a substantial bridge. At the bridge, watch for water ouzels, or American dippers. This chunky brown bird, which resembles a tailless robin, likes to dive in rushing water in search of small fish and insects. The superbly adapted dipper is able to walk on the bottom of streams, swim underwater, and fly behind waterfalls. After a dip, the ouzel hops on a rock and bobs up and down. Ouzels build their nests on rocky ledges, often within the spray of a waterfall, where their eggs are safe from predators. Look for the entertaining ouzel throughout the park, whenever you encounter a small, swift stream. Listen for its cheerful "zreet!"

Meet another trail junction and continue straight (west). Follow the trail as it curves north and look for a spur trail on the left, signed for Hidden Falls (located just before another bridge). The spur trail leads hikers 50 feet to the falls. Flanking the path is tall purple monkshood, a colorful flower whose petals resemble the robes of a monk. Watch on talus slopes to the left for yellow-bellied marmots and tiny pikas.

The pika (six to nine inches in length) is a round-eared relative of the rabbit. Except for its large, shiny black eyes, its appearance is distinctly unrabbitlike. Its tiny tail is lost in fur, and it most resembles a small guinea pig. This grayish ball of fur is most often spotted scampering acrobatically over talus slopes. Its rapid rock-hopping owes a debt to the "non-skid" coating of fur on the bottom of its tiny feet.

Hidden Falls does not come into view until you are standing right before it. The terrific 200-foot cascade is a wonderful surprise. Its rushing rivulets swell with snowmelt in spring and early summer. If it's not too crowded, the falls is an excellent picnic spot. For additional entertainment, look north to the rock face where climbing clinics are regularly held. For those with energy remaining, visit Inspiration Point, a 0.4-mile climb of about 250 feet from Hidden Falls. At Inspiration Point (Trip 42), hikers have lovely views east over Jenny Lake and Jackson Hole.

42 INSPIRATION POINT

Difficulty: moderate
Distance: 0.9 mile one way from the West Shore Boat Dock; 2.6 miles one way from String Lake Trailhead; 2.9 miles one way from the East Shore Boat Dock
Usage: very high
Starting elevation: 6,794 feet; elevation gain, 406 feet
Season: mid-May through early October
Map: USGS 7.5-minute Jenny Lake, WY

After visiting Hidden Falls, climb to Inspiration Point for a rewarding view of Jenny Lake and the mountains that surround Jackson Hole. From Inspiration Point, strong hikers can continue to Cascade Canyon for more terrific scenery and wildlife (Trip 43).

Follow the directions for Trip 41 to Hidden Falls. From the falls, return to the main trail and cross the bridge over Cascade Creek. Climb the steep switchbacks that hug the rock face. Proceed with care and watch children closely. In the 1930s, the Civilian Conservation Corps carved this trail from the granite as part of a huge trail-building project that contributed hundreds of miles of trails to the park.

As you ascend, pass lookouts with boulders irresistible to climbing children. To the west rises the striking trio of mountains called the Cathedral Group. From left to right are Mount Teewinot (12,325 feet), Grand Teton (13,770 feet), and Mount Owen (12,928 feet). Five-hundred feet above the valley floor, Inspiration Point affords great views of Jackson Hole. *Hole* is a fur trapper's term meaning "high valley." From this vantage point, you can see the ranges that surround the mostly flat "hole." To the northeast lie the Washakie and Absaroka Ranges, to the east sit the Mount Leidy Highlands, and to the southeast lie Sheep Mountain and the Gros Ventre Range.

From Inspiration Point, the whole of Jenny Lake is visible. Jenny Lake is the second-largest lake in the park, smaller only than Jackson Lake. Like Jackson Lake, Jenny Lake was created by a glacier flowing out of a canyon. About 12,000 to 15,000 years ago, consistently cool temperatures produced huge expanses of ice, or glaciers, on the Teton peaks. Gravity eventually drew the glaciers down the mountain. Taking routes of least resistance, the ice slid down river valleys, turning V-shaped valleys into flat-bottomed, U-shaped canyons. Glaciers pushed soil, boulders, and rock down the mountain like a child plowing sand with his hands. At the bottom, the glacier rested. All around the tongue of ice stood masses of debris, called moraines.

In time, temperatures warmed, the glaciers melted, and the moraines held the water of the melting glacier. Today the moraine still holds the lake's water, which is replenished each spring by fresh snowmelt. Glacier-born lakes lie at the mouths of nearly all the canyons in the Tetons; including Jenny Lake at Cascade Canyon, Leigh Lake at Leigh and Paintbrush Canyons, and Bradley Lake at Garnet Canyon.

From Inspiration Point, the trail turns west and enters Cascade Canyon, one of the prettiest trails in the park (Trip 43). Those returning should retrace their steps to the boat dock.

43   FORKS OF CASCADE CANYON   🝝🔺

Difficulty: strenuous
Distance: 6.5 miles one way from the East Shore Boat Dock (subtract 2 miles if boat shuttle is used), 5.4 miles one way from the String Lake Trailhead
Usage: high
Starting elevation: 6,794 feet; elevation gain, 1,057 feet
Season: June through September
Maps: USGS 7.5-minute Jenny Lake and Mount Moran, WY

This classic Teton hike offers the works: breathtaking scenery, abundant wildflowers, clear mountain streams, wildlife, and dramatic waterfalls. From Jenny Lake's

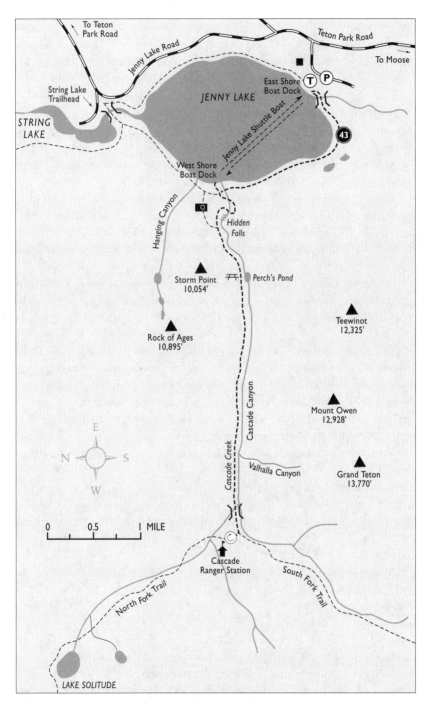

West Shore Boat Dock, a hike of only 1.6 miles takes you through the portals of the canyon to vistas of awesome beauty. The rest of the hike is easy; the trail rises only 600 feet on its 2.9-mile journey through the magnificent canyon. Cascade Canyon's only drawback is its popularity; it is essential to hike early to avoid crowds.

From Jenny Lake, hike to Hidden Falls and Inspiration Point as described in Trips 41 and 42. From Inspiration Point, the trail heads due west through dense forest. In 0.3 mile, the main trail intersects with a horse trail leading to the west shore of Jenny Lake in 0.4 mile. For variety, use this forested, pretty trail on your return to the boat dock. Those who start at the String Lake Trailhead can join the Cascade Canyon Trail via this horse trail (Trip 39).

Shortly after the horse trail junction, pass a rocky, or talus, slope on your right, one of many along the north side of the trail. Furry inhabitants include the indolent yellow-bellied marmot and the tiny, industrious pika. A marmot has yellowish fur on its belly and neck. Listen for their whistles, warning other marmots of your presence. This call earned them the nickname "whistle pig."

Unlike marmots, pikas do not hibernate. They spend the summer diligently gathering plants, scampering to and fro with mouths full of grass. Pikas spread the plants in the sun to dry and later build "haystacks" in dens beneath the rocks. In the dead of winter, pikas remain in their dens, subsisting on their dried bounty.

The talus slopes bear fruit for hungry hikers also. Wild red raspberry can be found among the rocks. Look for berries from late July through August on prickly stems with compound leaves of three to five ragged-edged leaflets. In moister areas of the canyon, find wild huckleberry (a bushy shrub two to three feet high) and grouse whortleberry (a delicate shrub six to eight inches tall). Both yield delicious reddish purple berries.

Continue west along Cascade Creek. Where the banks are thick with willow, look for moose. Moose relish willow twigs, and many retreat from the warm Snake River bottomland to browse in the cool reaches of the canyon. Often during the summer, moose sit in the shade of the willows. Spot them by looking for the dark horizontal line of their broad antlers among the vertical branches. Watch for moose also on the steep canyon slopes. Despite their awkward physique, moose are skilled climbers.

At about 0.6 mile from Inspiration Point, the canyon opens up in full grandeur. A glacier, moving down the mountain, scooped out this valley to create a flat-bottomed, steep-walled canyon. Its rocks glisten in the sun, "polished" by the tremendous weight and burnishing action of the sliding ice. Above the trail, the peaks rise nearly a mile. The south wall offers Teewinot Mountain (12,325 feet), Mount Owen (12,928 feet), and finally Grand Teton (13,770 feet). To the north stand Storm Point (10,054 feet) and Rock of Ages (10,895 feet).

About 0.7 mile from Inspiration Point, rockfall from Storm Point dammed

Crossing Cascade Creek, Grand Teton National Park

Cascade Creek, creating lovely Perch's Pond. This is a wonderful place to rest or wade. Look for rare but beautiful harlequin ducks and common mergansers. Female mergansers are large and handsome, with distinctively crested, bright reddish heads. Harlequin ducks are small but wonderfully marked. The white, slate blue, and reddish brown male wears his bright colors like a duck who has joined the circus.

The trail continues due west, alternately passing through trees, rock fields, and gorgeous flowered meadows. In July and August, the canyon explodes with color. Delight in red-orange Indian paintbrush, cream-colored columbine, delicate bluebells, purple fringed gentians, yellow goldenrod, and many more. The variety of color and texture is dazzling. Orange, green, and black lichen top trailside boulders. Dark green pines spiral up silvery ledges. Sparkling waterfalls fly down the canyon's south face.

About 3.5 miles past Inspiration Point, look to the south wall (left) for a ribbon of waterfall marking the location of beautiful Valhalla Canyon. Located 2,000 feet above the floor, the canyon is reached only by climbing the steep rock wall beside the waterfall. Once a place of mystical retreat for Native Americans, this canyon is now negotiated primarily by climbers assaulting the Grand Teton. Those bent on exploring this challenging and untrailed canyon must obtain a permit at the Jenny Lake Ranger Station and possess excellent cross-country climbing skills.

About 0.7 mile farther west, Cascade Creek forks. Cross its North Fork on a bridge and arrive in 0.3 mile at the Canyon Fork, a good turnaround point. To the left, the South Fork Trail rises steeply 2,500 feet in 5 miles to reach Hurricane Pass. The North Fork Trail is more popular, rising 1,200 feet in almost 3 miles through meadows and subalpine forest to lovely Lake Solitude (9,035 feet). Lake Solitude is a spectacular destination for hardy day hikers. In July, glacial lilies rim the lake and the view of the Grand from its north side is unparalleled. The hike is arduous, however, so be prepared. Because of years of overuse, camping is not allowed at the lake but is permitted about 1 mile below it.

Those returning to the trailhead should retrace their steps.

44 JENNY LAKE PADDLE

Difficulty: moderate
Distance: 4.5 miles round trip
Usage: high
Starting elevation: 6,794 feet
Season: late May to late September
Map: USGS 7.5-minute Jenny Lake, WY

Jenny Lake is unquestionably one of the most beautiful lakes in the world. Sitting at the foot of Cascade Canyon, the lake reflects the magnificent peaks that tower a mile and a half above it. Your experience at Jenny Lake can, however, be marred by midsummer crowds. To escape the mob, rent a canoe or kayak at the southeast end of the lake and paddle to postcard-pretty views of the Cathedral Group of Mount Owen, Teewinot, and the Grand Teton (12,928 feet, 12,325 feet, and

13,770 feet). If you arrive in the morning before the wind and the crowds, the sun will light up the snow-covered peaks' and the trip will be pure magic.

Bring your own boat or rent a canoe or kayak from the Jenny Lake Boating Company located at the southeast end of the lake at the ferry dock. From June to September 15, boats are available daily from 8:00 A.M. to 6:00 P.M. From May 15 to May 31 and September 16 to September 30, boats are available from 10:00 A.M. to 4:00 P.M. For additional information, call (307) 734-9227. To find Jenny Lake, enter the park via the Moose Entrance Station and drive north 6.7 miles on the Teton Park Road to the turnoff for South Jenny Lake. Turn left, drive toward the ranger station, and park in the large Jenny Lake parking lot. See Trip 39 for a map of Jenny Lake.

Your route around the lake may depend on the direction of the wind. If the wind is blowing from the west, for example, you'll want to hug the west side of the lake for the easiest paddling. If wind is not an issue, head east (right) from the boat dock. Paddling along the lake's eastern shore gives you gorgeous views southwest to the Cathedral Group. A paddle around the entire lake is about 4.5 miles, taking the average paddler around two hours. The west shore is generally quieter, with fewer hikers taking advantage of the trail that circles the lake (Trip 39). Also on the west side, there is an abundance of huckleberry bushes that ripen in late July through early August. (Berry-pickers must watch for black bears that frequent the area and enjoy the same bushes.)

You can choose to meander up the eastern or western shore and even picnic at one of the many choice spots along the shore. Along the lake's edge, boulders provide places to sun and Engelmann spruce, subalpine fir, and lodgepole pine provide ample shade. In the shallower, nearshore areas, paddlers will be amazed by the clarity of the water and, if the water is calm, there are terrific views of giant boulders below the surface, deposited by the glaciers that carved the lake. In fact, paddlers must watch for boulders to avoid unintended upsets. (This water is *cold*.) Paddlers can also try for lake, brown, brook, and cutthroat trout, as well as whitefish, in Jenny Lake. A permit is required, and the catch is limited to six fish per day. Thirty and forty pounders have been caught here.

Traveling toward the north end of the lake, the most striking sight to the west is the U-shaped opening marking the mouth of Cascade Canyon, carved by a glacier flowing east from the Teton Range (Trip 43). The sparkling granite walls comprising the canyon and the gleaming boulders at its mouth are the result of glacial polish, the buffing from the tremendous rubbing and pressure on the rocks by the glacier as it slid from the Teton peaks to Jackson Hole. In its wake, as it melted, the ice left a string of glacial lakes, such as Jenny Lake, and nearby Leigh and String Lakes (Trips 38, 39, and 40). Looking up into Cascade Canyon, you can see an active glacier on the north side of Mount Owen, south of the canyon.

The boat dock on the lake's west side marks the trailhead to Hidden Falls, Inspiration Point, and Cascade Canyon (Trips 41, 42, 43). A hike into Cascade Canyon is highly recommended for its stunning display of wildflowers, abundant wildlife, and unequaled scenery. A trek into the canyon is a whole-day endeavor, however, so it is best accomplished when you have a full day to enjoy it. In summer the Jenny Lake Shuttle crosses the lake every fifteen minutes. Consequently, paddlers should steer clear of the center of the lake to avoid the noise and wake of the ferry.

Jenny Lake's waters are too cold for swimming, but a post-paddle swim is highly recommended in nearby String Lake (Trip 40), approximately 3 miles north. For more paddling adventures, try String Lake and adjacent Leigh Lake; both offer excellent (and much more secluded) paddling.

Paddling on Jenny Lake, Grand Teton National Park

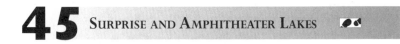

45 SURPRISE AND AMPHITHEATER LAKES

Difficulty: very strenuous
Distance: 9.6 miles round trip
Usage: high
Starting elevation: 6,732 feet; 2,960 feet elevation gain, plus a 200-foot climb up a pinnacle at Surprise Lake
Season: June through September
Maps: USGS 7.5-minute Moose and Grand Teton, WY

The first 3 miles of this tough trail are grueling and nearly unbearable on a hot summer's day. Yet the rewards of reaching two subalpine cirques, gorgeously set amid the rugged Teton Peaks is well worth the sweat; and the views at tree line are worth twice the effort. Pick a cool day, start early, and pack plenty of water.

To reach the Lupine Meadows Trailhead, enter the park at the Moose Entrance Station and drive 6.2 miles north on the park road to Lupine Meadows Road on the left. Turn left and drive 1.6 miles to the trailhead and parking area at the end of the road. Snow may persist at the highest elevations of this trail to midsummer.

The Lupine Meadows Trailhead is the launching point for climbs up the Middle and Grand Tetons, so you are assured of company on this trail. The trail first travels south across sage flats and then crosses a bridge over Glacier Gulch. About one mile from the trailhead, the trail turns west and climbs a moraine through lodgepole forest. At 1.7 miles, meet the Valley Trail that heads left (south) to Bradley Lake. Continue straight (west) and begin your steep ascent. The trail makes about twenty switchbacks as it rises and traverses the east-facing slope of the mountain between Glacier Gulch and Garnet Canyon. You are soon rewarded with excellent views of the Gros Ventre Range as well as a bird's-eye view of Jackson Hole. Directly below to the south are Taggart and Bradley Lakes. Below to the north is Jenny Lake. Keep your mind on the scenery as this trail gains more than 2,000 feet in 2.7 miles.

Meet a second trail junction at 1.3 miles from the Valley Trail Junction. The trail to the left (south) heads to Garnet Canyon. This is the turnoff for Grand Teton and Middle Teton climbers. To reach Surprise and Amphitheater Lakes, take the right fork and continue north on the switchbacks.

Remember this junction because the climb to Surprise and Amphitheater Lakes may inspire you to ascend a Teton peak. Most popular is the Middle Teton (12,804 feet), the third-highest mountain in the Teton Range. Despite its incredibly imposing appearance, this mountain can, nevertheless, be climbed in a single day on a "relatively easy scramble-up route" according to Exum Mountain Guides. Exum Mountain Guides, located in Grand Teton National Park, offer guided one- and two-day climbs up the Middle Teton, with or without porters to assist with backpack loads for the 6-mile trek to their camp in Garnet Canyon. For information, call (307) 733-2297, *www .exumguides.com.*

Climbing the Grand Teton (13,770 feet), the highest mountain in the range, is another story. It is *not* an "easy scramble" and should not be attempted by novices. The first recorded ascent of Grand Teton was on August 11, 1898. The first woman reached its peak in 1923. To get an idea of how steeply these mountains rise, note that the USGS Grand Teton 7.5-minute quadrangle is one of the few quadrangles that use 80-foot contour intervals instead of 40-foot intervals (the standard in the West). Climbing the Grand Teton typically requires two days. Nevertheless, the fastest time was clocked in 1983 at three hours and six minutes from the Lupine Meadows Trailhead to the summit and back! A good view of the Grand appears from the trail at about 4.4 miles from the trailhead.

At 4.6 miles from the trailhead, finally clear the trees and arrive at Surprise Lake (9,540 feet). The beautiful tarn, sometimes frozen well into the summer, is nestled beneath soaring, jagged peaks so characteristic of the Tetons. The Grand, Mount Owen (12,928 feet), and Teewinot (12,325 feet) are prominent. Surprise Lake got its name because the trail comes upon the lake very suddenly and from the valley floor there is no indication a tarn exists on this shelf. For the best views of the lake and surrounding mountains, take the trail to the left around the east shore of the lake to the lake's south side. From the top of the 200-foot pinnacle just southeast of the lake, there are truly outstanding views of the Teton Peaks. This may be the best view in the park.

To continue on the trail to Amphitheater Lake, walk along the north side of Surprise Lake. You need only climb 148 feet and 0.2 mile to reach Amphitheater Lake, lying at the foot of Disappointment Peak (11,618 feet). This beautiful peak got its rather sad name when a group of early climbers thought they could reach the peak of Grand Teton from this mountain. When they reached the top, they were surprised by the considerable gap between the two peaks. The trail continues along the eastern shore of Amphitheater Lake to climb a 150-foot ridge that overlooks Glacier Gulch and affords an impressive view of the huge glacier-carved U-shaped canyon below.

To return to the trailhead, retrace your steps. Allow plenty of time for the descent, and watch those knees.

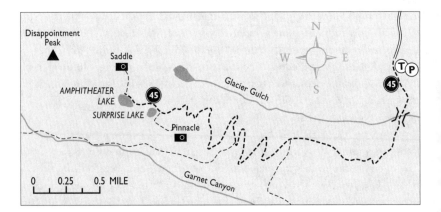

46 TAGGART AND BRADLEY LAKES LOOP

Difficulty: moderate
Distance: 4.7 miles round trip
Usage: moderate
Starting elevation: 6,625 feet; elevation gain, 650 feet
Season: late May through early October
Maps: USGS 7.5-minute Moose and Grand Teton, WY

Stark, beautiful, desolate, and teeming with life—the loop trail to Taggart and Bradley Lakes is all of the above! In 1985 the raging Beaver Creek Fire denuded the hillsides, revealing the awesome work of glaciers like nowhere else in the park. Don't miss this hike if your family is interested in fire ecology, geology, bird-watching, or fishing. For more information, pick up the Grand Teton Natural History Association's informative trail guide, available at the visitor center and from a dispenser near the trailhead. For colorful foliage, try this trail in autumn.

Enter Grand Teton National Park via the Moose Entrance Station and drive 2.7 miles north on Teton Park Road to the Taggart Lake Trailhead and parking lot on the left. Find the trailhead on the lot's west side.

Hike west across dry sage flats 0.3 mile to a fork in the trail. Take the right fork, the shortest route to Taggart Lake. This is prime habitat for playful Unita ground squirrels, which pop in and out of holes like furry jack-in-the-boxes. Larger holes (roughly football size) mark the excavations of badgers. Badgers dig elliptical holes resembling the sites of small explosions, with soil and debris spewed in all directions. A badger often appropriates a squirrel's tidy burrow, enlarging it for his wider dimensions after dining on its unlucky inhabitant. Unlike squirrels, badgers are primarily nocturnal and therefore seldom seen.

Sun-tolerant flowers brighten the trail. Prominent are "butter and eggs," with yellow and yolk-colored blossoms arranged on stalks one to two feet tall (an easy flower for children to recognize); purple rockcrest, a mustard sporting four small purple petals; blue harebell; and creamy buckwheat. The trail soon crosses rushing Taggart Creek and its tributaries. Look west for great views of the Grand Teton. The creek's moister environment supports thimbleberry, wild raspberry, mountain ash, and the following black bear favorites: snowberry, chokecherry, and, of course, bearberry.

The trail rises gently. Pass above a NPS corral, and then head west and follow Taggart Creek. Boulders and shade along the creek provide pleasant resting places. Where there are rocks, look for yellow-bellied marmots.

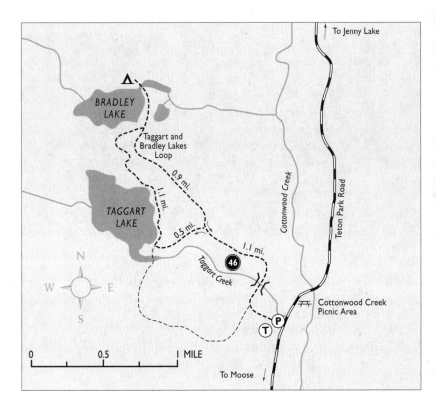

Marmots act like wealthy old tourists, spending the summer eating, sun-bathing, and sleeping. Find them foraging in the early morning, sun-bathing at midmorning, napping at noontime, sun-bathing again at midafternoon, and finally foraging again in late afternoon. By sunset, they are snug in their rocky burrows, asleep.

Throughout this area, the lightning-caused Beaver Creek Fire severely burned over 1,000 acres of one-hundred-year-old forest. Its burning released valuable minerals to the soil, generating a rush of new growth. Snowbrush ceanothus is one pioneer plant growing prodigiously beside the trail. Also known as "varnish bush," it was named for the shiny and sticky coating on its leathery leaves. In early summer, snowbrush bears showy clusters of small white flowers. Native Americans made a soap by rubbing the flowers in their hands with a small amount of water. Today, elk, deer, and moose browse its leaves. Quaking aspen also thrives in the fire-ravaged landscape. Easily identi-fied by its small fluttering leaves and whitish bark, aspen is often the first tree to come back after a fire, for its roots remain alive below the ground. The roots send forth replacement suckers that are nourished by the established root system. Because of the aspen's ability to "rise up from the ashes of destruction," it has been called the "phoenix tree."

Without the usual dense forest cover, hikers can fully appreciate the shape of the moraine they are climbing. About 15,000 years ago, a mammoth glacier rode down Avalanche Canyon (dramatically visible from the shore of Taggart Lake). After thousands of years, it finished its journey and fanned out at the mouth of the canyon, leaving a pile of unsorted rock and soil in front of its eastern edge (a moraine). As temperatures warmed and the glacier melted, the moraine held in the water. In this way, Taggart Lake was created, and in the same way glaciers created Bradley Lake and the other lakes along the base of the Tetons.

At a junction 1.1 miles from the trailhead, the trail levels. Take the left fork that meets Taggart Lake in 0.5 mile. Enter an area where young lodgepole thrive in the full sun. Lodgepole are specially adapted to fire; they produce two types of cones. Their serotinous cones (with a waxlike coating) open only at temperatures above 113 degrees F. The bursting of these cones in a fire produces up to 1 million seeds per acre!

Life thus returns almost instantaneously after a fire. As timbers cool,

Shore of Jackson Lake, Grand Teton National Park

birds and small mammals flock to eat the newly released seeds. Many take up residence in standing snags. Look for mountain bluebirds, northern flickers, a multitude of woodpeckers, gorgeous red-headed, yellow-breasted western tanagers, and, atop snags overlooking open areas, red-tailed hawks. Fire-generated openings provide fertile hunting grounds, and tall snags are ideal lookout-posts for the sharp-eyed hawks.

Arrive at beautiful, tree-rimmed Taggart Lake. Dazzling reflections of snow-capped peaks grace its waters. Boulders at water's edge make perfect picnic spots. Gaze up glacier-carved Avalanche Canyon and imagine the path of the ancient glacier. Don't miss Shoshoko Falls visible near the top of the canyon, 2,000 feet above the lake. Try angling for cutthroat and brook trout in the shallow waters. Then follow the trail north along the lake's eastern shore for about 0.5 mile.

To reach Bradley Lake, climb over another moraine at Taggart Lake's north end. On the way, notice aspen with raised black scars. In winter when food is scarce, elk eat aspen bark, occasionally killing trees if they girdle them. The trail rises up and over the moraine, and then switchbacks down to lovely Bradley Lake. Across the lake, U-shaped Garnet Canyon reveals the route of the glacier that created Bradley Lake.

Explore the east shore of Bradley Lake by continuing north on the trail, or start the journey back to the trailhead by bearing right (south) at the next trail junction. Backpackers can find a good campsite on Bradley Lake's north shore. To return home, climb over the moraine, and then hike southeast along its exposed ridge, gaining excellent views of the lakes. After traveling 0.9 mile from the junction, meet the main trail and bear left. The trail follows Taggart Creek back to the parking area.

47 MORMON ROW / KELLY LOOP ⌒

Difficulty: moderate
Distance: 14.75 miles round trip from Moose (12.25 miles from Antelope Flats Road)
Usage: moderate
Starting elevation: 6,490 feet; elevation gain, 300 feet
Season: mid-May through mid-October
Map: USGS 7.5-minute Moose, WY

This 14.75-mile bike loop gently courses through open country affording spectacular Teton views. Interesting stops along the way include the picturesque

"Shane" cabins and Kelly Warm Springs (bring a bathing suit). En route, watch for coyote, badger, red-tailed hawk, antelope, and especially bison. This is an excellent ride for strong young riders, for the elevation gain is minimal. This is also a fine ride for parents towing young children in bike trailers.

Most visitors start from the bike rental store at Moose Village, where children's bikes and trailers can be rented. For those who have their own equipment, the preferable starting point is the beginning of Antelope Flats Road, 1.2 miles north of Moose Junction on US 191-89-26. Find Moose 12 miles north of Jackson, off US 191-89-26. To find the bike rental store, take the first right after you leave US 191-89-26 at Moose Junction. To reserve rental bikes (highly advisable), call Dornan's Bike Rentals at (307) 733-2522.

If you're beginning in Moose, ride out to US 191-89-26, and then ride north (left) 1.2 miles to Antelope Flats Road. The highway is very busy, so use extreme caution. (Fortunately, this is the only section requiring highway riding.) To the east is Blacktail Butte (7,688 feet), a prime rock-climbing area. Several local climbing schools offer instruction for all ages there. Some of the trainees hanging 1,000 feet above the highway are preparing for the Grand Teton, where they'll be suspended 5,000 feet above the valley floor!

Turn east (right) on Antelope Flats Road. Stretching out in all directions are

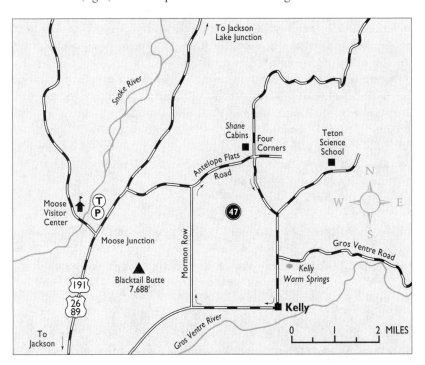

miles of dry sagebrush flats. Although the dusty gray-green landscape may first appear uninteresting, sage flats are teeming with life. Its inhabitants include badger, coyote, sage grouse, rabbit, pronghorn antelope, and bison. If you're not familiar with sagebrush, dismount and crush one of its leaves in your hand. It was named for its pungent scent, although it is not related to the herb. Its odorous leaves are a favorite winter food for sage grouse, mule deer, and pronghorn.

This is prime antelope habitat, so keep a sharp watch. Pronghorn are difficult to spot, for their tawny coat and white markings provide perfect camouflage. The pronghorn was named for its branching horns, common to both sexes, although larger on the male. In summer, hidden in the sagebrush are pronghorn fawns (often twins and occasionally triplets), born each spring in late May and early June. On hot days, groups of pronghorns rest in the shade of the sagebrush to avoid overheating. The best time to see antelope in the open is in the early morning and at dusk when they are foraging.

Nevertheless, pronghorn are likely to spot you long before you see them. Their exceptionally large eyes are especially keen; they can detect movement at a distance of 4 miles! When they detect danger, one pronghorn signals to another by raising its white rump hair. Others flare their hairs to spread the signal, and the entire herd disappears in the blink of an eye. A pronghorn can reach speeds of 60 miles per hour and leap 20 feet in one bound! Despite its speed and natural camouflage, the pronghorn's niche in the Greater Yellowstone Ecosystem is far from secure. Its handsome head is a popular hunting trophy, and its favored habitat is endangered by burgeoning residential subdivisions.

Continue east on Antelope Flats Road for 2.5 miles to crumbling cabins on the left side of the road. This is Joe Pfeifer's abandoned homestead, now part of Grand Teton National Park. Joe Pfeifer came to Jackson Hole in 1910 and built these cabins as a summer residence. His intent was to farm, but the quality of his views far exceeded the quality of his soil. Nevertheless, Joe hung on and eked out a subsistence each summer until 1948. The site is locally known as the *Shane* cabins, for the beautifully weathered buildings were used in the classic western film.

This is a *prime* bison grazing area. Riders may see a herd right by the road or even *in* the road. Be sure to stay at least 25 yards away. Watch the adjacent fields also for coyote, which hunt the numerous rodents of the sageflats. Close examination of the ground reveals countless burrows of ground squirrels and badgers. Coyote eat a wide variety of burrowers from shrews to rabbits as well as reptiles, frogs, and grasshoppers.

Continue 0.5 mile east of the cabins on Antelope Flats Road to Four Corners. To the left (north) the road leads to Teton National Forest. Straight ahead are private ranches. Take a right (south). This pretty stretch of road is

Riders on Antelope Flats Road

easy riding. Relax and enjoy the Gros Ventre Range that lies to the south and east. To the east (left), notice a sign for the Teton Science School. The school is known for its excellent summer naturalist camps for children. Ride for 2.5 miles to another junction signed US Forest Service Campgrounds. This is Gros Ventre Road; turn east (left) to visit Kelly Warm Springs.

Almost immediately look for a patch of green grass and find the pond on the south (right) side of the road, across from a parking area. This is a wonderful place for a rest stop. Fed by hot springs originating in the Gros Ventre Range, the water temperature is 75 to 85 degrees F year-round. Kelly Warm Springs is a popular local swimming hole and a favorite place for "frogging" (catch and release with nets, of course). The plentiful bullfrog tadpoles reach enormous proportions and will serenade you as you swim.

After a swim, ride west back to the main road. Then turn south (left) to continue the loop. Cycle a little over a mile to the small town of Kelly, hosting a small general store with great character. This is a good place to get a cold drink and a candy bar.

From Kelly, ride west. The line of cottonwoods to the left (south) indicates the path of the Gros Ventre River. After 2 miles, arrive at a junction with a gravel road, called Mormon Row, heading north. Turn north (right) on Mormon Row and ride 2.75 miles to its intersection with Antelope Flats Road. Along the way, look for red-tailed hawks perching regally atop tall snags and fence posts. Watch the sky also for their graceful, soaring circles. Mormon Row was named for the settlers who homesteaded this land in the early 1900s.

At the junction with Antelope Flats Road, turn west (left) to return via US 191-89-26 to Moose.

48 PHELPS LAKE OVERLOOK AND DEATH CANYON

Difficulty: moderate to Phelps Lake Overlook, strenuous to Death Canyon
Distance: 0.9 mile one way to Phelps Lake Overlook; 3.7 miles one way to Death Canyon
Usage: moderate
Starting elevation: 6,770 feet; elevation gain, 400 feet to Phelps Lake Overlook, 1,461 feet to Death Canyon
Season: late May through early October
Map: USGS 7.5-minute Grand Teton, WY

This is a marvelous hike, but it's tough. Even before the 1,000-foot climb to Death Canyon's portals, the trail gains and then loses 400 feet of elevation. Nevertheless, your efforts are handsomely rewarded, for Death Canyon is truly beautiful. Head there to picnic, camp, explore, or look for the plentiful moose that browse the canyon's creek. In summer enjoy the trail's profuse flower displays, and in fall admire its brilliant foliage. For an easier, but still scenic hike, turn around at beautiful Phelps Lake Overlook, just 0.9 mile from the trailhead.

From Jackson, drive north 12 miles on US 191-26-89 to Moose Junction. Turn left and drive about 1 mile to the Moose–Wilson Road. Turn left onto the Moose–Wilson Road and proceed 3 miles (watch for moose on the left) to a turnoff for White Grass Ranch on the right, also signed for Death Canyon Trailhead. Turn right (west) and drive 1.6 miles to the parking area. (The pavement stops after 0.7 mile. Cars with low clearance may park at pullouts along the road.) The trailhead is at the parking lot's west end.

Follow the trail west through lodgepole, spruce, and fir. Plentiful water creates a lush garden of flowers and shrubs. Why is there so much moisture here? The answer lies in the origin of the Teton Range. The Tetons were created by a cataclysmic uplift and sinking along the fault line lying at the eastern base

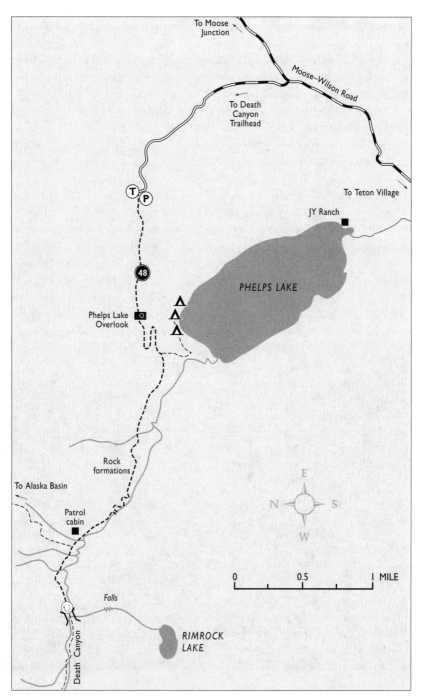

of the range. Along that fault, many thousands of years ago, the valley floor swung downward (as if there was a hinge on the valley's eastern edge) while the mountains swung up. Along the fault there are fissures and, just uphill from the trail, numerous underground springs. The springs bubble up through the fissures and run downhill to water this area.

Is this still an active earthquake zone? One Teton ranger suggested that this park be renamed "Grand Teton National Fault Park"! Experts believe that a significant earthquake along the fault could happen at any time. Historically, major ruptures have occurred every two thousand to four thousand years, and the last quake shook about four thousand years ago. Thus, the question is not if, but when, another major quake will rock this area.

Along the trail, note the numerous coneflowers, five feet tall in midsummer, each with a large brown cone atop a stout green stem. Native Americans used them to treat rheumatism by placing a large quantity in a hot bath. Other tribes boiled their stems to produce a yellow liquid for treating poison ivy. Coneflower was also widely used as an antidote for snakebite.

The trail continues west, climbing gently. Look for purple monkshood on tall stalks. Although it is quite poisonous, Native Americans successfully used monkshood to reduce fever. Today the same chemical is produced synthetically

Phelps Lake Overlook

and employed as a heart sedative. In medieval Europe, a closely related flower, wolfbane, was worn on necklaces to ward off werewolves.

Pass huge aspens whose bark has been sampled by elk. Climb moderately to several ancient Douglas-fir trees by the trail (three hundred to four hundred years old). Identify Douglas-fir by its pendant cones with their distinctive three-pronged bracts between the scales. Switchback up to reach the Phelps Lake Overlook, 0.9 mile from the trailhead. Enjoy the gorgeous view of the large, beautiful lake from this perch 600 feet above the water. Like other lakes at the base of the Tetons, Phelps Lake was created by the movement of a glacier. This viewpoint is located on the edge of its lateral moraine. At the south end of the lake is JY Ranch, owned by the Rockefellers. To the northwest is the portentous entrance to Death Canyon.

Descend the moraine in switchbacks weaving through aspen and mountain ash. Near the bottom of the moraine, 1.6 miles from the trailhead, arrive at a trail junction. The left fork descends to the lake and to excellent campsites at the lake's north end. Campsites are reached by continuing south 0.2 mile toward the lake. Turn left (east) at the next trail intersection and hike another 0.2 mile. Noncampers stay right for Death Canyon.

Enter pleasingly shady old growth. Pass beneath magnificent Englemann spruce and towering cottonwoods. As you travel northwest toward Death Valley Creek, the trail is enveloped by berry bushes. When the shrubs are full of fruit in late summer, make noise to avoid surprising black bears.

Next ascend steep and narrow switchbacks that climb over 1,000 feet. Strange and alluring rock formations guide your ascent. Look for the scowling head of a gorilla guarding the canyon entrance. Exposed along the trail are some of the oldest rocks on the surface of the earth. The violent uplifting that occurred eons ago unearthed this ancient stone.

Listen for the "bleat" of pikas on the rocky slope. The tiny "rock rabbits" spend their days gathering grasses and sedges. A five-ounce pika may gather up to fifty pounds of plants to store for the winter.

Pass a lovely spot by the creek where water cascades over rocks, and wild raspberries and flowers grow profusely. Stupendous views to the east include Phelps Lake and the Gros Ventre Range. Prominent on the eastern horizon is Sheep Mountain (11,200 feet), also called Sleeping Indian for its resemblance to the horizontal profile of an Indian chief with headdress.

At last, follow the creek through an area of large boulders where the trail finally levels. Stroll by clear pools, below sparkling cliffs, along grassy banks and colorful flowers. The effect is paradisiacal.

A little farther down the trail, willows by the creek create superb moose habitat. These immense creatures can eat fifty to sixty pounds of browse per day. Moose eat constantly during the summer for they remain in Grand

Teton National Park through the winter when food is scarce. Moose are well adapted for cold and can easily endure temperatures up to -40 degrees F. Their coat contains a layer of hollow hairs that acts as an effective insulator. Look creekside for moose, but don't neglect the slopes, for moose can climb quite competently. If your binoculars are handy, check the cliffs for human climbers as well.

At approximately 3.5 miles, arrive at a NPS patrol cabin. Just after the cabin, a spur trail to the left leads to a beaver dam. Look for conical tree stumps with teeth marks. At 3.7 miles, pass the junction with the Alaska Basin Trail. Stay left to explore Death Canyon.

The level trail travels along the beautiful valley floor. Dense vegetation undoubtedly hides numerous moose. Cross two tributary creeks, and then look for a lovely cascade on your left (south) flowing from Rimrock Lake, over 2,000 feet above the canyon floor. Next arrive at a bridge over the canyon's major creek. For backpackers, the camping zone begins on the opposite bank. This is a good turnaround point for families.

49 GRANITE CANYON

Difficulty: moderate to east end of Granite Canyon, strenuous to Rendezvous Mountain Trail Junction
Distance: 3 to 6.2 miles one way
Usage: low
Starting elevation: 6,400 feet; elevation gain, 600 to 1,600 feet
Season: late May through early October
Maps: USGS 7.5-minute Teton Village and Rendezvous Peak, WY

While Granite Canyon may not be quite as spectacular as the park's magnificent canyons to the north (Cascade, Paintbrush, and Death Canyons), this trail does provide beautiful forests, cascading creeks, good opportunities to see moose and deer, and more solitude than the more popular canyons. Hike the entire canyon to a flower-filled alpine meadow or trek just to the canyon's mouth. Either way, it's a delightful trail, convenient to Moose and Teton Village.

From Jackson, drive north 12 miles on US 191-26-89 to Moose Junction. Turn left and drive about one mile to the Moose–Wilson Road. Turn left onto the Moose–Wilson Road and proceed 5.9 miles to the signed Granite Canyon

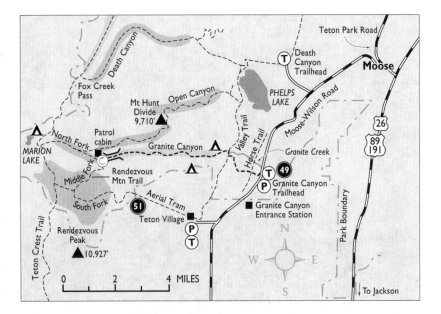

parking area on the right. From Teton Village, drive north 2.1 miles on the Moose–Wilson Road to the trailhead on the left, just 1 mile after the Granite Canyon Entrance Station.

The trail begins in an open, sunny sagebrush meadow dappled with lupine, paintbrush, cinquefoil, and harebells. Head west, walking in and out of small aspen groves. The meadows are gorgeous with waist-high wildflowers in midsummer. Snow-covered mountains lit by the morning sun define the eastern horizon. Just to the west-southwest, find the ski slopes of Rendezvous Mountain.

Cross a horse trail (Bearpaw Meadow to the right, Poker Flats to the left) and continue straight ahead. Soon enter the shade of pines and cross a small stream. The trail then climbs a bit above the stream and follows it, heading north. The stream stays on your right as you travel through forest where berries and pink mushrooms thrive in the shade.

At 1.5 miles from the trailhead, arrive at a Y junction. To the south (left), the Valley Trail heads to Teton Village. Take the right fork and continue north to cross a bridge over fast-running Granite Creek. Almost immediately cross a second smaller stream on a second bridge to arrive at another trail junction. The Valley Trail heads northeast (right) to Phelps Lake (Trip 48) and Open Canyon. Bear left (west) on the Granite Canyon Trail and travel along the north side of Granite Creek.

Canyon trail, Grand Teton National Park

Enter a drier and more open area where the trail steepens. Climb past rock piles where marmots and pika are frequently seen and enter the Lower Granite Canyon Camping Zone about 3.9 miles from the trailhead. Continue climbing past cascades and through dense vegetation on the canyon floor.

Keep an eye out for moose. You are almost certain to see tracks. In midsummer, you may spot a cow with her calf. Hikers in July would see a calf about one month old, and it would likely stay close to its mother. Bulls, however, do not usually remain with the mother and offspring. If you do spot a calf, don't linger. The mother is probably close by, and she will not hesitate to defend her young. When its mother is not by its side, a young moose calf, like elk calves and fawns, will remain motionless. Their stillness minimizes the dispersion of their scent and thus protects them from predators.

The trail continues to climb. Sounds of birds, rushing water, and wind dominate. The walls of Granite Canyon flank you, marked with bare areas where avalanches have swept away the trees. At approximately 5 miles from the trailhead, arrive at another bridge where a beautiful cascade falls from the canyon wall. This makes a good turnaround point for those seeking a moderate hike.

After 1.2 more miles on the ascending trail, you arrive at another bridge and trail junction. To the south, the Rendezvous Mountain Trail heads to the Jackson Hole Ski Area and aerial tram (Trip 50). Continuing straight ahead takes you past the Granite Canyon Patrol Cabin toward Marion Lake, a small subalpine lake resting at the base of Housetop Mountain. A much shorter hike southwest on the Rendezvous Mountain Trail leads to magnificent meadows filled with wildflowers between the south and middle forks of the canyon. At your pleasure, turn around and retrace your steps to the trailhead. The beautiful views on the return are of the Gros Ventre Range to the east.

You can experience the Granite Canyon Trail in an entirely different way by riding the Jackson Hole aerial tram from Teton Village to the top of 10,450-foot Rendezvous Peak and hiking down 12.4 miles through Granite Canyon. The 4,135-foot loss in elevation makes this a very challenging trip, but the opportunity to journey through the flower-filled alpine meadows on the back of Rendezvous Peak is a strong draw in midsummer. Catch the tram at Teton Village, 12 miles northwest of Jackson on the Moose–Wilson Road. The tram operates from 9 A.M. to 6 P.M. during the summer, and the trail is open after snow has melted at the summit to allow safe travel. Additional information on the trail and maps are available at the Village and from tram operators by calling (307) 733-2292.

50 RENDEZVOUS PEAK / ROCK SPRINGS BOWL LOOP

Difficulty: strenuous
Distance: 4.2-mile loop
Usage: moderate
Starting elevation: 10,450 feet; elevation gain, 1,000 feet
Season: early July through mid-September (snow may persist into July)
Maps: USGS 7.5-minute Rendezvous Peak and Teton Village, WY

In just ten minutes, the tram at the Jackson Hole Ski Area rushes hikers over 4,000 feet to the top of Rendezvous Mountain (10,450 feet). It's a painless way (despite a little sting to the wallet) to access a beautiful alpine environment and gain magnificent panoramic views.

Before setting out, heed the following precautions. Hiking at 10,450 feet is very taxing, so take it easy. Since wind and sun can cause rapid dehydration, carry water and extra food for energy. Before hiking, sea-level visitors should first acclimate themselves to valley elevation (6,200 feet). Families with children under ten may want to limit their hiking to the shorter Cody Bowl Trail. Also, bring raingear and warm clothing for the summit temperature is commonly 20 to 30 degrees below that of the valley and afternoon thunder-

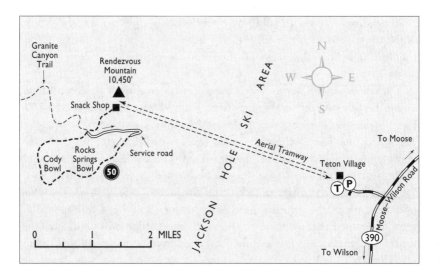

Hiking Rock Springs Bowl

showers are frequent. In addition, sturdy footgear is a necessity, for the slopes are steep and rocky. For information on tram schedules, fares, and trail conditions, call Jackson Hole Ski Resort at (307) 733-2292. Inquire also about the free naturalist hikes in both Rock Springs and Cody Bowl. Rest rooms and a snack shop are located on the summit.

Drive south from Jackson on US 89-191 to the turnoff for Wyoming Highway 22, just south of town. Turn west on Highway 22 and drive about 5 miles; then turn right onto Wyoming Highway 390 (Moose–Wilson Road) and drive 7 miles to the Jackson Hole Ski Area at Teton Village. Turn left into the ski area and drive to a parking lot opposite the clock tower and tram building. When you buy your tram tickets, ask for the Rock Springs interpretive brochure.

On the tram ride, look for moose on the steep slopes below. Although it may seem unlikely, moose are frequently seen. They climb the mountain to access the willow-choked streams of the canyons and to escape the heat and insects of the valley.

At the summit, exit the tram and head southwest. Pass the snack shop and continue southwest along the ridge. Arrive at the junction with the Granite Canyon Trail and descend to the left via the service road where you rapidly lose about 1,000 feet of elevation in switchbacks. Watch for the Rock Springs Bowl

Trail on the right heading south, at the end of the second switchback. Head right on the nature trail and consult the numbered guide for information on flora, fauna, and geology.

At this elevation, it is critical to avoid stepping on alpine flowers. A trampled alpine garden could take a century to grow back. Growth is slow when the growing season is only a few weeks long each year.

All alpine vegetation struggles to survive by growing close to the ground. Hikers, too, may wish to lay low and huddle together to avoid the wind, even in midsummer. Try a simple experiment with your children. Ask them to crouch down on the trail. They will feel a noticeable difference in the temperature close to the ground, for wind speed increases with its distance above the surface. Increased wind velocity brings greater wind chill and colder temperatures. To survive, alpine flowers must escape the wind because it robs them of heat and precious moisture, and it tears at them with blowing dirt, ice, and snow.

Follow the trail west up Rock Springs Bowl to Cody Bowl. Cody Bowl is the glacial cirque lying just above Rock Springs Bowl. In midsummer, melt-water forms a small lake in the bowl. From Cody Bowl, the trail heads back to the ridge. The ridge gives hikers a chance to experience a stand of *krummholz* (a German word meaning "crooked wood"). Krummholz describes trees living at or near timberline whose growth has been stunted by strong winds and severe cold. These trees may be one hundred years old, but they stand barely taller than a child. Before leaving the ridge, look east for marvelous views of the rugged Teton Range. To the north is an inspiring view of the Grand Teton. Also visible (from south to north) are Housetop Mountain (10,537 feet), Fossil Mountain (10,916 feet), Mount Meek (10,681 feet), and Battleship Mountain (10,679 feet). From the ridge, follow the service road back to the tram building for your return trip.

51 MOOSE–WILSON ROAD BIKE TRAIL   ⌃

Difficulty: easy, handicapped accessible
Distance: 13 miles round trip
Usage: high
Starting elevation: 6,200 feet; no elevation gain
Season: early May through late October
Map: USGS 7.5-minute Teton Village, WY

Teton Village is no longer just the base camp for Jackson Hole skiers. The village has become a summer recreation mecca, offering a climbing wall, horseback riding, bike rentals, mountain biking, hot-air ballooning, paragliding (solo and tandem), and an aerial tram providing easy access to alpine hiking (Trip 50). Teton Village is also the perfect place to catch the new bike trail on the Moose–Wilson Road. The paved trail stretches nearly 6.5 level miles. The easy ride is great for a short family outing.

Drive south from Jackson on US 89–191 to the turnoff for Wyoming Highway 22, just south of town. Turn west on Highway 22 and drive about 5 miles; then turn right onto Wyoming Highway 390 (Moose–Wilson Road) and drive 7 miles to Teton Village. Park in the large parking lot. Bike rentals, including provisions, are available at Teton Village.

Riding first north (turn left from the Teton Village entrance road), the bike trail passes open pastures and grazing cattle and horses. The pleasant ride comes to an end too soon after just 1 mile when you arrive at the park's Granite Canyon Entrance. After the entrance station, Moose–Wilson Road is narrow and not well-suited to family biking. Cycle back to Teton Village to continue your ride.

Riding south (right) from the entrance to Teton Village, the bike path

Biking the Moose–Wilson Bike Trail

extends about 5.5 miles. To your right, as you ride south, there are more fields of grazing cattle. These large open areas, on both sides of Moose–Wilson Road, are excellent places to watch red-tailed hawks riding the thermals and hunting for rodents in the fields. Red-tailed hawks are large brown raptors, about twenty-five inches long, recognizable by their white breast and rust-colored tail. They are excellent hunters and can spot a mouse from 100 feet in the air. The hawks eat a wide variety of small mammals, including mice, voles, shrews, moles, squirrels, chipmunks, rats, rabbits, opossums, muskrats, and skunks. In the spring, watch for the aerial courtship "dance" of the hawks. The hawks dive and roll in the sky, and even lock talons and free-fall with a potential mate before splitting apart to resume the dance. If the mating is successful, the male and female will build a nest together. The male hawk will then hunt for and feed his mate during the month that she must sit on their eggs.

Looking toward Rendezvous Peak to the west, you may also see paragliders catching thermals and drifting gracefully to the fields below. The exciting drop from Rendezvous Mountain is over 4,000 feet. Visitors without experience can try paragliding and hang-gliding by accompanying a trained pilot on a tandem flight. For information on Jackson Hole gliding, call (307) 690-TRAM. If money is no object and floating is irresistible, try a hot-air balloon flight over Teton Village. Arrange a trip with Wyoming Balloon Adventures at (800) 329-9205.

About 2 miles from Teton Village, cyclists arrive at the Lake Creek Rest Stop. Benches by the creek provide a pleasant picnic spot. After your rest, continue south on the trail less than a mile to the Aspens, a condominium development. If you haven't brought your own drinks and snacks, there is a deli here that can meet your needs. Shortly after the Aspens is a second development, Teton Pines. As you pass Teton Pines, observe the osprey nests atop tall poles above the water. Their large nests of sticks are used year after year and grow accordingly. Summer riders have a good chance of seeing osprey because the young remain in or near the nest for two months.

An osprey is a large bird of prey almost the size of a red-tailed hawk. An osprey, however, is darker brown, with a white breast and a dark stripe running through its eyes. You can recognize an osprey by the M-shaped crook of its wings in flight. Ospreys feed exclusively on live fish, which they catch with their long, hooked talons, diving feet first into the water. Ospreys were declared an endangered species in 1976 because widespread use of the pesticide DDT caused the shells of their eggs to thin and break before hatching could occur. Since the United States banned DDT in 1972, the osprey population has recovered and the bird has moved from its "Threatened" classification in 1983 to "Special Concern" in 1999. Ospreys are found on every continent in the world except Antarctica. Their position on the top of the aquatic food chain make the bird a good bellwether of the health of aquatic habitat, the state of the fish population, and the extent of environmental contamination.

The trail along the Moose–Wilson Road stretches about 7 miles from Teton Village to its junction with Highway 22. As you approach the highway, commercial development increases and the path becomes less scenic. At your pleasure, retrace your route on the bike trail and return to Teton Village.

52 NATIONAL ELK REFUGE

Difficulty: moderate
Distance: 6.8 miles one way
Usage: moderate
Starting elevation: 6,320 feet; elevation gain, 160 feet
Season: mid-May to mid-October
Maps: USGS 7.5-minute Cache Creek and Gros Ventre Junction, WY

The National Elk Refuge hosts no elk in summer, but it does provide a nice dirt road with spectacular Teton scenery. Ride in the early morning when car traffic is light and the temperatures are cool. At midday, the road can be hot, sunny, and quite dusty. In any season, carry an ample supply of water.

Drive or ride to the National Elk Refuge, located at the east end of Broadway Street, just past St. John's Hospital, 1 mile east of the Jackson Town Square. The Refuge Headquarters provides information on the refuge and is open weekdays, 8 A.M. to 4 P.M. The refuge entrance is just east of the headquarters.

The National Elk Refuge was established in 1912 to preserve the last winter range for elk in the Jackson Hole valley. Prior to its settlement in the late 1800s, the valley supported an immense elk herd, perhaps numbering as many as 25,000. But the town of Jackson and its surrounding ranches took over a large portion of the elk's historic winter range. By the early 1900s, thousands of starving elk wandered the streets of Jackson in search of winter forage. Their population plummeted as they competed poorly with local livestock for winter food. The Jackson Hole Museum displays stark photographs of the plight of Jackson's pre-refuge elk. The winter scenes depicted in the photos moved a concerned public to establish the 25,000-acre refuge, which protects about one-fourth of the elk's original range.

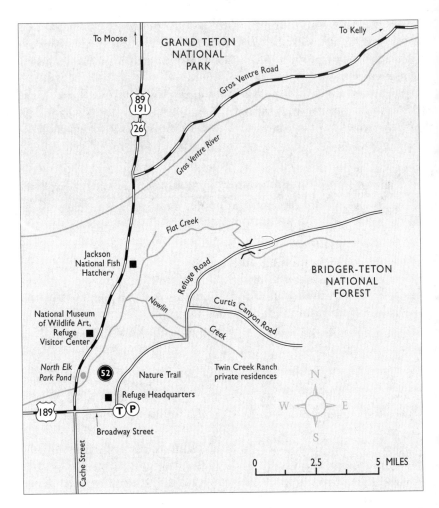

You won't see elk here in the summer, for they move north in April and early May to their high summer range in the Tetons and South Yellowstone. In late October and early November, the elk return to the refuge. All summer the refuge is irrigated to yield rich grasslands for the approximately 7,500 elk that winter there. When snow covers the grass, the refuge provides alfalfa pellets. A winter visit to the refuge includes a horse-drawn sleigh ride among the herds. In the rarified winter air, it is quite an experience to hear the musical rattling of the elk's huge racks as they spar in the silent, snow-covered valley. Access to the refuge for summer visitors is largely limited to the road. Although some of the refuge's creeks are open to fishing in August and September, many restrictions apply (check at refuge headquarters). Hiking and camping are not permitted within the refuge. Please obey all signs regarding access, and stay on the road.

Begin the ride by turning left (north) on the dirt road at the refuge's entrance. The good surface makes riding a real pleasure on the first 4.2 miles. Pass the Old Miller Place and ride to the east of sage-covered Miller Butte. At 2 miles, pass a nature trail where hikers are allowed to climb the slope to examine an elk exclosure constructed in 1993. The exclosure was put up to determine the elks' effect on local vegetation, particularly aspen. Inside the exclosure are numerous aspen seedings, whereas few seedlings survive on the unprotected slope, for the elk love to eat the young trees.

Continue to ride northeast, passing over Nowlin Creek. At 3.6 miles the road turns north and passes Twin Creek Ranch and some private residences. At 4.2 miles from the entrance, county maintenance ends and the road surface roughens.

At 4.5 miles, reach a junction with the Curtis Canyon Road to the right. Go straight (north). The road becomes rougher still as it heads north, but views west to the Tetons are spectacular. In summer, a subtle sprinkling of flowers brightens the dry meadow. At 7.8 miles from the entrance, reach McBride Bridge over Flat Creek.

Flat Creek and other refuge waters support a wild population of Snake River cutthroat trout, a unique variety of the cutthroat species and the only trout native to the area. There are also a small number of brook and rainbow trout. Because of road conditions, the bridge is a good turnaround point for young cyclists. Those who want to continue can ride 2.2 miles farther on fairly rough road to the refuge boundary. To return to the trailhead, just ride the road in the opposite direction.

If fisheries management interests you or your youngsters, a nice side trip is the nearby National Fish Hatchery on US 26-191 just north of the refuge. Holding tanks provide viewing of hundreds of young trout, aquarium tanks display additional species, and friendly hatchery personnel are available to answer all your questions. If your youngsters want to try fishing on the refuge, remember that the refuge's North Elk Park Pond is stocked with Snake River cutthroat and open to youths under age fourteen. The pond is located on the refuge along US 26-191.

APPENDIX A

RECOMMENDED READING

Build upon your family's experiences in Yellowstone and Grand Teton National Parks through excellent books on nature and regional history. The following list includes books that promote an awareness, sensitivity, and enjoyment of the environment. Most are available in park visitor centers.

The Yellowstone Association and Grand Teton Natural History Association are excellent resources for top-quality nature books for all ages. These non-profit associations sell a wide assortment of books at park visitor centers and through their mail-order catalogs. Contact the Yellowstone Association, P.O. Box 117, Yellowstone National Park, WY 82190, (307) 344-2293, *www .yellowstoneassociation.org* or the Grand Teton Natural History Association, P.O. Box 170, Moose, WY 83012, (307) 739-3606, *www.grandtetonpark.org.*

The following organizations also offer nature books by mail: The National Wildlife Federation, 1400 16th Street NW, Washington, D.C. 20036, (800) 432-6564; The National Geographic Society, Educational Services, P.O. Box 2118, Washington, D.C. 20013-2118, (800) 368-2728; and The Sierra Club, 730 Polk Street, San Francisco, CA, 94109, (415) 923-5500.

FIELD GUILDES FOR CHILDREN

Alden, Peter. *Mammals: A Simplified Field Guide to the Common Mammals of North America*. Boston: Houghton Mifflin Co., 1987.

Arnosky, Jim. *Secrets of a Wildlife Watcher: A Beginner Field Guide*. New York: Beech Tree Books, 1991.

Halfpenny, James C. *Scats and Tracks of The Rocky Mountains*. Guilford, CT: Globe Pequot Press, 2001.

Magley, Beverly. *Montana Wildflowers: A Children's Field Guide*. Helena, MT: Falcon Press, 1992.

Murie, Olaus J. *Animal Tracks. Peterson Field Guides*. Boston: Houghton Mifflin Co., 1974.

Peterson, Roger Tory. *Birds: A Simplified Field Guide*. Boston: Houghton Mifflin, Co., 1986.

————. *Wildflowers: A Simplified Field Guide to Common Wildflowers*. Boston: Houghton Mifflin, Co., 1986.

GENERAL NONFICTION FOR CHILDREN

Arnosky, Jim. *Crinkleroot's Guide to Walking in Wild Places*. New York: Bradbury Press, 1990.

Bryant, Jennifer. *Margaret Murie: A Wilderness Life*. New York: Twenty-first Century Books, 1993.

The Earthworks Group. *50 Simple Things Kids Can Do to Save the Earth*. New York: Universal Press Syndicate, 1990.

Foster, Lynne. *Take a Hike! The Sierra Club's Guide to Hiking and Backpacking*. Boston: Little Brown and Company, 1991.

Groons, Molly. *We Are Wolves*. Minnetonka, MN: NorthWord, 2002.

Jensen, Kate. *Chief Joseph: Leader of Destiny*. New York: Troll Associates, 1979.

Holdsworth, Henry. *Born Wild in Yellowstone and Grand Teton National Park*. Helena, MT: Farcountry Press, 2003.

Pollack, Jean Snyder, and Robert Pollack. *Common Campground Critters of the Mountain West: A Child's Guide*. Boulder, CO: Roberts Rinehart, Inc., 1987.

Robinson, Sandra Chisholm. *The Everything Bear*. Boulder, CO: Roberts Rinehart, Inc., 1992.

Robson, Gary D. *Who Pooped in the Park?* Helena, MT: Far Country Press, 2004.

Schneider, Bill. *The Flight of the Nez Perce*. Helena, MT: Falcon Press, 1992.

Turner, Erin. *It Happened in Yellowstone: 24 Fascinating Stories from the History of America's First National Park*. Guilford, CT: Two Dot Press, 2001.

PICTURE BOOKS

Arnosky, Jim. *Deer at the Brook*. New York: Lothrop, Lee & Shepard Books, 1986.

————. *Come out, Muskrats*. New York: Lothrop, Lee & Shepard Books, 1989.

dePaola, Tomie. *The Legend of Indian Paintbrush*. New York: G. P. Putnam's Sons, 1988.

Donahue, Mike. *The Grandpa Tree*. Boulder, CO: Roberts Rinehart, Inc., 1988.

Evans, Lisa Gollin. *An Elephant Never Forgets Its Snorkel*. New York: Crown Books, 1992.

George, Jean Craighead. *One Day in the Alpine Tundra*. New York: Thomas Y. Crowell, 1984.

Goble, Paul. *The Girl Who Loved Wild Horses*. New York: Aladdin Books, 1993.

Lopez, Barry. *Crow and Weasel*. New York: Harper Perennial, 1993.

Plumb, Sally. *A Pika's Tail*. Moose, WY: Grand Teton National History Association, 1994.

Robertson, Kayo. *Signs Along the River—Learning to Read the Natural Landscape*. Boulder, CO: Roberts Rinehart, Inc., 1986.

Seuss, Dr. (Theodore Geisel). *The Lorax*. New York: Random House, 1971.

FICTION FOR YOUNG READERS

Caduto, Michael J., and Joseph Bruchac. *Keepers of the Earth: Native American Stories and Environmental Activities for Children*. Golden, CO: Fulcrum, Inc., 1989.

George, Jean Craighead. *Julie of the Wolves*. New York: Harper & Row, 1972.

————. *My Side of the Mountain*. New York: E. P. Dutton, 1975.

Mowatt, Farley. *Never Cry Wolf*. Boston: Little Brown and Company, 1963.

Paulsen, Gary. *Dogsong*. New York: Bradbury Press, 1985.

Rawlings, Marjorie Kinnan. *The Yearling*. New York: Collier Macmillan Publishers, 1938.

Savage, Deborah. *A Rumour of Otters*. Boston: Houghton Mifflin Company, 1986.

Thomasma, Ken. Any of the following books published by Baker Book House, Co., Grand Rapids, MI: *Kunu:Winnebago Boy Escapes; Naya Nuki: Shoshoni Girl Who Ran; Om-Kas-Toe: Blackfeet Twin Captures an Elkdog; Pathki Nana: Kootenai Girl Solves a Mystery; Soun Tetoken: Nez Perce Boy Tames a Stallion*.

White, E. B. *The Trumpet of the Swan*. New York: Harper & Row, 1970.

Wilder, Laura Ingalls. *Little House on the Prairie*. New York: Scholastic Book Series, 1963.

PERIODICALS FOR CHILDREN

National Geographic World. National Geographic Society, P.O. Box 2118, Washington, D.C. 20013-2118. (800) 368-2728. Ages eight to fourteen.

Ranger Rick. National Wildlife Federation, 1400 West 16th Street NW, Washington, D.C. 20036. (800) 432-6564. Ages six to twelve.

Your Big Backyard. National Wildlife Federation, 1400 West 16th Street NW, Washington, D.C. 20036. (800) 432-6564. Ages three to five.

Zoobooks. Wildlife Education, Ltd. P.O. Box 28870, San Diego, CA 92128. Ages four to twelve.

BOOKS FOR PARENTS

Alden, Peter, John Grassy. *National Audubon Society Field Guide to the Rocky Mountain States*. New York: Chatileer Press, Inc., 2003.

Brown, Tom, Jr. *Tom Brown's Field Guide to Nature and Survival for Children*. New York: Berkley Publishing Group, 1989.

Cahill, Tim. *Lost in My Own Backyard*. New York: Crown, Publishers, 2004.

Cahill, Tim, and Tom Murphy. *Silence and Solitude*. Helena, MT: Riverbend Publishing, 2002.

Carson, Rachel. *The Sense of Wonder*. New York: Harper & Row, 1984.

Cornell, Joseph Bharat. *Sharing Nature with Children*. Nevada City, CA: Dawn Publications, 1979.

Lingelbach, Jenepher. *Hands On Nature: Information and Activities for Exploring the Environment with Children*. Woodstock, VT: Vermont Institute of Natural Sciences, 1986.

FIRST-AID BOOKS

Gill, Paul G., Jr. *Simon and Schuster's Pocket Guide to Wilderness Medicine*. New York: Fireside Books, 1991.

Lentz, Martha J., Steven C. MacDonald, and Jan D. Carline. *Mountaineering First Aid*. Seattle: The Mountaineers, 2004.

NATURAL HISTORY

Bach, Orville, Jr. *Exploring the Yellowstone Backcountry*. San Francisco: Sierra Club Tote Books, 1991.

Carter, Tom. *Day Hiking Grand Teton National Park*. Garland, TX: Dayhiking Press, 1993.

—. *Day Hiking Yellowstone National Park*. Garland, TX: Dayhiking Press, 1990.

Craighead, Frank C. *For Everything There is a Season*. Helena, MT: Falcon Press, 1994.

Craighead, Karen. *Large Mammals of Yellowstone and Grand Teton National Parks*. Yellowstone National Park: Yellowstone Association, 1991.

Eversman, Sharon, and Mary Carr. *Yellowstone Ecology: A Road Guide*. Missoula, MT: Mountain Press Publishing Co., 1992.

Fritz, William J. *Roadside Geology of the Yellowstone Country*. Missoula, MT: Mountain Press Publishing Co., 1992.

Halfpenny, James C., and Roy Douglas Ozanne. *Winter: An Ecological Handbook*. Boulder, CO: Johnson Books, 1989.

Halfpenny, James C. *Yellowstone Wolves in the Wild*. Helena, Montana: Riverbend Publishing, 2003.

Harry, Bryan. *Teton Trails: A Guide to the Trails of Grand Teton National Park*. Moose, WY: Grand Teton Natural History Association, 1987.

Henry, Jeff. *Yellowstone Winter Guide*. Boulder, CO: Roberts Rinehart Publishers, 1998.

Marschall, Mark C. *Yellowstone Trails: A Hiking Guide*. Yellowstone National Park: Yellowstone Association, 1990.

Olson, Linda L., and Tim Bywater. *A Guide to Exploring Grand Teton National Park*. Salt Lake City: RNM Press, 1991.

Raynes, Bert. *Birds of Grand Teton National Park and the Surrounding Area.* Moose, WY: Grand Teton Natural History Association, 1984.

Schmidt, Jeremy, and Steven Fuller. *Yellowstone / Grand Teton Road Guide.* Jackson Hole, WY: Free Wheeling Travel Guides, 1990.

Shaw, Richard J. *Plants of Yellowstone and Grand Teton National Parks.* Salt Lake City: Wheelwright Press, 1981.

Wilkinson, Todd. *Yellowstone Wildlife.* Minocqua, WI: Northword Press, Inc., 2004.

Wuerthner, George. *Yellowstone: A Visitor's Companion.* Harrisburg, PA: Stackpole Books, 1992.

BOOKS ABOUT BEARS

Herrero, Stephen. *Bear Attacks: Their Causes and Avoidance.* New York: Nick Lyons Books, 1985.

Schullery, Paul. *The Bears of Yellowstone.* Boulder, CO: Roberts Rinehart, Inc., 1986.

APPENDIX B

CONSERVATION ORGANIZATIONS

The following organizations share a common goal of working to maintain and preserve the Greater Yellowstone Ecosystem. All welcome your support.

The Yellowstone Association
P.O. Box 117
Yellowstone National Park, WY 82190
(307) 344-2296, *www.yellowstoneassociation.org*

The Yellowstone Association is a nonprofit organization serving Yellowstone National Park and its visitors through support of educational, historical, and scientific programs. The goal of the association is "to educate the public to a better understanding and appreciation of the Yellowstone area and what it represents in terms of our historical and natural heritage." The association publishes quarterly newsletters and serves as a clearinghouse for a vast number of books, maps, videos, and posters concerning Yellowstone. In conjunction with the Yellowstone Institute, the association sponsors an impressive schedule of multiday courses on Yellowstone's natural history. As well as helping to support the significant contributions of the Yellowstone Association, association members also receive quarterly copies of the NPS newspaper and a fifteen percent discount on publications sold in park visitor centers or ordered through the association.

Greater Yellowstone Coalition
13 South Wilson, P.O. Box 1874
Bozeman, MT 59771
(406) 586-1593; *www.greateryellowstone.org*

Founded in 1983, the Greater Yellowstone Coalition has grown to more than 6,000 individual members and more than 110 member organizations. Its mission is "to preserve and protect the Greater Yellowstone Ecosystem and the unique quality of life it sustains." The coalition publishes a substantial quarterly newsletter that informs members of regional issues including proposed private developments, governmental actions, wildlife news, and habitat issues. Included in the newsletter are "EcoAction Alerts" aimed at involving the membership in the decision-making process. The coalition also holds annual meetings, outings, educational programs, and provides additional publications.

Joining the coalition is an excellent way to keep informed of a wide realm of issues affecting the Greater Yellowstone Ecosystem. For membership information, write or call the coalition at the above address or number.

Yellowstone Park Foundation
222 East Main Street, Suite 301
Bozeman, MT 59715
(406) 586-6303; *www.ypf.org*

The Yellowstone Park Foundation is a nonprofit organization created by a group of concerned citizens, working with the National Park Service, to preserve, protect, and enhance Yellowstone National Park. The Foundation funds projects and programs that are beyond the financial capacity of the Park Service. Without the generous support of private citizens, foundations, and corporations, these projects would be unfunded.

Grand Teton Natural History Association
P.O. Box 170
Moose, WY 83012
(307) 739-3406; *www.grandtetonpark.org*

The Grand Teton Natural History Association (GTNHA) operates impressively stocked bookstores in visitor centers in Grand Teton National Park, Bridger-Teton and Targhee National Forests, and the National Elk Refuge. Bookstore profits support significant educational, interpretive, and research efforts in the national park and forests. The association also publishes free educational and informational leaflets obtainable within the park. A mail-order catalog of books, maps, and pamphlets about Grand Teton may be obtained by writing to the association at the above address. Association members help support the essential services of the GTNHA to Grand Teton National Park and receive a fifteen percent discount on all publications and bookstore purchases.

Grand Teton National Park Foundation
P.O. Box 249
Moose, WY 83012
(307) 732-0629; *www.gtnpf.org*

The Grand Teton National Park Foundation is the only nonprofit organization dedicated exclusively to raising money for projects that protect, preserve, and enhance Grand Teton National Park. Look for their products throughout the park and in the Jackson Hole area. Your membership will help fund park projects.

The Teton Science Schools
P.O. Box 68
Kelly, WY 83011
(307) 733-4765; *www.tetonscience.org*
Teton Science Schools is a nonprofit educational organization that provides and encourages experiential education in natural science and ecology while fostering an appreciation for conservation ethics and practices. The Greater Yellowstone Region serves as their outdoor classroom and model for year-round programs that offer academic, professional, and personal benefits to students of all ages. As well as other educational adventures for children and adults throughout the summer, the School offers year-round wildlife expeditions that provide close-up wildlife viewing and natural history interpretation of Greater Yellowstone's wild animals in their natural habitat.

INDEX

ABOUT THE AUTHOR

Lisa Gollin Evans received her B.A. from Cornell University and her J.D. from Boalt Hall School of Law. Evans works in the field of environmental law, most recently for the Clean Air Task Force, a national nonprofit environmental organization based in Boston. Evans believes that respect for and stewardship of the environment grows from a child's positive experiences in natural areas. The best way to create tomorrow's environmentalists is to expose children to the wonders, beauty, and excitement of nature. Her series of guides helps families put her ideas into practice and make the most of their wilderness vacations. Her books include *Rocky Mountain National Park: A Family Guide; Lake Tahoe: A Family Guide; An Outdoor Family Guide to Acadia National Park;* and *Sea Kayaking along the Massachusetts Coast*. Evans has also written an award-winning nonfiction children's book, *An Elephant Never Forgets Its Snorkel* (Crown), which was named an Outstanding Science Book for Children in 1992 by the National Association of Science Teachers and the Children's Book Council. She lives with her husband and three daughters, Sarah, Gracie, and Lilly, in Marblehead, Massachusetts.

THE MOUNTAINEERS, founded in 1906, is a nonprofit outdoor activity and conservation club, whose mission is "to explore, study, preserve, and enjoy the natural beauty of the outdoors. . . . " Based in Seattle, Washington, the club is now the third-largest such organization in the United States, with 15,000 members and five branches throughout Washington State.

The Mountaineers sponsors both classes and year-round outdoor activities in the Pacific Northwest, which include hiking, mountain climbing, ski-touring, snowshoeing, bicycling, camping, kayaking and canoeing, nature study, sailing, and adventure travel. The club's conservation division supports environmental causes through educational activities, sponsoring legislation, and presenting informational programs. All club activities are led by skilled, experienced volunteers, who are dedicated to promoting safe and responsible enjoyment and preservation of the outdoors.

If you would like to participate in these organized outdoor activities or the club's programs, consider a membership in The Mountaineers. For information and an application, write or call The Mountaineers, Club Headquarters, 300 Third Avenue West, Seattle, WA 98119; 206-284-6310.

The Mountaineers Books, an active, nonprofit publishing program of the club, produces guidebooks, instructional texts, historical works, natural history guides, and works on environmental conservation. All books produced by The Mountaineers Books fulfill the club's mission.

Send or call for our catalog of more than 500 outdoor titles:

The Mountaineers Books
1001 SW Klickitat Way, Suite 201
Seattle, WA 98134
800-553-4453
mbooks@mountaineers.org
www.mountaineersbooks.org

OTHER TITLES YOU MIGHT ENJOY FROM
THE MOUNTAINEERS BOOKS

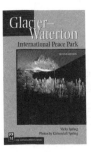

Glacier—Waterton International Peace Park, 2nd Edition
Vicky Spring & Tom Kirkendall
Get the most out of this world-famous park with t.
guidebook on the many outdoor activities available

**Walking the Big Wild:
From Yellowstone to the Yukon
on the Grizzly Bear's Trail**
Karsten Heuer
Join the author and his dog on their
2,200-mile walk in the wild.

**Yellowstone to Yukon:
Freedom to Roam**
Florian Schulz
The dream is a connected eco-system through
Norh America's Wild Heart—see what this
means and learn why it is important.

BEST HIKES WITH CHILDREN SERIES
Find the guidebook for your area—hikes that appeal to pint-sized
hikers, as well as their parents.